Smarter Investing

PEARSON

At Pearson, we believe in learning – all kinds of learning for all kinds of people. Whether it's at home, in the classroom or in the workplace, learning is the key to improving our life chances.

That's why we're working with leading authors to bring you the latest thinking and the best practices, so you can get better at the things that are important to you. You can learn on the page or on the move, and with content that's always crafted to help you understand quickly and apply what you've learned.

If you want to upgrade your personal skills or accelerate your career, become a more effective leader or more powerful communicator, discover new opportunities or simply find more inspiration, we can help you make progress in your work and life.

Pearson is the world's leading learning company. Our portfolio includes the Financial Times, Penguin, Dorling Kindersley, and our educational business, Pearson International.

Every day our work helps learning flourish, and wherever learning flourishes, so do people.

To learn more please visit us at: **www.pearson.com/uk**

The Financial Times

With a worldwide network of highly respected journalists, *The Financial Times* provides global business news, insightful opinion and expert analysis of business, finance and politics. With over 500 journalists reporting from 50 countries worldwide, our in-depth coverage of international news is objectively reported and analysed from an independent, global perspective.

To find out more, visit **www.ft.com/pearsonoffer/**

Tim Hale

Smarter Investing

Simpler decisions for better results

Third Edition

Harlow, England • London • New York • Boston • San Francisco • Toronto • Sydney • Auckland • Singapore • Hong Kong
Tokyo • Seoul • Taipei • New Delhi • Cape Town • São Paulo • Mexico City • Madrid • Amsterdam • Munich • Paris • Milan

Pearson Education Limited

Edinburgh Gate
Harlow CM20 2JE
United Kingdom
Tel: +44 (0)1279 623623
Web: www.pearson.com/uk

First published in Great Britain in 2006 (print)
Second edition published 2009 (print)
Third edition published 2013 (print and electronic)

© Tim Hale 2006, 2009 (print)
© Tim Hale 2013 (print and electronic)

The right of Tim Hale to be identified as author of this work has been asserted by him in accordance with the Copyright, Designs and Patents Act 1988.

Pearson Education is not responsible for the content of third-party internet sites.

ISBN: 978-0-273-78537-8 (print)
978-0-273-78966-6 (PDF)
978-0-273-78967-3 (ePub)
978-1-292-00756-4 (CourseSmart)

British Library Cataloguing-in-Publication Data
A catalogue record for the print edition is available from the British Library

Library of Congress Cataloging-in-Publication Data
A catalog record for the print edition is available from the Library of Congress

The Financial Times. With a worldwide network of highly respected journalists, *The Financial Times* provides global business news, insightful opinion and expert analysis of business, finance and politics. With over 500 journalists reporting from 50 countries worldwide, our in-depth coverage of international news is objectively reported and analysed from an independent, global perspective. To find out more, visit www.ft.com/pearsonoffer.

10 9 8 7 6 5 4 3 2 1
17 16 15 14 13

Cover design by Dan Mogford
Typeset in Stone Serif 9 point by 3
Printed in Great Britain by Henry Ling Ltd., at the Dorset Press, Dorchester, Dorset

NOTE THAT ANY PAGE CROSS REFERENCES REFER TO THE PRINT EDITION

For Emma, Tilly and Betsy who make my life so rich.

Contents

Foreword

This is the third edition of *Smarter Investing* and emerges as stock markets around the world return to levels last seen prior to the 2008 market collapse. Nothing material has changed in either investor psyches or market behaviour since the last edition four years ago. Investors who showed good discipline have made solid returns. Those who were carried away with market noise have generally had lower returns and may find themselves anxious about when and how to return to the market.

If you are concerned about how money is invested you should read *Smarter Investing*. If you are responsible for, or are the beneficiary of, moneys invested to meet your or your family's future needs, you must read *Smarter Investing*. It matters not whether you are a 'do-it-yourself' investor or you are employing others to make investment decisions for you. In both cases you will be richer and more capable of critically judging the options available to you if you do read it. Whether you like it or not, the quality and enjoyment of your future is likely to be heavily determined by investment decisions. You fail yourself and your family if you leave those decisions naively to others or rely on chance.

Tim Hale has distilled, into less than 300 easy-to-read pages, the building blocks to help you to construct an investment portfolio that meets your needs. He puts together a solid case for low cost, low turnover investments that are easily understood. It is the most coherent and well constructed argument that I have come across in more than 40 plus years working in the financial services industry.

We know that investing is an uncertain activity. What Tim does is tell you why and how to build portfolios which have the greatest likelihood of achieving your goals. This does not mean that they come with a guarantee of portfolio performance. The financial world is too fickle for that. You might be the one in 50 or the one in 100 that will not be happy with your results. However, what you will learn from this book will leave you unsurprised by the portfolio returns and outcomes over time. You may be disappointed in the results but you should know that they are possible.

There are two distinct parts of Tim's argument. One is concerned with helping you solve a very personal issue: how much investment risk you should take on in your investment portfolio. The second gives you a practical 'how to' strategy for both constructing and managing your portfolio over time.

So how much investment risk should you take? Tim shows that you need to quantify and prioritise three competing expressions of risk in your life: risk required, risk capacity and risk tolerance (sometimes called risk appetite).

Risk required is the amount of risk associated with the return required to achieve your goals. You might want to live well in retirement, travel internationally on a regular basis, support your children and give generously to charity. You would not be unusual if you needed to take a reasonable amount of risk in your investments to do so. Most of us do not have sufficient existing or potential assets to meet our preferred future spending from cash-like returns. One of the basic laws of capitalism is that shares in businesses will, in the longer term, give you a higher return than lending money to a bank or government. So for those needing a higher return than cash or bonds, investment in shares is necessary. The downside is that there is a possibility that some of the companies you invest in might fail outright whilst others will vary in value and dividend over time. In simple terms shares should give a higher return than cash but with greater likelihood of variation above and below.

Risk capacity is the amount of money you could lose without putting your important short and long term goals at risk. Risk tolerance is best understood as the amount of financial risk you would naturally be comfortable with taking, all else being equal. Risk required and risk capacity vary with individual circumstances over time whereas risk tolerance is an enduring and generally persistent personal trait.

So here's the rub. Rarely do all three line up. More often than not the risk you need to take (risk required) is more than you could afford to take (risk capacity) and more than you normally prefer to take (risk tolerance). Which is the dominant one for you? What is the right mix? Many individuals would prefer to say this is just too hard. But you and your family will live the outcomes of these decisions and they must be made based on your values and priorities, not someone else's. It's just not fair to your family to leave it to someone else to decide. Worst of all do not leave it to a common risk profiler or portfolio picker. These are usually idiot quizzes offered by lazy life companies, indolent fund managers and apathetic financial advisers. More akin to the more lurid women's magazines' astrology predictions than science, they seek to box unsuspecting investors into such groupings as 'You are a balanced investor seeking inflation protection, tax efficiency and regular income' from the answers to half a dozen unrelated questions. They might just as easily say 'You are an Aquarian. You like new floats, holidays by the sea and highly liquid investments'.

While it might seem a little difficult to define and establish the portfolio that best suits you, this turns out to be relatively straightforward compared to the challenges of managing that portfolio over time as markets move, the media bays and as a consequence your confidence waxes and wanes. More often than not individual investors make the mistake of buying at the top of the market and selling at the bottom. Tim first gives you the underlying disciplines to build a solid portfolio that meets your needs and secondly tells you how to minimise the behaviour that results in poor investment performance in the longer term.

The best thing about Tim's arguments is that they are almost invariably supported by both hard evidence and intuitive common sense. In summary they are: invest in things you understand, use transparent, cheap and predictable products and control yourself when markets move strongly. Whether you manage your own investments or use a financial adviser your responsibility to yourself and your family demands that you read and make sense of his arguments.

Paul Resnik
Melbourne
August 2013

Paul Resnik has had many roles in the financial services industry over the last 40 years including setting up a national financial advisory practice in Australia, an asset management business, a life insurance company and many retirement income products. He has spent the last 20 years developing practical solutions to better match portfolios to investors' needs. He is a co-founder of FinaMetrica which scientifically assesses financial risk tolerance for investors in more than 23 countries.

About the author

Having read Zoology at Oxford University, Tim went straight into the city, working for Standard Chartered in Hong Kong in their corporate banking division for four years. Following his MBA in 1991, he joined Chemical Global Investors in London – a global investment boutique – that was part of Chemical Bank. This later became part of Chase Asset Management, which in turn has subsequently been subsumed into JP Morgan Asset Management. He worked for Chase Manhattan until the turn of the millennium in London, Hong Kong and New York.

Driven by his experience of the difficulties that many investors face trying to invest sensibly, he set up Albion Strategic Consulting in 2001, which has forged a niche working with a small group of high-quality financial planning firms in the UK helping them to establish and manage a robust, risk-focused and low cost, passive approach to investing for their wealthy clients.

He lives in Devon with his lovely wife and two beautiful daughters and enjoys the moors, the beaches and cycling in the South West. He can sometimes be spotted on his paddle board in the Exe estuary heading for a sun-downer at one of the waterside hostelries.

Preface

When the first edition of the book was published in 2006 the global equity markets had recovered much of their losses following the technology stock driven crash of 2000–2003 – a period during which the UK market fell by over 45%. The global economy was booming, as were house prices; everything seemed rosy. Yet by the time the second edition was published, readers and investors had suffered the trauma of the credit crisis and the demise of Lehman Brothers and a range of other near collapses, such as RBS and Lloyds, which were saved only by the largesse of the UK taxpayer. The UK market fell during the period November 2007 to February 2009 by over 40%, and the economy was deeply in recession.

By the time of this third edition, we have suffered through the Eurozone crisis (which may well raise its ugly head again), double dip recession, quantitative easing (printing money), record low interest rates and the signs of a few shoots of recovery. Equity markets in 2013 have roared ahead, pricing in better future earnings.

What does all this tell us? Not a lot really, other than we have virtually no idea what lies ahead of us in the next few years, and no one else does either. You'll find lots of opinions but, inevitably, no real certainty. But that is how it has always been and will always be for investors. Our crystal balls are very clouded and are of little use in predicting the short-term direction and timing of market moves.

So what has changed since the last edition of the book? Well, not the underlying thesis of the book. The only sensible solution as an investor is to try and build a robust investment portfolio that delivers you with the long-term rewards of capitalism – either as an owner of companies (equities) or as a lender of capital to governments and companies (bonds) – and has the capacity to weather whatever storms the markets suffer both over the short and the long term.

A truly effective way to capture the returns on offer is through using low cost funds that seek to replicate the returns of the markets (known as passive funds or sometimes index trackers), and the global empirical evidence in support of this approach grows steadily. The highly challenging task of identifying fund managers who have the skill to beat the market in the future, and living with them once selected, is best left to others – their chance of success is exceptionally low as the increasing body of evidence in this edition demonstrates.

The value of a simple yet robust portfolio, executed using passive funds is strikingly evident: from the height of the market in January 2000, just before the technology driven crash, to April 2013, an investor in a portfolio comprising 60% global equities and 40% high quality bonds would have experienced a return that more than doubled their portfolio before inflation.[1] The purchasing power of this portfolio (i.e. after inflation) grew by 40%. That's a pretty solid achievement given that the money invested in the UK's FTSE All Share Index or held in cash just about maintained their purchasing power. Structure, fortitude and discipline are the keys to success, not trying to pick the next hottest thing or trying to time when to be in or out of the market.

What has changed, and changed for the better, since the previous edition is the number and quality of passive fund providers and sensible passive products available to retail investors. The arrival of Vanguard has caused a revolution in product and huge pressure on pricing which is all great from a Smarter Investor's perspective. It is now easy to construct and administer a robust and well-diversified portfolio using online broker platforms. The implementation section of the book provides insight into some of the funds that investors can research to fill each slice of their portfolio pie.

The nature of financial advice has changed too. On 1 January 2013, a new regime came into being that effectively bans all commission payments by providers to advisers. Advice has never been free to those who took it, they just never had to write the cheque directly. The only money that an adviser can receive today must be agreed directly with and paid to them by their clients. In one step (but a quite painful step in many ways for the advice industry and its suppliers) the severe conflicts of interest and tyranny of function of commission-based advisers has been struck away – not before time. That said, a small number of high quality, financial planning firms have been charging client-agreed fees for many years. Remember that good advice will pay you back many times over your lifetime.

And finally the structure of the book has changed too. I have tried to get readers to the portfolio construction process a bit quicker and to place some

---

[1] Includes small allocations to emerging markets and value and small cap equities. The bonds are split evenly between UK index linked gilts and shorter-dated UK gilts. Costs of 0.8% a year were deducted to reflect the materially higher costs that index funds incurred in the early years and the portfolio was rebalanced once a year.

of the more planning type calculations and thinking into the appendices. I have also placed greater emphasis on how the portfolios can be executed in practice, both in terms of the fund opportunity set that the reader can look into, but also in terms of how portfolios can be administered. Finally, there is quite a lot of new empirical evidence supporting the Smarter Investing approach, which is well worth reviewing.

I hope that you enjoy it and find it to be of value as you build a robust, disciplined and simple-to-execute investment strategy for your future.

Tim Hale
Exeter, United Kingdom
2013

Author's acknowledgements

Writing is an adventure. To begin with, it is a toy and an amusement. Then it becomes a mistress, then it becomes a master, then it becomes a tyrant. The last phase is that just as you are about to be reconciled to your servitude, you kill the monster and fling him to the public.

Winston Churchill

Again, to those who asked me to write a pamphlet, this third edition is yet another step closer – I should be there by the tenth edition!

Thanks to the editorial and production teams at Pearson – including Chris Cudmore, Eloise Cook and Natasha Whelan – who have been instrumental in shaping and delivering this improved edition. Your ongoing support is appreciated. Thanks to Siân Lamb at my end who tackled the proofs and amendment task with fortitude.

I would also like to thank my clients for their unerring support and friendship that makes going to work everyday fun – they know who they are. Their continual challenge and pressure to make sure that what they are doing is the best they can do for their clients, is my spur.

Thanks too, to all those who have bought previous copies of the book and have kindly commented on it in blogs, on Amazon or sought me out in person. I truly value your comments and feedback.

The personal support to me of the 'passive' community has been remarkable too. It is a very open part of the fund management business populated by exceptionally bright professionals, and entirely devoid of the ego, hubris and overconfidence of some parts of the fund management industry. The free access to research, analytical tools and the generosity of time and intellectual capital of many people never ceases to astound me. It is truly appreciated.

Finally to all those individuals, industry firms and professionals who are striving to help themselves and others to invest more sensibly and fairly – 'press on regardless' – as the legendary Jack Bogle would say!

Publisher's acknowledgements

We are grateful to the following for permission to reproduce copyright material:

Cartoons

Cartoons on page 88 and page 160 from www.dilbert.com, reproduced with permission.

Figures

Figure 1 in Appendix 1, Figures 11.3 and 11.5 from MSCI (http://www.msci. com/), reproduced with permission; Figure 11.4 adapted from *Credit Suisse Global Investment Returns Sourcebook,* Credit Suisse AG (Elroy Dimson, Paul Marsh and Mike Staunton 2013) Copyright (c) 2013 Elroy Dimson, Paul Marsh and Mike Staunton.

Screenshots

Screenshot on page 237 from http://www.sensibleinvesting.tv/ (c) sensible. tv, used with permission from Barnett Ravenscroft Wealth Management.

Tables

Table 4.2 from FTSE International Limited ("FTSE") © FTSE 2013, "FTSE®" is a trade mark of the London Stock Exchange Group companies and is used by FTSE International Limited under licence. All rights in the FTSE indices and/or FTSE ratings vest in FTSE and/or its licensors. Neither FTSE nor its licensors accept any liability for any errors or omissions in the FTSE indices and/or FTSE ratings or underlying data. No further distribution of FTSE Data is permitted without FTSE's express written consent; Tables 4.3 and 4.4 from Vanguard 2012, 'Active managers' performance against market benchmarks, www.vanguard.co.uk (c) The Vanguard Group, Inc., used with permission; Table 7.3 from MSCI (http://www.msci.com/), reproduced with permission ; Table 11.2 from Barclays Equity Gilt Study 2012, reproduced with permission.

In some instances we have been unable to trace the owners of copyright material, and we would appreciate any information that would enable us to do so.

Introduction

I.1 Why did you pick this book up?

I imagine it is because you know that maybe all is not as good as it should be in terms of getting your investment life in order. Maybe you feel that you ought to start investing for your future, but feel at a loss where to start. Perhaps you feel that your money should be working harder for you, but are unsure what to do, or are not sure how you should invest your pension contributions, surplus income, an inheritance or your bonuses. Read on if you have a suspicion that what you are doing at present is not optimal. It is an important business that deserves some of your time.

Most of us do not build our own houses or service our own cars, but increasingly we have to take on the responsibility for investing money without any formal training. You may well have some questions on your mind:

- What type of investments should I get involved in?
- What should my portfolio look like?
- How would I go about building this portfolio in practice?
- What do I need to do to service my investments?
- Should I seek advice? If so, who can I trust?

This book is a chance to arm yourself with what you need to know to answer these questions yourself.

What this book will do for you

- Develop a simple set of rules to make your investment decisions by (or to understand those suggested by your adviser).
- Help you to control some of your demons that will tempt you into being a bad investor.
- Help you broadly to define what you want to achieve from your investing.
- Help you to construct a portfolio that meets your financial needs.
- Help you to construct a sensible portfolio of investments that you can live with.

■ Suggest some practical ways of being an efficient, good investor.

■ Provide some practical pointers about using advisers and products.

■ Help you to relax and enjoy your investing responsibilities.

1.2 Some eye-openers to get you thinking

A good place to start is by looking at some facts that should make you sit up and take notice. If they do not, then either you are a very well informed investor, or you need to go away, drink a strong cup of coffee and start again. Do not despair though if you are shocked, because the solution to smarter investing is straightforward and this book shows you how. Smarter investing is simple investing – a mantra we will return to time and again. Perhaps now is the time to begin to commit to doing things differently and so avoiding some of the pitfalls that many investors fall into, including: failing to invest in the first place; investing too little to have any real chance of achieving your goals; asking too much from your portfolio; and chasing last year's best performing markets and managers –a fool's errand.

Eye-opener 1: It is not too hard to be a great investor

It is actually quite easy to be a great investor. Have faith in capitalism; there may be stormy weather at times, but capitalism is a pretty effective system for creating wealth. Own global capitalism (i.e. companies) by owning a global equity index tracker fund that puts as much of the market return that it generates in your pocket, not someone else's. As a balance, lend your money to the UK government with their promise that they will preserve its purchasing power for as long as they borrow it (inflation-linked investments), plus a little more, or even just hold cash. Get this balance right, execute it with the lowest costs and hold the balance firm over time. That's about it. This book shows you how.

Eye-opener 2: The market beats the 'average' investor

Over the long term the market will beat the majority of investors, professional or otherwise. This is a mathematical fact, not supposition. The market is made up of all investors; as such, the return of the average investor is by definition the return of the market before costs. After paying professionals to manage money, administration costs and costs associated with the buying and selling of shares, the average investor's return will inevitably be below that of the market. In the UK, investment professionals trying to beat the market represent the majority of investors, so for all of them to beat themselves is not possible. You might be surprised to hear, that of the £706 billion invested in funds in the UK (Investment Management Association, 2013), around 85% of the money is invested in strategies that try to beat the market. A lot of people will lose out – fact. Not everyone can be a winner. In the USA around 65% of institutional money is trying to beat the market return.

Eye-opener 3: The average investor is terrible at investing

In the USA, during the twenty-year period to 2010, the average individual investing in US equity funds generated an annual return of around 4% (Dalbar, 2011), while the market delivered a return of a little under 10%. This occurred because investors chased returns, moving from the funds they were in to those that seemed to be performing better, destroying their wealth with this buy-high and sell-low strategy. Such behaviour in all likelihood applies to investors around the world, not just those in the USA. Investors are simply throwing away wealth. Although there has been some criticism of the methodology, the unarguable fact remains – investors undertake wealth destroying investment activity driven by emotion. A recent piece of research (Meyer et al., 2012) on German private investors who managed their money on a DIY basis using online brokerage accounts revealed that the average investor underperformed the market by a whopping –7.5% a year, before costs.

Research on UK investors (Schneider, 2007) reveals that they also chase fund managers who have performed well, with the same unfortunate consequences. From 1992 to 2003, investors' returns were around 2% per year below the return delivered by the funds they were invested in as a consequence of the timing of their entry and exits into the funds. On average, UK equity funds underperformed the market (FTSE All Share) by around 2% per year. In total that means that the average fund investor received a return around 4% a year below the market. That is approximately equivalent to the entire reward that you can expect for owning equities rather than placing a deposit.

Eye-opener 4: The market beats most professionals

Recent research from the UK marketplace (Vanguard, 2012) reveals that around 75–100% of professional managers – depending upon which bond and equity fund categories one is looking at – failed to beat the market over the fifteen years to the end of 2011. That is a pretty terrible outcome for the high fees they charge.

Eye-opener 5: Industry costs are excessive

The average 'on the road' cost of a UK equity fund exceeds 1.5% a year, although this may well come down in the new era that was ushered in on 1 January 2013, where pricing has become more transparent and unbundled, separating out the cost of fund management from the cost of distribution and administration. In the long run equities have produced a real return, i.e. after inflation, of around 5% a year over the past 113 years or so (Barclays, 2012). In the long run, the industry croupier takes almost 30% of your returns. Is that really fair or sensible? As the title to Fred Schwed's classic book about New York's Wall Street asks: *Where are the Customers' Yachts?* (Schwed,1995).

Eye-opener 6: Past performance tells you almost nothing

A track record of good past performance for a specific fund provides few clues as to whether performance in the future will be good or bad. Performance in most cases appears to be random over time. As an investor, it is extremely hard continuously to outsmart all the other smart people trying to outsmart you. Some investors will get it right, either through luck or judgement, some of the time, but very rarely all of the time. You probably need fifteen to twenty years of performance data to be able to differentiate between the two. Yet for most investors, short-term past performance is the sole criterion for selecting a manager. How are you going to choose a good manager to manage your money without using performance data? If you find a way, let me know.

To be fair, a small handful of managers, such as Warren Buffett in the USA, have excellent track records as a result of outstanding skills and investment processes. The challenge, as you will see, is picking them in advance.

Eye-opener 7: Picking winners is hard

Looking for a manager who will beat the market for you over the next twenty or more years is like looking for a needle in the proverbial investment universe haystack. There are around 2,000 UK domiciled funds from which to choose and around 30,000 across Europe that you could potentially choose to invest in. Where on earth would you start trying to pick the wheat from the chaff? Here's a challenge to mull over – a piece of research (Bogle, 2007), covering a thirty-five year period in the USA, revealed that of 355 US equity mutual funds in 1970 only 3 (less than 1%) delivered statistically significant and consistent performance through to 2005. Now that should get the alarm bells ringing. For all the claims of the market-beating active management world, the emperor has no clothes!

Eye-opener 8: Many will be poor in their retirements

People in their twenties spend around £150 a month on booze and cigarettes yet only half save anything and of these, half save less than £50 a month according to a Birmingham Midshires Bank survey (2004). *Carpe diem.* The magnitude of the problem in the UK is immense. Only 2.9 million people contributed to workplace pensions (Office for National Statistics, 2011) – the lowest number ever since records began in 1953. The average contribution rate (as a percentage of salary) in private sector schemes was 2.8% for employees and 6.6% for employers, which is well below the minimum of 20% or more of salary needed to provide a half decent pension. The average pension pot (after a tax free sum has been taken) was around £26,000 (Association of British Insurers, 2011). Given today's annuity rates, this would buy a 65-year-old man around £900 of income a year, protected from inflation or £1,500 without any inflation protection. That doesn't sound very encouraging. My advice – do not be one of them.

Eye-opener 9: You can easily avoid these pitfalls

Hopefully, I now have your attention and we can focus on the task of making sure that you avoid the many investment pitfalls that lie in wait for the unsuspecting investor, not by any complicated investing strategy, but by doing a few plain, easy-to-understand things, well. Please read on.

I.3 Why am I qualified to write it?

While I am not a fund manager by trade (thank goodness), my career has revolved around the process of advising wealthy individuals and advisory firms on their investment strategies. I have probably heard most of the crazy notions that investors have about investing, discussed many of the old chestnuts they argue about, which we will throw around too, and had the privilege to meet and listen to some very smart and experienced investors.

Today, my company, Albion Strategic Consulting, focuses on helping-wealth advisory boutiques to provide valuable, clear and well-articulated investment advice to help clients meet their lifetime spending goals. I spent many years thinking that there must be a better way to try to educate investors than the tools and books that the industry provides; in the end I decided to tackle the issue myself, both through my business and this book.

1.4 How this book works

The basic principle of this book is to provide a clear and balanced view of investing and some simple rules and practical tools to help you to make your own decisions. It will provide access to research, data, concepts and hotly contested debates that are central to the industry and from which good investing rules arise. It provides an understanding of investment ideas at a level that you decide and is broken down into five parts:

Part 1: Smarter investing basics

This is a foundation course on investing. It introduces some of the basic things that you need to understand before you go any further. Failing to take these basic concepts on board may prove to be very costly. If you are familiar with them, there is no harm in spending a few minutes in bringing them into the forefront of your thoughts. Even if you intend to employ an adviser to help you with your investment programme you should make sure that you understand the concepts that are raised. It is rounded off with twenty investing tips, although I urge you to read beyond this point!

Part 2: Smarter thinking

Here, you will build a simple and practical investment philosophy to develop rules that give you the highest chance of success in your investing, avoiding the many pitfalls set by the industry. It also provides an insight into the bad-investing demons that tempt you towards poor investment practices. Your emotions have the potential to destroy your wealth.

Part 3: Smarter portfolios

The concept of building a smart but simple portfolio is covered and an insight into why equities and bonds form the structural core of this portfolio, is provided. The chapter helps you to identify the types of investment that probably make sense to include and points out others you would do well to avoid. A number of portfolio choices – from low risk to high risk options – are provided along with detailed insight into what each would be like to own, both on the upside and the downside.

Part 4: Smarter implementation

It is no good getting to this stage of the book and failing to do anything because you are swamped by choice when you put the book down. This part of the book arms you with some down-to-earth advice and ideas about how to put into action what you have decided upon in Part 3, right down to website and product provider details.

Part 5: Smarter insight

The final section puts a bit more meat on the bones of the asset classes that have been considered and either included or excluded in the Smarter Portfolios. Understanding why we have steered away from a number of asset classes will hopefully help you avoid falling to the siren voices of the investment industry. Understanding why you own what you own and feeling comfortable with both the down and the upsides will help you to live with these components through the bad, as well as the good, times.

An apology to active managers

I want to make clear that this book is not meant to be a direct assault on active managers or their efforts. There are some very smart and hardworking people in the industry, but that just raises the bar for all in a game of winners and losers. Rarely is an industry so brutally cruel on its skilled and dedicated participants, and rarely too are the chances of success (from an investment perspective) so stacked against them throughout their careers. As you will see from the evidence, hard-working and smart does not necessarily translate into outperformance of the market after costs, the measurement of success in this industry.

There are undoubtedly a few managers who outperform over long periods of time as a consequence of their superb skills. I congratulate them.

References

Association of British Insurers (2011) from: Private Pensions Table 17 (www.pensionspolicyinstitute.org.uk).

Barclays Equity Gilt Study (2012).

Birmingham Midshires Bank survey (2004).

Bogle, John C. (2007) *The Little Book of Common Sense Investing*. John Wiley & Sons.

Dalbar, Inc. (2011) 'Quantitative analysis of investment behavior', press release (http://dalbarinc.com/).

Investment Management Association (2013) February 2013 figures (www. investmentfunds.org.uk).

Meyer, S., Schmoltzi, D., Stammschulte, C., Kaesler, S., Loos, B. and Hackethal, A. (2012) 'Just Unlucky? – A Bootstrapping Simulation to Measure Skill in Individual Investors' Investment Performance' (6 June) (http://ssrn.com/ abstract=2023588).

Office for National Statistics (2011) *Occupational Pension Schemes Survey 2011* (www.ons.gov.uk).

Schneider, L. (2007) Diploma thesis: 'Are UK fund investors achieving fund rates of return?', submitted in July 2007, Fachhochschule Kufstein, Tirol, Austria.

Schwed Jr., F. (1995) *Where are the customers' yachts?* 3rd edn. New York: Wiley.

Vanguard (2012) 'The case for index fund investing for UK investors' (www. vanguard.co.uk).

Smarter investing basics

A foundation course for the rest of the book. Understanding a few basic investment ideas and spending a few minutes thinking about them will give you the basis on which to move forward and design and implement your own portfolio. The chapters in this part of the book include:

Chapter 1: Simplifying the confusion

To many investors, the world of investment can seem both confusing and complicated; yet it can be reduced down to a simple process. Product proliferation, conflicts of interest and market noise are the culprits. Identifying and filtering out the industry's noise is a good place to start.

Chapter 2: Covering the basics

What is smarter investing actually about? Your understanding of a few simple concepts will allow you to focus on the really important issues. For some, this may seem trivial, but take a look anyway because it really is important stuff that you cannot afford to misunderstand or ignore.

Chapter 3: It only takes a minute

In recognition of the fact that some readers may not be able to find the time to read the whole book in one sitting, this chapter provides a summary of the rules, tips, hints and guidelines that you should be following. In fact, applying these ideas will put you at the forefront of investors, although you may well be doing the right things but without necessarily understanding why. I strongly urge you to read beyond this chapter.

1

Simplifying the confusion

It would not surprise me if the world of investing seems a confusing and complicated place; the number of investment choices is vast and making sense of it all may be daunting. Fortunately, it need not be so.

1.1 Choices, choices, choices

The menu of potential investments has the capacity to leave many new to the game mesmerised by choice; a little like when you go into a restaurant and have to choose what to eat from a menu ten pages long. Dishes on offer include bank deposits, corporate bonds, investing in China, UK companies, gold, property, commodities, the USA, Japan, stamps, wine and vintage cars to name but a few. Your choice is as wide as it is confusing. Do not worry though; this book narrows down the menu to a sensible one-pager and gives you help on what to choose.

As already mentioned, in the UK there are around 2,000 funds (unit trusts or OEICs) registered for sale that you can choose from, and around another 30,000 in Europe! That's a lot of choice. Add in over 1,000 Exchange Traded Funds or ETFs (products that are like funds but which are listed on stock exchanges and you buy and sell like equities), 900 new structured products issues in 2011, and over 700 investment trusts and you can quickly see the enormity of the selection decision.

To make things worse, you face a constant barrage of noise and information from the industry, in its widest sense, trying to influence what you should be doing with your money. This 'advice' comes from a wide range of sources. Journalists write articles in the Sunday papers along the lines of 'Is now the right time to be investing in [substitute the flavour of the month]?' creating a convincing spin on what to do with your money. Unfortunately it is usually just a return-chasing story encouraging you to jump out of one investment that is doing badly into one that is currently doing well – not a good strategy, as we saw in the Introduction. Fund managers advertise their spectacular market-beating returns over the past three years for a chosen fund, or laud their market-beating 'star' manager in the press. Financial advisers all seem to have their list of 'best performing managers'. Even the TV news gets in on the act with its valueless daily comments that the 'Footsie Index of the leading 100 shares was up 47 points today' or 'The pound fell by a cent against the dollar'. The magazine racks in the newsagents are full of investment magazines that provide stock and fund tips, the bookshelves groan with books on investing that try to teach you about how to pick stocks, day trade, make a million and time when to be in or out of markets, and your poor postman delivers sacks full of junk mail on what ISA to pick before April comes around again. Throw in the thousands of search results from a Google search on any investing topic, and if you weren't already confused, you are now!

The natural response to this confusion is to think about employing someone to unravel the mess and help make the decisions for you. This may well be a sound thing to do, provided you find the right person. Yet here too, uncertainty reigns: investors' confidence in the advice industry has taken a beating from a series of scandals and broken promises, from pension and endowment mortgage misselling to Equitable Life reneging on the payment of its annuity promises to some pensioners. It is not really surprising that many investors do not know which way to turn for advice they can trust.

Finally, let's not forget the stock market crash of 2000–2002 and 2007–2008 when the market fell by more than 45% and 40% respectively, which bruised a good few investors and brought real meaning to the term 'risk'. You can quickly understand the temptation to put investing in the 'I'll deal with that later' category; but face the problem you must and this book is a good starting point.

1.2 How did we get here?

A potted and generalised history provides an insight into how this complexity has arisen, and why the noise from the industry has been turned up so dramatically in the past few years. We can then work out how we can try to make your investing a calmer, simpler and more enjoyable process.

The best way to invest has shifted dramatically

This is really a story about the way in which the best means of investing has evolved. Many investors seem to believe that beating the market is the goal of their investment programme, somewhat ignorant or blind to the fact that the world of investing is one of winners and losers and that costs (in the form of fees, commissions and taxes) result in more losers than winners in aggregate. The active management industry has done a good job in encouraging them to do so, and will try to do the same to you. Today, the battle for investors' money rages around whether you should try to beat the markets through active decision-making, or simply try to capture the market return as closely as possible, adopting a buy-and-hold strategy, as you will see. It is a question of where the probabilities of success lie in your favour. This is how the story unfolds.

The stockbroking model is on its last legs

Before the early 1970s, investors had little option but to buy securities through stockbrokers, or employ a stockbroker to manage a portfolio for them, an optimal way of managing money at the time. Information about companies was disseminated largely in print, and portfolio reporting was commonly just a list of stocks showing their purchase and current prices. Online trading, powerful computers and financial software were still science fiction. Brokers usually made money based on transaction fees, thereby encouraging the churning of investors' portfolios. This was fine at the time, but is not the best option today. Most stockbrokers are moving towards annual fee-based models, as investors wise-up, but 'all-in' fees remain too high.

Professionally managed 'active' funds

Fortunately, the world has moved on. In the 1970s the mutual fund market-place in the USA and other markets around the world, began to take off. Professional active managers looked after collective pools of money for a large number of investors, providing diversification by holding a wide number of securities, and a professional eye dedicated to watching over your money. Some managers provided individually managed investment services aimed at more wealthy clients.

Fund managers are remunerated via a management fee, calculated as a percentage of assets managed, so their interests are more closely aligned with their clients than the old stockbroking model. For many, this rightly became a better option than using a broker or investing on their own. These managers strove (and still do) to beat the markets and their peers by making active investment decisions – hence the term 'active managers'. With annual management fees of 1% to 2%, this can be an expensive business, unless the manager is able to cover their costs and more. The problem with being paid good fees based on assets is that it has placed the gathering of assets as a higher objective than investment quality, in some firms.

The index fund challenges active management

A few visionaries in the USA began to question the blind belief that professionals could consistently outperform the markets and cover their increasing fees. They began to explore whether there was a better way of investing by simply replicating a market index rather than trying to beat it. Empirical research seemed to indicate that it made sense. The first index (tracker) portfolios were born in 1973 and run by Wells Fargo and the American National Bank of Chicago. This happened many years later in the UK, as seems the case with most investment developments.

In the 1970s and 1980s computers were a scarce resource and analysis of data from the money management industry was largely confined to academics. The advent of cheap processing power in the early 1990s provided the means to analyse large amounts of data, the means to run market-replicating portfolios efficiently, and via the internet, disseminate information and monitor and administer a portfolio.

Index investing has slowly become mainstream, overcoming hurdles as extreme as the charge of being unpatriotic, levelled against it in the USA (no American should accept that they can't beat the markets!) and the vociferous attacks on them by the active management industry, which continue today. Recognition in the institutional world, and increasingly by individuals in the USA and more slowly elsewhere, has created significant challenges for the active management industry. Today, a battle exists between the two camps.

The rise and rise of product engineering and hot air

Over the 2000s the investor has been faced with an ever-increasing barrage of product engineering by investment banks and investment managers. Opacity, high costs and unidentified and unquantified risks were taken on by investors sold on a convincing story by a conflicted industry. Products such as structured notes were revealed not to be without risk. Ask anyone whose capital was guaranteed by Lehman Brothers (around $8 billion of investors' money was allegedly in these structures). Hedge funds failed to deliver their 'skill-based' returns and were revealed in the main to be selling market exposures at usurious prices, enriching themselves at the expense of gullible investors. No more gullible than those professionals who 'approved' and invested in Madoff's $50 billion Ponzi scheme, uncovered at the back end of 2008 – that list is long and undistinguished.

The time has come for transparency, value for money and the fulfilment of the fiduciary responsibility of all in the industry including fund managers, product development and marketing teams, and advisers. The outlook for impartial fee-based advice and evidence-based, transparent passive investing has never been so promising, or important to us.

DIY investing

The ability to buy, and in many cases trade, funds and other securities online has grown dramatically in the past decade. A growing band of DIY investors are seeking to use the information and technology to manage their own investments. While this may be a sensible route for an experienced and rational investor, it is likely to be a very expensive option for many investors who do not have a sensible investment philosophy and approach. It is not the financial costs that are the problem – in fact, from a financial cost perspective this may be a highly effective way to invest – it is the emotional costs of being sucked into rising markets and panicked out of falling markets (the reverse of what one should logically do) that has the potential to damage investors' wealth. As we saw earlier, German DIY investors lost around 7–8% on average, every year, relative to the market, before costs. If the professional fund managers find beating the market hard, it is a bit optimistic to think that we can do so as some sort of a hobby.

1.3 Battling for investors' money

The active management industry works on the premise that the markets can be beaten, after costs, and over the long term. We will test the efficacy of this premise in some depth a little later on in the book, where you can make up your own mind. Each manager has to believe that they will be the winner and can persuade investors to believe the same. Unfortunately, the mathematics doesn't work. Market-return replicating managers, on the other hand, defend their position on logic and abundant empirical evidence, as you will see.

Even so, the active management industry has been remarkably successful, remaining as the default choice for the majority of individual investors, often by default. It has several weapons that it uses remarkably effectively to maintain its dominant position, evidenced by the fact that today the vast majority of individual and institutional money remains in active beat-the-market strategies in the UK.

- The first and most legitimate claim is that picking and investing with an active manager who beats the market can have a very substantial positive effect on your investment outcome, compared with just gathering the market return by owning an index fund. I wholeheartedly agree. Yet, this powerful claim that plays on the hopes and emotions of investors fails to point out the fact that your chances of identifying such a manager upfront are simply too long for most individual investors to consider as a core strategy.

- Second, human beings tend to be impressed by short-term success and treat it as a proxy for long-term success, which makes them believe that they can pick the long-term winning managers by looking at two or three years of outperformance. Short-term performance tells you next to nothing, I'm afraid, as you will find out. Canny product selection by managers means that most firms always have one or two good stories to sell.

- Third, for investors who may be confused but are trying their best to be sensible, choosing a reputable firm to manage their money, which is staffed by bright people as most investment firms are, with a seemingly strong recent track record, appears like the safest thing to do and is a convenient way of passing on their investment responsibilities to someone else.

- Fourth, the industry has incredible firepower to influence investors. Marketing and branding strategies are backed with big bucks. In the USA, in 2000 at the high of the technology bubble, media advertising alone came to around $1 billion (Bogle, 2001).

1.4 Reducing confusion and complexity

Imagine that the top edge of the triangle in Figure 1.1 represents your current interface with the market. It is crowded, noisy, confusing and all based on the premise that if you are smart, and have access to enough information, you can beat the market, or at least choose a manager who can. The lower layers give you an idea of the resources that are positioned

Noisy, complicated, confusing, stressful

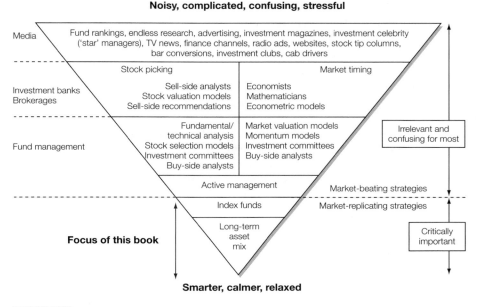

Figure 1.1 **Turning down the volume***

* Unless otherwise stated, all data analysis that appears in this book is by Albion Strategic Consulting.

in the industry that is trying to beat the market – smart, hard-working, diligent, well-paid but like alchemists of old trying to do the impossible. Remember that all the layers are being paid for by you, the investor, in one way or another.

The position this book takes

The premise of this book is that you can avoid most of the noise by focusing on the tip of the triangle. This is concerned with building and holding a sensible portfolio that gives you the greatest chance of success, not because you want an easier life, but because that is what the empirical evidence and logic tells you is the right thing to do.

In support of this position, a pertinent observation was made in the 2001 Myners Report commissioned by the government to look at pension plan management in the UK:

'A particular consequence of the present structure is that asset allocation – the selection of which markets [long term], as opposed to which individual stocks, to invest in – is an under-resourced activity. This is especially unfortunate given

the weight of academic evidence suggesting that these decisions can be critical determinants of investment performance.'

That's why this book focuses on constructing the right mix of investments above all else, followed closely by making sure that you capture the bulk of the returns that are on offer from this mix. It is as simple as that.

Three unassailable benefits accrue if you take this route:

- You dramatically reduce the noise and confusion associated with investing, which is predominantly focused on which stocks to invest in and whether to move your mix of investments around over time, with the hope of doing better than your long-term chosen mix.

- By avoiding the noise as your default position, you provide yourself with the greatest chance of success in meeting your investment goals. You are stacking the odds in your favour and you can't ask for more than that. The alternative, active management, is a high pay-off proposition with a low chance of a successful outcome for most individuals.

- You narrow the choices that you need to make dramatically, making it easier to identify products that have a very good chance of delivering what you want them to, and have little portfolio maintenance to do.

That sounds a lot easier, doesn't it?

References

Bogle, J. C. (2001) *After the fall: what's next for the stock market and the mutual fund industry?* Bogle Financial Markets Research Center (www.vanguard.com).

Myners, P. (2001) *The Myners review of institutional investing in the UK.* HM Treasury.

2

Covering the basics

Let's start by getting some basic concepts straight. These form the foundations on which you will build an investment programme. While you may be familiar with some or all of them, it makes sense to cover the ground, because they are so important. Even if you feel that you are reasonably well versed in the basics, it is never a bad idea to refresh your thinking.

2.1 What is smarter investing?

As you saw from the Eye-openers in the Introduction, there is a lot of bad investing about, so it is important to make sure that you and I are on the same page when it comes to what we think smarter investing is about. For some, investing is about buying and selling investments through an online brokerage account, feeling that they are in control and enjoying the buzz from the excitement of the markets; for others it is about deciding where to put their money based on which markets will do better in the next year or two, often using funds to reflect their ideas. For a few, it means putting money into an interest-bearing account, because they are cautious and want to preserve the money that they have. Smarter investing is not any of these things.

Smarter investing is not about saving

There is nothing wrong with saving, i.e. putting your money into a interest-bearing account if you either want to maintain a small contingency reserve for bad times or have a specific short-term goal that you need to accumulate cash for. However, if you have quite a few years until you need this money, one of the cardinal sins is to be recklessly prudent and 'save': placing your money on long-term deposit with a bank or building society makes little sense. The future wealth that you give up as a result is likely to be significant, as is the risk that unexpected inflation will eat up the spending power of your money.

Some individuals, having spent considerable time and effort in accumulating wealth in their business lives, for example, may decide that simple wealth preservation is what they want to achieve. That's fine: however, they still face the erosion of their money by inflation if they do not act sensibly – long-term saving is simply not an intelligent option. Savers have lost over 10% of the value of their purchasing power over the past three years (to 2012) – hardly a 'safe' place to be.

Investing is not about gambling with your money

When markets are going up, a combination of self-confidence and excitement encourages people to get involved in investing, particularly on their own – just witness the growth in online broking accounts in the late 1990s and the obsession with property in the 2000s. The buzz and excitement of seeing your money growing every day you log into your account is a powerful drug, and reinforces people's self-confidence to play the markets. The bull market of the 1980s, 1990s and mid–2000s influenced many people's perception of what good investing is about. Yet they conveniently forgot that a rising tide raises all boats. Many got caught up in the notion that it was about making significant money over the long term, defined as two to three years, and if you had any nous, you could beat the market. Always remember short term is two to three years and long term is twenty-plus years.

Online trading, day trading and a plethora of expensive, complicated and ultimately wealth-destroying products rode on the back of the euphoria of the raging bull. That is gambling and ends in tears for most, except for a few who get lucky. Gambling, unlike investing, is looking for long shots with high payouts and this includes: cards, horses and roulette; dipping in and out of the markets; trying to pick stocks that will outperform the market based on some sort of analysis, or guesswork; or picking professionals who you think will be able to beat the markets, and switching between them, as one falters and another shines. This may be a surprise, but as you will see in this book, you are entering a casino if you adopt such an approach, and one in which the croupier has a big fat hand in your pocket. The bank always wins in the long run.

One of my favourite quotes on the problems that investors face when trying to decide what is investment as opposed to what is speculation (gambling) comes from Fred Schwed's book (1995) on the brokerage industry:

'Investment and speculation are said to be two different things, and the prudent man is advised to engage in one and avoid the other. This is something like explaining to the troubled adolescent that love and passion are two different things. He perceives that they are different but they don't seem quite different enough to clear up his problems.'

Throughout this book you will get plenty of guidance to clear up any problems you may have.

Smarter investing is a dull process

Smarter investing is the boring process of deciding what you want your money to do for you in the future, putting your money into a mix of investment building blocks that has a good chance of getting you there, using products that allow you to keep as much of the market returns you make in your pocket rather than giving it to the industry croupier, and sticking to your planned mix through thick and thin – no chasing last year's winning markets or managers please! In a nutshell that is it. How dull! Where's the excitement in that? My advice to you is that if it is excitement that you want, book a turn on the Cresta Run with some of the money you make from being a smarter investor.

As you can see in Figure 2.1, good investing is about aiming for pay-offs you can survive with, along with chances of achieving them you can live with, not shooting the lights out with a wild bet or being certain of an unacceptably poor outcome.

Good investing is about playing the probabilities in your favour for every investment decision that you take. To know where the favourable probabilities lie requires a basic knowledge of the markets, an insight into the research that has been done, and a good dose of common sense.

Figure 2.1 **Focus on the middle ground**

2.2 Smarter investing – ten things to know

Perhaps not that surprisingly, few people are particularly interested in investing. After all, who cares whether a company's dividends are growing or how much a five year government bond is yielding today. Most are more interested in getting on with life, enjoying time with family and friends, pursuing careers or enjoying a relaxed time in retirement. The truth is, however, that decisions we make relating to our investments may well have a profound impact on our lifestyles today and tomorrow.

In this book you will find few complicated algorithms, calculations, forecasts or models for allocating assets between building blocks – just the application of standard investment rules, common sense and a determination to keep things simple, not for simplicity's sake, but because that is fortunately what the empirical evidence tells us we should be doing.

So how much do you really need to know to be able to make the most of your investment programme? Luckily, the answer is not much. What you really need to know is enough to spot when things do not make sense. Below are some tips and a few mental tick boxes to help.

Tip 1: Investing is a 'get rich, slow' process

However much we would all like to get rich quickly (or stay rich) the reality is that investing is a rather long-term and boring process that uses the power of compounding across time to magnify the two steps forward, one step back journey that participating in the markets will result in. The underlying nature and magnitude of those steps is explored further in Tip 3 below.

Yet much of what is taken for investing (the good chance of getting rich slowly), is not investing but more akin to gambling (the low odds of getting rich quickly). These activities include trying to pick 'winning' stocks, attempting to time when to be in or out of the equity markets, chasing the latest star fund manager or hot market (what is it this week, gold, commodities, emerging markets?), spread betting, horse racing, roulette etc.

It is not about saving either, as set out above.

Good investing is about owning a sensible, highly-diversified, low-cost and stable portfolio, put in place for the long term, and which is rebalanced back to its original mix from time to time. It is also about having the fortitude to keep 'on message' when the markets feel extreme on both the down and the upsides. A bit boring, sometimes emotionally challenging, but effective.

Mental tick box 1: Remember the tortoise beats the hare.

Tip 2: Harness the power of compounding and time

Compounding, as I am sure you are aware, is the effect of interest-on-interest. For example, a portfolio of £100 that compounds by 10% a year rises to £110 in year one, to £121 in year two, £133 in year three and so on. The effect of compounding returns is central to investing success and goes hand-in-hand with time. Its effects are exponential. Albert Einstein is commonly credited with the often-quoted statement that:

'[Compounding] is the greatest mathematical discovery of all time.'

Table 2.1 illustrates some simple rates of return compounded over different periods of time.

As you can see, compounding and time make a significant difference. While the difference between £100 compounded at 8% versus 10% over five years is only small (£147 versus £161), over forty years you would lose out on over half of your potential future wealth, i.e. £2,172 instead of £4,526. You may think forty years is a long time but if you start investing at twenty-five and retire at sixty-five you have clocked up forty years. A favourite quote of mine about time and compounding comes from Sidney Homer in *A History of Interest Rates* (Homer and Syllar, 2005), a book far more interesting than it sounds.

'One thousand dollars left to earn interest at 8% a year will grow to $43 quadrillion in 400 years, but the first hundred years are the hardest.'

Good investors always try to keep money in their portfolios for as long as possible.

Table 2.1   **Value of £100 with compound interest over time**

Rate	5 years	10 years	20 years	30 years	40 years
2%	£110	£122	£149	£181	£221
4%	£122	£148	£219	£324	£480
6%	£134	£179	£321	£574	£1,029
8%	£147	£216	£466	£1,006	£2,172
10%	£161	£259	£673	£1,745	£4,526

Mental tick box 2: You should always be aware that any money that you withdraw, any income you receive from your investments and spend instead of reinvesting, pay out in tax, or in management fees, brokerage commissions, initial fees, etc., is going to cost you dearly in the long run because it will not benefit from compounding over time. Seemingly small differences make big differences in the long run.

Tip 3: It is not rocket science – there is one big decision

At its very simplest, there are only two things that you can do when investing your money. The first is to become a part owner in a company. That is what equity investing is. The rewards that you receive are the regular dividends the company pays in cash, and the hope that the strategy of the company is a strong one and this will be reflected in growing profits, and a rise in the price of its shares over time.

The second is to lend your money to someone, be it an individual (not usually recommended), a corporation or a government. In return, investors receive interest (usually referred to as a coupon) and their capital back at the maturity date of the loan. Loan instruments are often called 'fixed income' securities, because the interest is fixed at the outset, or, alternatively they are called bonds. In general, the higher the risk of not getting your money back and the longer the time you lend your money for, the higher the rate of interest you will expect to be paid by the borrower. When you next place a bank deposit, remember that you are lending your money to the bank. Perhaps in this context, Icesave's and Northern Rock's high deposit rates were telling a useful story – their strategies were risky.

The fortunes of a company are highly uncertain over time, which can result in wide movements in the price of a company's shares as the market absorbs the latest release of information and how this will impact on the company's future earnings. On the other hand, the cash flows of bonds are known, as is the maturity date. Bonds are generally less risky than equities, but with lower expected returns as a consequence. In a corporate collapse, equities owners lose their money before bondholders.

'£50 billion wiped off shares today!' (and other nonsense)

Investors the world over tend to be very influenced by what is happening in the equity markets today, rather than placing this in the context of longer-term history. The press help to whip up this emotional short-term focus, making investors feel unsettled. Headlines such as *'Unprecedented*

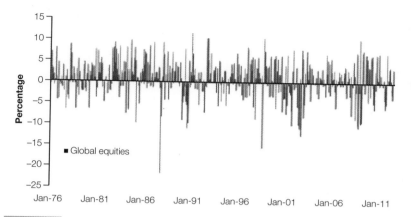

times in the market', *'It is different this time'* and *'£50 billion was wiped off shares today'* certainly do not help. But markets are always like this, that's how they work and will always work. Study Figure 2.2. What do you notice? Probably that today's *'unprecedented'* volatility of equity markets is not different to the past and therefore neither unprecedented, nor unexpected. That's what equity investing is like. Over the longer-term, the dividends paid and the growth in corporate earnings (the economic return of equity investing) will shine through the noise created in a dynamic, forward-looking market.

If you cannot stand the heat, get out of the kitchen

The simple message is that if this volatility scares you to death, then you need to balance the upside of being an owner, by lending some of your money to high-quality borrowers (such as the UK government or strong companies) for a relatively short period of time. Figure 2.3 clearly shows that this is a lower risk option, and therefore likely to deliver a lower return, over time.

The most critical decision that you will make in your entire investment programme is finding the balance between the two that is right for you. This balance is a consequence of your emotional capacity for taking risk, your financial capacity to suffer losses, and your actual financial need to take risk. This is an area that any good adviser spends considerable time discussing and evaluating with their clients.

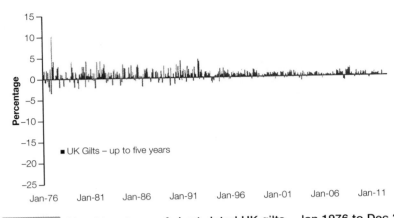

Figure 2.3 | **Monthly returns of short-dated UK gilts – Jan 1976 to Dec 2012**

Refining exactly what you should own, and to whom you should lend takes some insight, but is simply an important finessing of this initial portfolio decision by your adviser.

> **Mental tick box 3:** Make sure that you fully understand what the right balance between ownership and lending (equities and bonds) is that makes sense for you. Understand too, what your investment journey will look like.

Tip 4: Do not put all your eggs in one basket

The future is uncertain and nobody has a crystal ball that can accurately predict what it holds. This is never more true than in the investment markets. It doesn't take Einstein to work out that placing all of one's investment eggs in one, or just a few, baskets makes little sense. Diversification is simply good practice and should be employed widely in any investor's portfolio. Diversification takes place at several levels.

The first is that as an owner of a company the value of your investment is beholden to the specific fortunes of that company. The owners of BP, for example, found that out when it suffered the catastrophic oil spill in the Gulf of Mexico in 2011. Owning a broad number of oil companies would have smoothed returns. But the oil sector faces its own sector-specific risks so it makes sense to diversify by sector, by owning the UK equity market more broadly. The trouble is that the UK is less than 5% of global economic output (and less than 10% of market capitalisation i.e. the value of its stock market) and the companies listed on the market have biases towards sectors such as financial services and energy. It probably makes sense to have a material allocation to other developed and emerging markets too. Equities, while expected to deliver higher returns than bonds, deliver no certainty that they will do so, although the odds increase over time. Diversifying away from equities and holding other assets such as bonds makes sense.

As John Bogle, founder of Vanguard, a leading, global investment firm, says:

'Asset allocation [the mix of your investments] is not a panacea. It is a reasoned – if imperfect – approach to the inevitable uncertainty of the financial markets.'

Mental tick box 4: Is your portfolio well diversified at all levels? Remember that owning a number of funds does not necessarily mean your portfolio is diversified. Look through the fund structure at the underlying investments to see if you are diversified broadly enough.

Tip 5: Capturing the market return is a valid objective

Human nature drives many of us to try to win at whatever we do, or at the very least to aim to be above average. The majority of fund managers fall into this category, which in itself raises an obvious paradox – not everyone can be a better than average driver (or fund manager).

The problem that most investors suffer from is that they have not thought clearly about the definitions of 'winning' and 'average'. They usually regard winning as generating returns from their investments that beat the market, and often employ fund managers who try to do so. The personal finance pages of the Sunday papers bear testament to this fund/manager picking affliction. The supposition is that the market bogey is an easy one to beat, or at least it is easy to pick a fund manager who can. Where this falls down is that it is not easy! The assumption that markets do not work very well and that mispricing opportunities can be picked up profitably by the skilled (who themselves are easily identifiable), is incorrect.

The problem is that the market is a highly competitive place, and drives prices quickly to fair value. The empirical evidence, in a broad array of studies, across multiple markets, shows that beating the market, after costs, through skill and not luck is exceptionally rare. That would not matter if they could be identified, in advance, with a high degree of certainty. The ranking lists in the Sunday papers, based on short-term performance, are certainly not the solution.

The definition of being average needs some thought too. Viewing 'average' as being the return of the market pushes investors emotionally towards a 'try-to-beat-the-market' strategy. Yet all investors are the market and after the costs deducted after trading with each other, the average trading investor (i.e. an 'active' manager) will be below the market return by the average level of the costs incurred. The mathematics stipulates therefore that the market will beat the average active fund trying to beat the market. The empirical research supports this. As a consequence, capturing the market's 'average' return, as closely as possible, becomes a worthy goal.

> **Mental tick box 5:** Be sceptical of 'market-beating' performance promises and claims. Do not underestimate how hard it is to pick a market-beating fund today, for the years ahead. Remember that the market's 'average' return beats most professional managers and is a worthy goal.

Tip 6: If it looks too good to be true, it probably is

There are no dead certainties in investing apart from the fact that any product that appears to deliver great returns with low risks has a high chance of disappointment, usually in the form of a material reduction in the value of your investment.

There are two main types of products that fall into this category: a fraud wrapped up in a good story, and a bet wrapped up in a good story. Beware the snake-oil salesman. The recent Ponzi scheme fraud perpetrated by Madoff was a classic case of someone with the 'gift of the gab', a semblance of credibility, a complex strategy that few investors understood (apparently a split strike conversion strategy, whatever that is) and an air of exclusivity and secrecy.

The second is usually something that sounds so fantastic that you get sucked into the upside and blinded to the risks (e.g. the true cases of firms peddling freeholds to apartment blocks in Beirut at the height of the troubles there, or repossessed homes in Florida). Alternatively, it is an investment strategy that is akin to picking up pennies in front of a steam roller. Good until you stumble. Any risk-return asymmetry is illusory.

Mental tick box 6: If you get excited about a specific opportunity, stand back, take a deep breath and ask yourself where the catch is. Return and risk are always closely related. Ask yourself why, if the opportunity is so great, is someone trying to sell it to you? Surely they would keep it all to themselves. Remember that the investment world is full of great story-tellers.

Tip 7: Investment costs truly matter

In investing, costs matter because they are a drag on (a) achieving the market return, which is the goal of a 'passive' manager, or (b) beating the market, which is the goal of an active manager. From an investor's perspective, the outcome differential between the actual outcome and what could have been achieved at lower costs, may be substantial over long periods of time due to the negative effects of compounding these costs year on year. A pound of costs saved this year, is saved again next year, and the year after, and this is guaranteed. The extra money saved remains in your portfolio and compounds with time.

Recent research by Morningstar – a firm that makes a living providing star ratings for mutual funds – provides a useful insight: costs (as defined by a fund's total expense ratio or ongoing charges) are a better predictor of future performance than even their own 'star' rating system.

'If there's anything in the whole world of mutual funds that you can take to the bank, it is that expense ratios help you make a better decision. In every single time period and data point tested, low-cost funds beat high-cost funds.'

Passive funds are very cost conscious, while actively managed funds are less so, as they believe they will add skill-based returns in excess of the costs they incur. In fact, passive costs have fallen considerably in the past three years – you can now access a UK equity 'tracker' fund for a TER of around 0.2% to 0.3%. On the other hand active costs have been rising in the UK and across Europe. In fact 90% of all active funds reporting changes in fees (Lipper, 2012) in Europe (including the UK) reported upward movements.

Mental tick box 7: Never embark on an investment strategy without knowing exactly what cost drag you will be incurring. Always ask whether there are any other costs of any kind that you will suffer. Costs really matter. In investing, you get what you do not pay for, as Jack Bogle would say.

Tip 8: Manage yourself as tightly as your investments

Human beings are all afflicted with minds that battle between being reflective and being intuitive. Unfortunately, with an investor's hat on, the intuitive side of the brain wins on many occasions, resulting in panic and elation as markets fall and rise. If the intuitive mind dominates in making investment decisions, then investors risk damaging their wealth, usually by buying at the top in a state of euphoria and greed and selling out at the bottom in blind panic. The difference between the published return of a fund and the return an investor receives based on when they enter and exit a fund, illustrates whether investors are good or bad at timing markets. The evidence is that investors across the board are overwhelmingly bad at doing so, giving up somewhere between 1% and 3% a year (Phillips, 2011).

The key to success lies in a number of areas. The first is to own a portfolio that is well diversified across markets and asset classes. The second is a clear understanding of the journey and acceptance of the fact that it will be two steps forward and one step back and occasionally two steps back and one step forward. Finally it is about putting in place an investment process that mitigates some of the sources of leakage from the portfolio due to emotional, rather than rational, decision making. This includes regular rebalancing of portfolios back to their original mix on a regular basis, selling out of assets that have performed well and re-investing in assets that have done less well – a systematic, contrarian investment process.

> **Mental tick box 8:** Accept that you are prone to emotional pressures that drive you to do the wrong thing at the wrong time. Learn to be comfortable with the diversified portfolio that you own. Lean heavily on your adviser, when you need support at times of emotional, investment-related weakness.

Tip 9: There are no perfect answers

Let me tell you that there are no perfect answers to investing and this book does not seek to provide any. But there are better and worse solutions. It is simply about making some sensible choices around the risks that you want to take and those that you wish to avoid to make sure that you build yourself an investment portfolio that gives you what you believe is the highest chance of success to achieve your goals and should protect your wealth in poor markets.

We cannot see into the future, yet we have to make assumptions about a range of events; many of the measurements that we make and use in coming to decisions vary depending on the time periods we are looking at; and the process of forecasting is littered with the bodies of those who have tried. Add to this the fact that we are all emotionally different as investors and the science of investing quickly becomes the art of common sense.

What we do have on our side is the ability to learn from history, to read and evaluate the empirical research that exists, to maximise the use of all the things that we know to be proven and minimise uncertainties that we know have the power to divert us from achieving our goals.

> **Mental tick box 9**: Just remember that common sense and rational thinking are your friends and that emotions and spurious accuracy are your enemies.

Tip 10: Do not worry about what you cannot control

In life in general, too many people spend too much time worrying about things that they cannot control. Examples from the investing arena would include things like how the economy is performing, the collapse of the Eurozone, hyperinflation, deflation, how the markets are going to perform this year and over 30 years, how their fund manager is going to perform relative to the market. The essence of Smarter Investing is to control the things that we have the power to control, to help us to live through the very uncertain future (both good and bad) that being part of a dynamic, challenging capitalist global economy will throw at us.

The trick is to position your portfolio to try to weather a range of outcomes. As an example, we can weather the risk of the UK economy performing poorly in the future, by owning companies that are domiciled and operate outside of the UK, we can also mitigate the risk of poor equity performance generally by owning commercial property and offsetting this risk more materially by owning high quality, shorter-dated bonds. What we cannot do is look into our crystal balls to try to manage short-term risk by altering the shape of our portfolios by trying to control those uncontrollable scenarios – yet that is what many people believe.

> **Mental tick box 10:** If you can control an outcome, worry about it if you have to, but then control it (e.g. the uncertainty of an active manager's performance can be controlled by not taking manager risk by owning an index tracker fund). If you cannot control an outcome (the prospects for the UK economy) take strategic long-term decisions

▶

to mitigate a negative outcome – then accept that you have done all you can to manage this uncertainty and then stop worrying.

Remind yourself that your (and any adviser or fund manager's) crystal ball is very cloudy!

In summary: do these things exceptionally well

Smarter investors realise that investing is not about trying to be an economist, or knowing how to read a company balance sheet, or having the ability to pick and choose when to be in or out of markets, or what stocks to buy or sell. What they do know is that their mix of assets has a good chance of delivering them a successful outcome and will not lose them too much if things do not go as planned. They ruthlessly pursue options that increase the chances of success: they stick with their mix, avoid chasing returns, try to gather a market return rather than trying to beat the market, and eliminate costs in whatever form they take to keep their money in their pockets. They focus ruthlessly in pursuing these few things exceptionally well. That's all there is to it!

References

Homer, S. and Syllar, R. (2005) *A history of interest rates*. 4th edn. New York: Wiley.

Lipper (2012) Lipper data reported in Marriage, M. (9 April) 'Little take-up of "low-cost" active funds', FTfm p. 12.

Morningstar (2010) 'How Expenses and Stars Predict Success' (www.morningstar.com).

Phillips, D. (2011) 'Five Lessons from 25 years' (Business & Wealth Management Forum, Interviewer), 15 October (www.morningstar.com).

Schwed, Jr. F. (1995) *Where are the customers' yachts?* 3rd edn. New York: Wiley.

3

It only takes a minute

When I originally talked to friends and colleagues about my plan to write a book, the unanimous response was: 'Great, but please make it a pamphlet'. They are to a large extent right. The 80/20 rule applies in investing – you gain 80% of what you need to know from only 20% of the effort. To that end, the summary below provides a brief list of some of the guidelines commonly used in the investment industry when giving advice.

These tips can help you to become a better investor by way of a kind of investing by numbers, without a real understanding of why or the consequences of the actions you take. They may help you to avoid some of the pitfalls that lie in wait. Some use gross oversimplifications and assumptions about your personal circumstances, but, by and large, they will put you in the right ballpark.

I hope that the list at least makes you ask yourself whether this is how you are currently investing. But only by truly understanding what you are doing and why, will you be able to bear the emotional pressures that force many investors to destroy their wealth. I encourage you to use this section as an aide-memoire for later.

If you have not begun investing yet, then better late than never. The effect of time will be hugely beneficial to you through the power of compounding, i.e. the effect of interest-on-interest. The longer you give it the more powerful it becomes. Time also gives you a greater chance that the investments you choose will act as you hope they will rather than as the exceptions to the rule that inevitably occur over the shorter term, from time to time. Invest whenever you have the cash to do so, regularly if possible.

3.1 Twenty tips for smarter investing

First of all ...

1 *Have faith in capitalism*: It may not be the fairest system, but it has a pretty good track record of creating wealth. Believing that the rewards of capitalism will flow through to you, either as the owner of many companies via your equity investments, or as your role of lender via your bond holding, is a good start. Equities are higher risk than bonds and you should expect a higher rate of long-term return as a consequence. If you cannot or will not buy into this – shut the book now!

Choosing your mix of investments

2 *Investment period:* Decide how long you can invest each pool of money for, whether it be pension, nest egg or school fees. Getting this right is very important. A mismatch between your mix of investments and your investment period could result in either having to sell investments when markets are down to meet your obligations, or giving up potentially higher levels of future money by being too conservative if your investment period is actually longer than you say it is.

3 *The mix of investments (your asset allocation):* At the end of the day, it is the mix of investments that you own that drives your portfolio returns (along with keeping as much of this as you can by keeping other people's hands out of your pockets). As already discussed, finding the right balance between ownership (equities) and lending (bonds) is key. Messing around with this mix once it has been decided, by trying to pick market-beating investments or managers, will add little, for most. Choosing this mix carefully is the first step towards smarter investing. It is a function of your emotional ability to suffer losses, your financial capacity to suffer losses, and the need you have to take risk to achieve the returns you need to fulfil your financial goals.

4 *Rules of thumb for defining your mix:* A couple of simple rules provide a sensible starting point for deciding the appropriate mix between equities and bonds, the building blocks of your portfolio. Both provide similar outcomes. Think about them carefully.

Rule 1: Own 4% in equities for each year until you need the money as defined by your investment period above and own bonds for the rest.

Rule 2: If this money represents general funds to support your future lifestyle, own your age in bonds and the rest in equities. Own more in equities if you are more aggressive and able to weather market falls, or more in bonds if you want more certainty of your outcome.

These mixes are based on the probabilities that equities and bonds will perform something like they have over the long run. You could, however, be one of the unlucky investing generations for whom markets stink; it is a possibility. Only you can decide whether you can tolerate such an outcome. If not, you may need to be less aggressive (by owning more bonds), save more, invest longer or scale down your expectations.

5 ***Be conservative in your estimates of future returns:*** It is far better to be conservative about the returns your portfolio will generate than to be overly optimistic. If you pay in more and expect less, most surprises will be on the upside – a far more pleasant place to be than the flip side. Going forwards, if bonds deliver a return higher than inflation, and equities deliver a return of more than 4–5% above inflation, count yourself lucky.

Practical investing

6 ***Diversify using funds or equivalent baskets of investments:*** Own your bonds and equities through some sort of pooled fund vehicle, such as an OEIC (open ended investment company) in the UK. This allows you to own a large number of securities to spread the risk of any one security being a duffer and damaging the value of your investments.

7 ***Do not try to beat the market, be the market:*** Buy index funds, known as tracker funds in the UK, that seek to track the market as closely as possible, or similar products such as exchange traded funds, usually referred to as ETFs. Do not try to move in and out of different building blocks just because the story for one sounds bad and for another good. Accept that trying to beat the market is a mug's game for most investors.

8 ***Own the broad (total) equity market:*** Your equity fund should reflect the broad base of companies that make up the market as a whole and not one or a few sectors of it. In the UK this would be the FTSE All-Share index, which covers the whole market. In the USA this may be an index such as the Wilshire 5000. For a more global approach own a globally diversified fund, based on an index like the

MSCI World Index. Look for words like *total market* or *broad market* when selecting products.

9   ***Own high-quality domestic bonds:*** Your bond investments should be high quality. Look for the words 'investment grade'. If you see the words 'high yield', 'high income', 'extra income', 'sub-investment grade' or 'junk' avoid them. The safest bonds are issued by the government and are called gilts in the UK and treasuries in the USA. Corporate bonds should be investment-grade only and generally rated AA or above on average. If the threat of inflation worries you, allocate some of your bond holding to index-linked (inflation proof) gilts issued by the government. Own bond funds that have a shorter maturity (the time until the bonds are repaid) as they are less volatile and balance the high volatility associated with equities.

10 ***Reduce costs at all times:*** As costs, which include initial fees, management fees and brokerage charges, destroy your wealth, always buy cheaper product equivalents. Never buy any product until you are sure of the stated and hidden costs. Never pay an initial fee for investments. Understand what a *total expense ratio* or *ongoing charge* is and always check what it is for each investment that you consider owning. Today, you can own a broadly diversified global equity fund for less than 0.5%.

11 ***Do not buy products you do not understand:*** If products are confusing or opaque, which includes most insurance-wrapped products such as with-profits endowments, and guaranteed or principal-protected products, avoid them. If you cannot understand it, do not invest in it. If it looks too good to be true – it is – it is just that you have not identified where the catch is.

12 ***Beat the taxman – legally of course:*** Make use of all legal tax breaks. In the UK, like many other countries, there are breaks on contributions you make to your pension, tax-free investment wrappers, such as ISAs and capital gains tax allowances. Make sure you are using these to the best effect and get independent advice if you need to. However, make your investment decisions first and then seek to maximise the tax advantages.

On investing for retirement

13 ***How much to contribute:*** You need to save regularly to build a suitable pot and it may surprise you just how much this is for a half-decent retirement. Start early.

Rule 1: Save £1 in £6 for retirement: If you are saving for your retirement invest 15% to 20% of your gross salary every year of your working life. If you do not, be prepared to have a quiet retirement. You need to balance the pleasurable and gratifying feeling of spending today with what feels like the nebulous and remote comforts of investing for tomorrow. In effect, you are buying all of your future fun today, with a little help from the markets and compounding to get you there.

Rule 2: Your age less twenty-five: If you are starting later in life then your contributions, as a percentage of your gross salary, should be equivalent to your age less twenty-five years, for an income in retirement that is half to two-thirds of your final salary – a scary thought for many! Alternatively, invest half your age as a percentage of your gross salary in your retirement savings pot.

These all come out to a similar level of contributions. The resounding message is the same: saving fifty quid here or there is not going to do it for you; retirement investing needs to be a systematic and financially significant process.

14 **Lifecycle investing:** As you approach retirement make sure that you take the investment mix (point 3) into consideration. If you really want to protect your wealth from equity market falls and inflation as you approach retirement, own *index-linked bonds* and hold them to maturity, this being the date you need the money as cash, which may be when you retire or when you buy an *annuity*. Alternatively hold it in cash (although this has bank risk and inflation risk).

15 **Taking an income from your portfolio:** If you need to take an income from your portfolio and you do not want to run out of money before you die, withdraw a maximum of 4% per year from your portfolio. A portfolio that is half bonds and half equities over the long term has a good chance of returning inflation plus 3% to 4%. So, withdrawing 4% should, if you are lucky, allow you to maintain the purchasing power of your capital and thus your income. Be sensible; if you have a sustained run of bad markets you may need to rein in your spending. To up your chances, only withdraw 3%.

Ongoing maintenance

16 **Maintain the mix:** Rebalance the proportion of equities and bonds back to your plan (points 3 and 4, above) if they are out of line by more than a tenth of the value of your total portfolio. If you are a regular investor you could redirect new cash flow to the

underweight investment to rebalance the portfolio. Check that the bond and equity investments have performed in line with the broad markets they reflect. If they have not, find out why. If the answer is unsatisfactory, then replace them with a better option.

Controlling your emotions

17 **Stick with your mix through thick and thin and avoid chasing returns:** One of the greatest risks to good investing is you. Hold tight when markets get bumpy, as they inevitably will. Remember buying high and selling low is the worst, but most popular, investment strategy. Never chase what seems like better performance with another type of investment or manager. Investors tend to be prone to emotional excesses that cloud their judgement both as markets go up and as they inevitably come down. Staying calm and staying the course is easier said than done, but is critical.

18 **Do not look at your portfolio too often:** Try to avoid looking at the value of your investments more than once a year. Any more than that and you will begin to get short-termist and jumpy about irrelevant short-term market movements.

19 **Avoid the noise:** Do not be taken in by articles that begin 'Is now the right time to be investing in …?' Ignore most of what you hear and read about the state of the markets, as most of it is nonsense and fluff – interesting but unimportant. Much of it is telling you to be happy or distraught at the wrong time. Generally it makes you covet investment products that have already gone up in price: a bizarre yet real emotion. Also, remember that if a product or idea looks too good to be true, it is too good to be true. If you get offered any sort of product that provides high returns for no risk or low risk to your capital, then look very carefully and reject it. Free lunches like this just do not exist in investing.

And finally

20 **Pay for truly independent advice if you need it:** If any of this confuses you, get independent advice. Employ a fee-based financial planner who will manage your wealth on an ongoing basis over time and help you through some of the tough decisions that you face, both today and in the years ahead.

Since 1 January 2013 all advisers now have to agree with you the full and transparent fees that they will charge you. They are no longer allowed to receive product-driven fees and commissions as they used to be, without you knowing or without them being part of the fees that you agree with the adviser upfront. Anything above 1% per year on your invested assets is getting costly. Most likely you will also need to pay for the technology platform through which your assets are administered. This will add another 0.2% to 0.5% to your costs.

It may seem expensive but in the long run good advice will pay for itself many times over. Do not give up your future lifestyle for the cost of good advice upfront. Question it if it is markedly different from the points above. As a starting point, go to the Institute of Financial Planning's website, www.financialplanning.org.uk, and choose a fee-based Chartered Financial Planner or Accredited firm to meet and discuss your issues.

Ask questions of your adviser that relate to your chances of meeting your goals such as: 'What are the chances of me not running out of money before I die if I withdraw £50,000 a year from my portfolio?' If they cannot give you a satisfactory answer, go elsewhere.

If you need more meat on these bones, then read on – after all, that is why you bought the book.

2

Smarter thinking

Perhaps one of the biggest mistakes that investors make is focusing on 'doing' rather than 'thinking' about investing or their own behaviour in relation to it. Before we talk about *what* you should invest in, it is critical that you formulate some simple rules about *how* you should invest. To that end, the following two chapters provide an insight so you can come up with some guiding principles to help you make decisions and curb your emotions on your investing journey.

Chapter 4: A smarter investment philosophy

Defining and believing in a set of investing rules lies at the heart of successful investing. Although you cannot control how the markets will perform during your investment lifetime, you can stop throwing money away needlessly. Much of the industry noise, either directly or indirectly, encourages you to do just that. Having some clear guidelines through which to filter the nonsense from the valuable is the key. By the end of this chapter you will have formed a clear set of rules to live your investment life by.

Chapter 5: Smarter investment behaviour

Without doubt, one of the hardest aspects of investing is having the courage to stick with an investment plan when times get tough, as they undoubtedly will from time to time. Failing to curb your emotions will be costly – one of the few things you can truly guarantee as an investor. This chapter helps to identify some of the pitfalls that you face. Understanding them is the first step to avoiding them. Take a long, hard, look at yourself.

4

A smarter investment philosophy

Too often, investors fail to spend enough time trying to sort out what will work and what will not work, but instead dive into the markets and end up being thrown around, chasing returns and damaging their wealth. To avoid being one of them, you need to determine a set of guiding rules and beliefs that will provide the basis for making astute investment decisions. These rules form your investment philosophy. This will become the central perspective from which you evaluate all investment options and ideas, providing a filter to eliminate the industry noise and help focus on what is truly important. By the end of this chapter you should have a pretty good idea of what it should be. This book can guide you, but at the end of the day you need to convince yourself, based on the evidence.

4.1 Investing in a philosophy-free zone

Many people go about their investing in a philosophy-free manner, with no firm guiding beliefs about what they should, and perhaps more importantly, should not be doing. Without a sound investment philosophy you risk making some simple, fundamental mistakes. Common symptoms of philosophy-free investing include:

- Not having thought clearly about what you really want to achieve with your money.
- Not having set up a long-term plan for the mix of investments that you will use. Investing is a journey, which needs to be planned.
- Chasing returns and entering a cycle of buying high and selling low, which is a certain recipe for wealth destruction, based on short-term market and emotional pressures.
- Buying high-cost products in the vain hope of professionals beating

the market and incurring switching costs by moving funds, when disappointed by the outcome. In my experience, investors rarely stick with a fund that has done poorly for more than 2–3 years.

■ Believing in your ability to pick an outstanding manager. For some reason many investors believe that they have the skills to select one of the very few managers who will outperform the markets consistently over the years by looking at an advertisement.

■ Choosing a manager who has a low probability of beating the market in the long term and a high probability of losing out to an index fund tracking the market, because the promised upside opportunity looks and feels better.

I am sure that you have never done any of these things! (But most likely you will have done.) Just draw a line under where you are and start from here.

A true, yet almost unbelievable, example

The noughties (2000–2009) are sometimes referred to as the 'lost decade' for US investors – as their home stock market ended the decade more or less where it started. But the best performing US mutual fund over the ten years to the end of 2009 (The CGM Focus Fund) delivered a return of 18% per annum – a quite remarkable outcome – $1,000 dollars invested at the start of the period would have risen to over $5,000. Yet the average investor received a return of minus (yes, minus) 11% a year (Laise, 2009). Truly.

This is a prime example of the lack of an investment philosophy in action: in 2007 this commodity-based fund returned 80% and, as a result, in 2008 investors poured a staggering $2.6 billion into the fund. Commodity markets reversed and the fund fell by almost 50% and investors withdrew around $750 million of the money that remained. Buy high – sell low!

4.2 The foundations of your philosophy

The time has come to build yourself a smart philosophy that gives you the highest chance of achieving your investment goals. This is not a difficult process. It is a matter of looking at the evidence and weighing up where you have the greatest probability of success and acting accordingly. Your resulting investment philosophy is the set of rules that you can use to guide you through the decisions you face.

Establishing your philosophical mindset

The best place to start as you begin to establish your philosophy is with the central message in Charles D. Ellis's superb book *Winning the Loser's Game* (Ellis, 2002) as it provides the mindset that you will need to adopt in all the decisions that you face through your investing lifetime: that the ultimate outcome of investing is determined by who can lose the fewest points, not win them. It is as simple as that!

I cannot stress how important and central this subtle statement is to your future wealth and financial security. When you look at investment success in this light, it becomes a lot easier to devise a set of rules that will give you a high chance of success – actions that revolve around minimising the chances of eroding the returns that your portfolio mix as a whole can generate for you. If you persist with the view that success comes with winning points by beating the market you are on a very complex, angst ridden road to likely failure, as you will see. In the pages ahead, you will be able to review for yourself the evidence that will hopefully make you believe in this simple statement as well.

Throughout this book we will ruthlessly apply this philosophy. First, though, we need to see why it is this philosophy, alone, that forms the basis of smarter investing.

Your starting point is your long-term mix of assets

As an investor, the choices include assets such as cash, bonds, equities, property, hedge funds, gold, art, commodities and stamps, each of which has its own return characteristics and risks. Depending upon what you are trying to achieve with your money, and the time frame you can invest for, you can put together a sensible mix of investment building blocks that will provide you with a reasonable probability of achieving your goals.

The mix that you choose will determine the level of potential returns of your investment programme, the chances that an acceptable outcome will be achieved, such as having enough income in your retirement, and how bumpy the investment road that you take is likely to be. Getting this mix right is critical.

The chosen mix is often referred to as your long-term *investment policy* or *strategic asset allocation*. All sophisticated investors have investment policy statements that set out exactly what this long-term strategy is – you need to do the same. We will not try to answer what this mix is for you until we reach Part 3 of the book, where we will explore the process you need to go through to decide what it is in some depth. Let us explore instead the fundamental philosophical questions that all investors face.

Should you try to beat the returns from your mix?

The central tenet that will underlie the investment philosophy is whether or not you believe that you have a *reasonably high chance* of beating the returns that your long-term investment policy portfolio will generate (simply through buying and then holding it), by making investment decisions during your investment lifetime that move your portfolio away from this long-term mix of investments, asset classes and securities.

Ultimately you face a choice: either try to identify an active manager who, through either personal skill or a robust investment process, adds returns relative to the market, which in the long term could be highly beneficial, or simply make sure that you capture the bulk of the market returns on offer. It comes down to your chances of success. Smart investors always make decisions that maximise their chances of being successful. Make up your own mind where you stand by the end of this chapter. Three potential ways exist to beat your investment policy mix.

1 Improving returns by moving between asset classes

The biggest decision you face and the one that is most likely to govern the success of your investment programme is whether you always keep your investment policy mix constant or whether you move money around to take advantage of investments that are performing, or appear likely to perform, well and sell those that are performing or are anticipated to perform poorly.

Moving your mix around to try to beat the returns from a static mix is called *tactical asset allocation, investment strategy*, or *market timing*. Proponents of this approach are *market-timers*. Seeking to add returns over and above those expected from your long-term investment policy from market timing, is often referred to as being a *top-down approach*. Such a strategy 'looks down' on the portfolio and moves chunks of it around either at the asset class level, for example between bonds and equities, between countries or at the sector level by preferring, say, the oil sector of the economy over the financial sector. The jargon is worth remembering, as it is the common language of managers and advisers. Much of what you read in the papers is about market timing decisions such as: 'Should you be investing in Japan (or read: oil, timber, art, wine, etc.) at this time?'

2 Improving returns by picking better securities

Irrespective of your answer to market timing, you also need to decide whether or not you believe if it is possible consistently to pick (or ignore) individual stocks or bonds, generically referred to as securities, that will beat those that make up the market as a whole. This process is known as *stock selection* for equities, or *security selection* in generic terms. Proponents of this approach are referred to as *stock-pickers*. Because it focuses on the smallest element of decision-making, stock-picking is referred to as a *bottom-up approach*. TV pundits, stock-tip columns and investment magazines and stockbrokers are the conduits of stock-picking noise.

3 Improving returns by picking market-beating managers

You may feel that you cannot achieve the first two options above yourself, as you have neither the expertise nor the time to do so, but you may feel that you have a good chance of selecting a manager who does, or finding an adviser who can find one that can. It is tempting to be drawn into the comfort of passing the responsibility over to the professionals, who after all should be best placed to beat the market, as they spend their lives working with valuation models, work with bright colleagues, meet and analyse

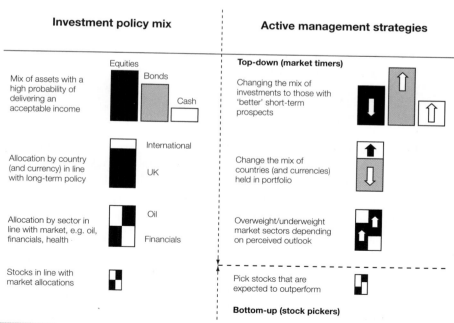

Figure 4.1 **Ways to try to beat a long-term buy-and-hold strategy**

companies, and have good access to information. Surely if anyone can beat the markets, they can?

Figure 4.1 illustrates how active managers attempt to beat the returns from a long-term investment policy mix of investments.

The route you choose is a question of probabilities

Managers who believe that they can beat your investment policy mix returns by market timing and security selection are known as *active managers*. The funds they manage are known as *actively managed* funds.

Investors who do not believe that they can improve upon investment policy returns through market timing or security selection are referred to as *passive* or *index investors*. Using the word passive is a misnomer, at least when it comes to managing funds that try to replicate, rather than beat, markets, i.e. index-tracker funds, as you will see later.

The difference between an active and a passive approach is actually about the probability of success, not skill, intelligence or hard work of those involved. Passive managers believe that the odds of success, through capturing as much of each market's available gain as possible, for your given mix, and thus losing the fewest points, lie in their favour. Active managers, on the other hand, believe that they can win points because they have superior insight and the ability to use information better than others in the market, and their process and people will allow this superiority to be sustained into the future. As you will see shortly, the probability of being successful is higher through avoiding losing points than trying to win them.

The attraction of active management is similar to that of smoking. It lies in a hope of beating the odds and enjoying a lifetime of rewards, despite that fact that the probabilities of financial and physical ill-health are high in both cases, in aggregate. As human beings, we seem to have an innate sense that we will escape the probabilities and be the lucky winners. After all, many people gamble on the lottery, despite the odds that a thirty-five-year-old man buying a lottery ticket on a Monday has a greater chance of dying than winning the jackpot!

For some reason, we hate to be considered average. We seem to aspire to want to be winners, which is fine if it is winning an egg and spoon race, but dangerous in the less-than-zero-sum game that we play as investors. In investing, there is nothing wrong with being average if by average you mean achieving the market return for your buy-and-hold portfolio, as you will see.

The problem with many investors is that they are attracted to active management because they have not thought through the issues clearly, and have not seen or read the evidence that exists that helps them to decide which course of action is likely to be best for their investing health. Others see the evidence, which is now widely available, but still cannot stop themselves from being attracted to trying to beat the markets. This is compounded by our propensity erroneously to value short-term success as a good proxy for long-term success, abrogate investing responsibility to others, and to be influenced by the apparent absolute (as opposed to relative) levels of expertise that reside in investment firms. Fortunately, you have the opportunity to see the evidence and weigh up the probabilities yourself.

Before we begin the process of establishing which approach has the greatest chance of success, you need to be aware of the zero-sum game that actively trading investments represents in aggregate.

Understanding the zero-sum game

As we unravel the chances of success from adopting either a passive or an active approach to your investing, you need to make sure that you understand the game that is being played by active investors in aggregate who are trading securities between each other. It is a zero-sum game, assuming that we ignore for the moment the significant issue of costs, where one investor's gain is another investor's loss. For every winning position, there has to be a corresponding losing position, relative to the market. Factoring in the costs of investing, it becomes a significantly less-than-zero-sum game.

If you buy a share at a certain price believing it will rise faster than the market, and it does, you win and the person who sold it to you loses – you cannot both be right. Take a look at the simple market in Table 4.1, which consists of just two investors, me and you, and two shares, ABC plc and XYZ plc. As you can see, the combined returns over one year of our two-stock market must be the market return. You win and I lose relative to the market.

The same applies for all investments. So, if you sell equities and buy bonds, again it has to be a zero-sum game before costs. Only one of the seller or buyer of the bonds can win in the short term. In order to believe that you can be one of the few who can consistently win over time at someone else's expense, you have to believe the following:

■ You are superior to the average investor, and are able to access and interpret information in a way that others cannot, in order to make market-beating decisions.

Table 4.1   **We can't both be winners**

	My portfolio	Your portfolio
Start of year	ABC plc (1 share)	XYZ plc (1 share)
Price	£100 per share	£100 per share
Trade	I buy XYZ plc from you for £100	You buy ABC plc from me for £100
Performance during year	XYZ plc up 10%	ABC plc up 20%
Portfolio value at end of year	£110 = **10%** (absolute)	£120 = **20%** (absolute)
Market performance	Total market value now £230 instead of £200 = **15%**	
Relative to market	Loser with −**5%**	Winner with +**5%**

- There are enough consistently dumb investors to be the losers funding your wins.

It should therefore come as no surprise that the investment management industry has more than its fair share of overly confident and prima donna fund managers throwing tantrums, computers and phones around the trading desk (all of which I have seen). To believe that they have the key to above-average wealth generation is a powerful drug, particularly given the talent of their peers in competitor firms. Not to believe it means that your professional worth is meaningless.

Who are the losers that make winning possible?

That is a good question, given that in the UK professional active investment managers make up the majority of all investors by assets, the losers by definition, are likely to include a fair number of this group. Perhaps it is the small minority of individual investors, who are providing the huge market beating opportunities for all the professionals. Do not bank on it.

A study of 60,000 individual investors in the USA trading their own brokerage accounts, a group that is at most risk of being persistent zero-sum-game losers, found that the average gross return, i.e. returns before costs, was more or less in line with the market return (Barber and Odean, 1998). So, as a group, these individuals are not being fleeced by the institutional managers, who you would expect to be the consistent winners. The German market research referenced earlier suggests that DIY investors may be the patsies to some extent.

4.3 The path to establishing your philosophy

Whether active management can beat the markets with a reasonably high chance of success over the long term, and is thus a philosophy worth adopting, depends on resolving three questions:

■ Can active managers beat the markets after costs?

■ If so, do some managers beat the markets consistently over time based on skill rather than luck?

■ Third, do you have a reasonable chance of identifying them in advance?

Remember that we are not trying to answer these questions with specific examples where a forecast has been right, or a particular manager who has performed well over the past few years. What you need to decide for yourself is whether you can be *reasonably confident* that there is a *high chance* that you can identify and exploit anomalies consistently over time, or find a manager who can. If you believe that this is a tough thing to achieve, then you need to adopt a 'lose the least number of points' strategy. As simple as that! The rest of this chapter deals with answering these three questions, the outcome of which will drive your core beliefs and the rules by which you will manage your money.

4.4 Can active managers win?

Obviously the short answer is 'yes'. Inevitably, as active managers manage portfolios of stocks that are different to the market, they will deliver returns different to the market, both on the up and downside. The more interesting question is really 'Can active managers deliver persistent skill-based performance that can be identified with a reasonable degree of certainty, in advance of when it is needed (rather than with hindsight)?' To answer this question, we need to review some of the evidence on the active management industry's success or otherwise. First, though, consider the following logical argument that immediately puts the active manager's case on the back foot, with the probabilities favouring a passive (index) approach.

Passive investors will beat the majority of active investors

As we have discovered in the zero-sum game above, all investors are the market. So, the average investor will generate the market return before fees, transaction costs and taxes. In the real world these costs cannot be avoided so the average active investor must inevitably be below the market by the amount of these costs. If index funds have lower costs than the average active investor, which is most often the case, then they will beat the average active manager by the difference between these costs. Index funds will thus beat the majority of active funds over the long run. That is simple mathematics, not supposition. As Professor William Sharpe (1991), a Nobel Prize winning stock market economist, puts it:

'The laws of arithmetic have been suspended for the convenience of those who pursue their careers as active managers.'

Opportunities abound for the active manager

Active managers have a wide range of opportunities to deliver above-market returns: many asset classes to switch between; the choice of domestic and non-domestic markets and currencies; and a very wide number of securities to pick from. On the face of it, the scope is there for them to outperform. The question is whether they can do so after costs, with a high chance of success from an individual investor's perspective.

The allure of market timing as a route to active returns is easily apparent. Let us look at a simple scenario. In Figure 4.2, the annual return for UK cash, bonds and equities over the past twenty years or so are ranked from highest to lowest. The first thing you see is that, over this short period, the rankings of each jump all over the place. Surely it cannot be that difficult to work out which investments are likely to do well and which are likely to do badly? Surely a paid professional manager with their access to market information, economists, analysts, MBAs, etc., should be able to work it out?

To a believer in market timing, this is great news. Their superior skills and insight should provide them with the opportunity to move into and out of these investments to the benefit of their clients. To be able to do so successfully implies success in forecasting future asset prices.

As a simple exercise, let us look at what the consequences are of being right and being wrong. Take two market timers, Ms Lucky and Mr Unlucky, who both have £100,000 to invest at the start of 1990. The former calls the market right, investing all of her funds in cash in 1990. On New's Year's Eve 1990 she decides to move all of her money into equities and she continues to get these market calls right, through to the end of 2012, receiving the full returns of the top line. Mr Unlucky on the other hand chooses the loser's line each time. Ms Lucky would have ended up with over £1.3 million and

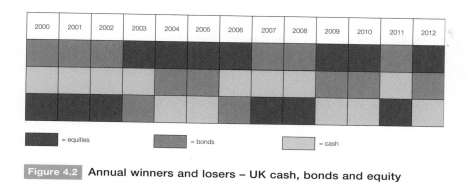

| 2000 | 2001 | 2002 | 2003 | 2004 | 2005 | 2006 | 2007 | 2008 | 2009 | 2010 | 2011 | 2012 |

■ = equities   ■ = bonds   ■ = cash

Figure 4.2 **Annual winners and losers – UK cash, bonds and equity returns**

Mr Unlucky would have lost money and ended up with less than £40,000 of his original £100,000 when the effects of inflation are factored in.

So, the rewards are there if you can get it right and the trade-off looks good. Can you get it right though? It seems so tempting to give it a go but research points strongly towards a conclusion that even most professionals struggle to do so. If you had simply held 50% equities and 50% bonds (and rebalanced your portfolio back to this mix at the start of each year) you would have built your £100,000 to over £270,000.

No costs have been deducted in this simple example, but the point is made. Time markets at your peril.

Winning points from market timing is very tricky

In the next few pages you should be acting like a jury and asking yourself whether beyond reasonable doubt, active management can beat the markets consistently. If you believe it can, then active management is for you, and good luck to you. If there is a level of reasonable doubt in your mind then you need to drop any notion of a points-winning philosophy and adopt a lose-the-fewest points philosophy. Here are some of the hurdles that you face:

Forecasting is notoriously difficult to get right, consistently

As economic forecasts are the basis for making forecasts about markets and securities, an active investor needs to be able to make consistently above-average forecasts to win. Wide scepticism by many acknowledged investors, backed up by empirical evidence, tells us this is so. Here are a couple of sceptical quotes about economists and forecasting to set the tone. The first I have always loved, its source unknown to me:

'An economist is an expert who will know tomorrow why the things he predicted yesterday didn't happen today.'

The second is attributed to Ray Marshall (LeBaron et al., 1999), a former US labour secretary, and is an example of the healthy scepticism that we all would do well to adopt.

'When it comes to forecasting, there are only two kinds of economist, those who don't know, and those who don't know they don't know.'

Your forecasting average needs to be Bradmanesque

A study in the USA (Sharpe, 1975) using data from 1929 to 1972 (and others since) estimated that if you employed a market-timing approach, moving your money between equities and short-term bonds, you needed to call the up markets and down markets over 70% right throughout this period just to make the same return as buying and holding equities. That's a steep hurdle to set. In addition, the study calculated that even if an investor managed to avoid all declining markets and to get back into half of the rising markets, they still would not have beaten the return of the market. In reality the hurdle is higher because no tax or transaction costs were included in these numbers.

Each decision you make actually requires two decisions

As the research above indicates, you need to be smart enough to make the call when to get out of the markets and to make the call when to get back in. If you have even a 50% chance of getting one decision right, you only have a 25% chance of getting two consecutive decisions right and so on. You need to be pretty consistently good at forecasting to be successful.

You need to act very quickly to win

To make matters tougher, many investors underestimate the rapidity and magnitude of the movements that markets make. Look at Table 4.2, which uses the FTSE All-Share Index as a source of data. It demonstrates that if you miss the best fifteen days, in over twenty-six years of trading, you miss out on over 50% of returns (9.6% if you hold the market, but only 6.1% if you miss these days). Miss the best twenty-five days, which is still less than 1% of days, and you lose out on over 70% of all the returns of the market (4.4%), which is less than the return on cash during this period (6.5% p.a.). In this simple analysis, costs and taxes are ignored, which would only make the picture worse. As you can see, not only do you have to make two

| Table 4.2 | Missing just a fraction of good days can be very costly |

	Value of £100	Annualised return %
Invested at all times	£1,089	9.6%
Top 15 days missed	£462	6.1%
Top 25 days missed	£308	4.4%

Source: FTSE International Limited ("FTSE") © FTSE 2013, "FTSE®" is a trade mark of the London Stock Exchange Group companies and is used by FTSE International Limited under licence. All rights in the FTSE indices and/or FTSE ratings vest in FTSE and/or its licensors. Neither FTSE nor its licensors accept ant liability for any errors or omissions in the FTSE indices and/or FTSE ratings or underlying data. No further distribution of FTSE Data is permitted without FTSE's express written consent.

decisions as to when to move out of the market and back again, but also the exact timing of each move is critical.

Being right is quite a challenge. Being wrong can be very costly. The odds of success are beginning to stack up against you.

Alternatively, you need to be lucky

Napoleon's response of 'send me lucky generals' when asked what type of generals he needed to turn things round against the English, could apply to the type of market-beating strategy to adopt when choosing active fund managers.

In the past decade or so, particularly with the rapid expansion of the financial media, the cult of the star investment manager has grown. In fact it probably takes less than three years of market, or peer-beating performance and some good public relations to make a star manager and be pushed into the limelight as the new 'guru'. Yet how can we tell whether this performance is down to skill or judgement?

A lucky run is probably what you get more often than not when you employ an active manager on just a good short-term track record. Imagine that there are 300 funds investing in the UK equity market and each manager at the start of each of the past three years had made a decision to allocate a portion of the fund into cash or not – a market-timing decision. Just by flipping a coin you would expect around forty of them to get the correct answer (300 × 50% × 50% × 50%). That's more than 10% right. Marketing departments can now use these 'exceptional' results to push product and support the case for active management. Sure, some may be geniuses but most will just be lucky over a short period. The problem is can you tell which is which?

The hurdles faced by active managers are significant

To be a successful active manager, you need to be able to forecast well, get a high percentage of your forecasts right, get your timing spot on as markets move so rapidly and with such great magnitude, or just be one of the lucky few. The hurdles to success are high, but that does not matter if you or managers out there have the ability to overcome these hurdles consistently and you can identify who they are in advance. So, do they exist and can that be done? Just how difficult this is, is revealed by a recent piece of research (Cuthbertson et al., 2006) that shows that only around 1.5 % of UK equity funds demonstrate positive market timing ability. Despite the claims made by the active management industry, the evidence simply does not support their wishful thinking.

This is nicely summed up in the comments made by John Bogle (2003), one of the patriarchs of losing-the-fewest points investing. He founded Vanguard, one of the USA's largest managers, which focuses on index investing to replicate the market.

'A lifetime of experience in this business makes me profoundly sceptical of market timing. I don't know anyone who can do it successfully, nor any one who has done so in the past. Heck, I don't even know anyone who knows anyone who has timed the market with consistent, successful, replicable results.'

Winning points through security selection is no easier

Quite a few active managers would happily go along with the proposition that trying to time markets is difficult, and put little effort into trying. They do, though, believe that they can beat markets by picking stocks. They are, however, up against a concept known as market efficiency. The concept is a simple one. It suggests that all known relevant information is incorporated in the current price of a security. Collectively, all the individual shares aggregate to form the market, which as a consequence is efficiently priced. Intuitively, the more analysts, journalists, brokers and lenders dig around companies, the more likely it is that all information is known about them. Some research estimates that new information is fully priced within sixty minutes (Chordia et al., 2003). As such, in an efficient market it is hard to find securities that are anomalously priced. The price of the security will only move again on any news that is unanticipated. Price movements are therefore random in their nature.

You would, in this case, not expect to achieve continuing superior profits from investment decisions that you make because any short-term market-beating investment ideas, reflecting the mispricing of assets, would be quickly spotted by all the other smart professionals and the misalignment between price and value would disappear. If a market is efficient, you would conclude that it should be difficult to beat it, particularly after all costs are taken into account. Rex Sinquefield, an economist and proponent of index investing, provides his own humorous slant on the debate:

'So who still believes that markets don't work? Apparently it is only the North Koreans, the Cubans and the active managers.'

This theory is known as the Efficient Market Hypothesis or EMH and is eloquently described in the seminal text *A Random Walk Down Wall Street* by Burton G. Malkiel, which I would recommend you to read if you want to pursue this topic further.

Academics and professional investors argue endlessly about the degree to which markets are efficient. Some mine data for anomalies, which others seek to disprove. They are fortunate to have the luxury of time to do so. Burton Malkiel's overall conclusion, as you will see from active manager returns illustrated later, is hard to disagree with (Malkiel, 2000).

'I remain sceptical that markets are systematically irrational and that knowledge of such irrationalities can lead to profitable trading strategies. Indeed, the more potentially profitable a discoverable pattern is, the less likely it is to survive. This is the logical reason one should be cautious not to overemphasize the apparent departures from efficiency.'

For the rest of us, we do not have to prove whether markets are efficient or not. What we should be interested in is whether, after all the costs incurred in investing are accounted for, any inefficiencies that exist can be exploited by active managers to generate market-beating returns consistently over time. To draw a conclusion we need to look at the track record of active managers as a collective group, to see if they do. We study the evidence a little later. Signs of efficiency include a narrow dispersion of longer-term returns between the top and bottom managers, as no one has a truly sustainable advantage or disadvantage. On this basis, the fixed income markets are reasonably efficient, as are equity markets such as the USA and the UK.

Active managers invariably claim that their market-beating approach will work better in less-efficient markets, such as small company stocks or small overseas equity markets, as they theoretically have the ability to exploit these inefficiencies. However, always remember that even in markets where information is deemed to be less than perfect, if the anomalies cannot be exploited to exceed the transaction costs involved with investing in them, then active management for you or me is worthless. Transaction costs are significantly higher in smaller, less efficient, markets, negating much of the benefit. Remember that they are still playing in a zero-sum game, but with higher costs.

What does the research tell us?

The reality is that research suggests that few investors outperform the market portfolio consistently over time, especially after transaction costs and taxes are taken into account. The magnitude and consistency of this research, from a wide number of angles, supports this emphatically. Let us look at the case more closely.

Even major investors have failed the active test

Some of the world's most renowned market timers have not been able to keep up their good track records. The credit crisis provides a good example in John Paulson, the founder of Paulson & Co, a hedge fund firm in the USA, best known as the man who executed 'the greatest trade ever'. During the run up to the credit crisis, he built up his exposure to credit-default insurance contracts – based on his firm's deep understanding of the market and its risks – which would pay out on the collapse of the subprime mortgage market in 2007. It is reputed that he made around $4 billion for himself on that trade alone. Despite the 158% rise in his Advanced Plus fund in 2007 and some gains in subsequent years, in 2011 he lost more than 50% of the fund and it is rumoured almost another 20% in 2012, taking macro-bets on sovereign bonds issued by Eurozone governments.

There is little doubt that Paulson and his team had deep insight into the subprime market and could see the opportunity to exploit its subsequent demise. However, the old behavioural trait of over-confidence appears to have struck, as the firm moved into other, less familiar markets.

Luck versus skill is always hard to discern, even in those who have achieved extraordinary returns in the past.

Other notable examples of just how difficult it is to exist: John Meriwether's Long Term Capital Management, complete with two Nobel Prize winning economists, threatened to drag down the global financial system with it – the company had a $100 billion balance sheet when it got its view on Russia wrong and markets behaved out of line with expected, at least in their eyes, norms.

Then there was Jeff Vinik, formerly of Fidelity, who made one of the largest market timing mistakes recorded on the largest mutual fund in the world,

The Magellan Fund. The latter's demise was recorded in *BusinessWeek* (Sparks, 1997).

'When Jeffrey N. Vinik ran Fidelity Investment's huge Magellan Mutual Fund, he was known for his large – and often short-term – bets on stocks and sectors. Vinik's record was stellar – until the end of 1995, when he shifted a big chunk of the $50-plus billion portfolio into bonds. Not smart. Rates rose, returns collapsed, and he departed in June, 1996.'

Most active UK equity funds were beaten by the market

We can come at this from another angle, by looking at how many actively managed UK funds beat the market. A recent piece of research (Vanguard, 2012) provides a comprehensive review of how well active managers have performed against their market benchmarks (i.e. whether they were delivering positive incremental returns for the fees that investors pay) over the fifteen-year period to the end of 2012. The research looked at funds available to UK investors in a number of broad categories and sought to identify the percentage of funds that were outperformed by the benchmark stated in the fund's prospectus. It also takes into account the funds that have been closed or merged during the period. The underlying data used in the research was obtained from Morningstar. The stark reality is that the vast majority of active managers have failed to live up to their promise, as Table 4.3 so clearly demonstrates. It provides clear evidence that adopting a passive approach to investing is worthy of consideration for the vast majority of investors.

As ever, the issue that remains is that even with these very high 'market-beating promise' failure rates, there are some managers who beat the benchmark over this fifteen-year period. If this outperformance can be shown to persist and a means exists to identify these managers ahead of when they are needed (not with hindsight), then an active approach should be considered. We will explore this question a little later in this chapter.

Table 4.3   **Percentage of active funds beaten by their benchmarks (after survivor bias)**

Equities	UK	Europe	Eurozone	USA	Global	Emerging
15 years	73%	83%	80%	87%	93%	79%
Bonds	UK divers.	UK govt.	Global	US divers.	EUR divers.	
15 years	90%	92%	100%	100%	100%	

Source: Vanguard (2012) © The Vanguard Group, Inc, used with permission.

Evidence from other European markets

The Norwegian government has established a fund that collects some of the revenue from its oil reserves to be held for the benefit of future generations of Norwegians (it is a shame that the UK government did not have the courage or foresight to do the same). This fund is actively managed (i.e. it is trying to beat the market). Research was conducted on this fund (Ang et al., 2009) to see how well it was performing. The key finding was that despite being given an active mandate, the lead manager failed to run an active fund, with 99% of the outcome attributable to the fund's long-term mix of assets (asset allocation strategy). The authors of the research stated:

'Recent theory and empirical evidence suggests that some fund managers do have talent and out-perform market benchmarks before fees. However, little of that superior ability filters through to the ultimate investors in those funds with after-fee returns and alphas being, on average, zero or negative ... we cannot find any statistical evidence of significant active outperformance ... A significant part [70%] of the very small component of the total Fund return represented by active return is linked to exposures to a number of well-recognized systematic factors.'

Converting this into English: the active fund managers used by the fund failed to deliver on their promise as a team to beat the market.

The authors also concluded:

'In light of the relative importance that factor exposures already play in the Fund's returns, we suggest that the Fund consider a framework that more explicitly recognizes the structure of its return generating process via investment in factor benchmark portfolios.'

Again, translating this into plain English: they might as well have used index (passive) funds to gain exposure to the risks and thus rewards they wanted to attain. As you will see later, this is exactly the approach that this book takes.

Finally, analysis of mutual fund performance in Spain between 1991 and 2008 (Fernandez, 2009) reveals that only 18 of the 1,025 funds (<2%) with ten years of performance data outperformed the relevant index benchmark.

Evidence from the USA

Where to start? The evidence is both compelling and abundant. The majority of active managers fail to deliver on their promise. One useful and regular piece of research (SPIVA, 2013) provides similar results to the Vanguard research in the UK. It demonstrates that a shade under 70% of all US domestic equity funds were beaten by their benchmark and mid- and smaller sized company funds did even worse (90% and 82% respectively). Bond funds fared little better. The previous year's research paper (SPIVA, 2012) came to the following paraphrased conclusions:

- The only useful trend over five years is that a majority of active equity and bond managers lag their appropriate index.

- The perception that indexing is likely to be a better option in more efficient markets such as large cap, and active management is better in less efficient markets such as small cap and emerging markets. To quote: *'is not supported by the data'*.

- Claims by active managers that they are favoured by bear markets as they can hold cash and defensive positions is not borne out in the two market crashes during the past ten years. To quote: *'the opportunity does not translate to reality'*.

Investment policy outweighs investment strategy

A classic study (Brinson et al., 1986) relating to actively managed US pension plans and the role of long-term policy versus short-term active management decisions concludes that:

'Investment policy dominates investment strategy, explaining on average 93.6% of the variation in total plan returns.'

This has also become one of the most misquoted pieces of research in investment academia. When I started work in the industry, I too was led to believe that an investor's total return was therefore about 90% due to asset allocation and 10% due to active decisions. What it refers to is the variation, i.e. changes in returns over time, not what proportion of total return is attributable to investment policy. You would be amazed how many people still misquote this study.

The relevance of this study is that it implies that even sophisticated players implicitly accept that it is difficult to beat markets and constrain their active decision-making. A similar study was undertaken in the UK looking at 300 pension funds (Blake et al., 1999). It concluded that:

'Strategic asset allocation accounts for most of the time-series variation in portfolio returns, while market timing and asset selection appear to have been less important.'

Where do you stand now?

The evidence against using active management as a high probability points-winning philosophy is mounting up: markets are competitive and probably reasonably efficient; forecasting has some serious hurdles to success, few active managers appear able to do it consistently; and research studies show that the majority of managers fail to outperform the index (and index funds) over the longer term. In its favour there appear to be a few managers who do. As a rational investor the probability of success lies in favour of an index approach over active management at this point.

4.5 Do a few managers outperform over time?

If, however, some managers do have exceptional skills that allow them to beat markets, rather than luck, and they can consistently use these skills to generate outperformance (after all costs) of the markets over long periods of time, then employing them to manage your money would make sense as each incremental point is extremely valuable, when compounded over time. A few do, and the UK's most celebrated manager is Anthony Bolton, with a remarkable track record (see the box at the end of this chapter), although his experience of managing his China fund since he stepped down from his original funds has been less than spectacular. Perhaps you could do this by picking funds with persistent past performance, as a guide to future performance. Let us see whether this is the case.

Testing whether performance persists

Significant amounts of research have been undertaken to test whether investment managers' performance does persist over time. In other words: are the few who outperform over one time frame the same managers who outperform over subsequent time frames? If performance persistence exists, then you could act on that information. Two recent and comprehensive reviews of the literature on performance persistence have been published, the conclusions of which are laid out below. The first was a paper commissioned by the Financial Services Authority, the UK's industry regulatory body (Rhodes, 2000). The conclusion that was reached was as follows:

'The literature on the performance of UK funds has failed to find evidence that information on past investment performance can be used to good effect by retail investors in choosing funds. The general pattern is one in which investment performance does not persist. Small groups of funds may show some repeat performance over a short period of time. However, the size of this effect and the

fact that it is only short-lived means there is no investment strategy for retail investors that could be usefully employed. The results of the US literature are similar.'

This is further indication that the UK market is pretty efficient, or that any inefficiency cannot be profitably exploited. If it were not, some managers would have been able to generate long-term persistent records of performance due to their superior skills. Bear this in mind the next time you see an advertisement in the paper for a stellar fund.

The Vanguard research paper (Vanguard, 2012) looks at this issue. It ranked 384 active UK equity funds into five peer-group, risk-adjusted performance quintiles in the five years to the end of 2006. If strong performance is based on persistent skill then one would expect a high proportion of funds in the top quintile in the initial period to continue to be in the top quintile in the next period. If the outperformance were simply due to luck, one would expect the top quintile performers in the first period to be spread evenly between the other quintiles in the second period.

Two key insights can be derived from this research (see Table 4.4):

▪ Performance does not persist. The even distribution of funds ranked in each quintile (in the first period) across the five quintiles in the second period suggests that outperformance is likely to be by chance i.e. no skill.

▪ A very high level of funds go 'missing' across all quintiles, indicating that poor performance tends to persist.

Additional research (Busse et al., 2008) from the institutional fund management world supports the thesis that active management is a tough game. It studied performance persistence amongst 1,384 institutional investment managers, representing $4 trillion of US plan sponsor assets.

Table 4.4   **Performance persistence – what persistence?**

To 2006	Quintile – Period 2: to 2011					
Quintile	Highest (1)	High (2)	Medium (3)	Low (4)	Lowest (5)	Missing
1	16%	14%	10%	13%	23%	23%
2	19%	8%	16%	12%	10%	34%
3	13%	15%	19%	19%	9%	26%
4	16%	22%	7%	20%	9%	26%
5	4%	10%	12%	17%	18%	40%

Source: Vanguard (2012) © The Vanguard Group, Inc, used with permission.

The conclusion: no evidence of performance persistence in winners or losers.

'The lack of risk-adjusted excess returns and the absence of persistence, support the efficient market hypothesis. Therefore one policy prescription might be that plan sponsors should engage entirely in passive asset management.

Are longer-term outperformers lucky or skilful?

Earlier you saw that luck might well play a part in short-term market beating track records of some managers.

In the event that investment performance of active managers was down to luck rather than skill, one would expect these returns to be 'normally' (bell curve) distributed. In a seminal piece of work Mark Carhart (1997) demonstrated that manager returns were similar to randomness less costs, i.e. a bell curve shifted to the left. He also revealed that active management adds additional uncertainty as it exhibited a greater chance of large losses. Persistence was evident in very few outperformers, but higher in terms of underperformance. In other words, bad funds tended to remain bad.

A skilled active manager should be able to generate returns in excess of the level of returns expected from a portfolio of equivalent market risk. The risk that the manager takes over and above that inherent in the general market, for example by choosing a few specific equities to hold in the portfolio, can be measured. If you work out the ratio of the excess return (known in the industry as *alpha*) to the excess risk taken on (known as *residual risk*), you can get a measure of how well an active manager manages money. In plain English, it describes the active bang of return they get for their active buck of risk they take. This is known as the *information ratio*.

A number of studies have calculated the information ratio of top-quartile managers, which tends to be around 0.5 on a gross basis. After fees and costs this is likely to be considerably lower. The point I am getting to is that for an information ratio of 0.5 you need sixteen years of data for you to be 95% sure that the returns are due to skill rather than luck. At 0.33, which may be nearer reality for these 'top' managers after costs, you would need thirty-six years of data. At 0.2 you need one hundred years. The reality is that you rarely get more than five years of data, let alone twenty.

A recent piece of research (Cuthbertson et al., 2008) shows that of 675 UK funds only nine (less than 2%) showed positive market-beating skills. That's hardly a number to base your investment strategy on.

Who can tell as managers move around so frequently?

As food for thought, you may want to ponder on data from the UK relating to fund manager turnover on funds, which is quite staggering: a quarter of fund managers have been in their current role less than one year, half have been with their present funds for under two years, only a third have been with the same fund for three years or more and alarmingly fewer than one in five for more than five years! Few have served twenty years. Just whose track record are you looking at?

In fact a few truly talented managers do exist

This part of the book may sound like a bit of an indictment of the whole active management industry. It is not meant to be. It is just meant to convince you that as an average investor, like me, you are unlikely to have the time, inclination, data or skills to evaluate active managers, or try to invest actively yourself. You can see for yourself that even sophisticated institutional investors find it a pretty daunting task. As a rational investor you need to make decisions based on the likelihood of long-term success, and therefore should adopt a lose-the-fewest points strategy.

There are some exceptional managers in the investment business, some of whom have moved to hedge funds or continue to manage funds or investor portfolios. An example of a long-term outperforming manager in the UK was Anthony Bolton who ran the Special Situations fund at Fidelity – but now you have found him, unfortunately he has retired from the fund! Take a look at the box at the end of this chapter to see just what a remarkable job he has done and to see what challenges investors faced sticking through the tougher periods the fund suffered along the way. It took a brave investor to reap the benefits.

4.6 Can you identify them in advance?

At this point you have the answers to the first two questions posed. You know that your mix of investments drives your portfolio returns, and the probability of capturing most of these returns lies in favour of a passive strategy rather than using active managers. You also now know that you cannot use past performance as a guide to picking future winners. As a result, you now have little to go on if you still want to use active managers.

Even if we can find a manager who can demonstrate fifteen years of outper-formance, based on skill, and/or a robust investment process rather than luck, the problem is that it is highly unlikely that they will be around for the next twenty years or more that *you* need them. They will be long gone to their beach houses in the Bahamas. If you cannot use something simple such as past performance to choose managers, you have a problem. Waring and Siegel (2003) sum this problem of manager selection up well in a recent paper where they state:

'Each investor has to develop his or her own methodology for forecasting manager alphas … if you don't think that you can do this, maybe you should not hire active managers.'

Even some of the world's largest and most sophisticated pension plans are index funds for at least some of their assets, such as the California Public Employees' Retirement System (CalPERS), who oversee more than $200 billion of assets. A few successful institutional investors, such as the Yale University Endowment managed by David Swensen and his team, use their proprietary insight, access to information and managers, and evaluation skills (combined with much hard work) to build an entire portfolio of high quality active managers. That may be fine for them, as they are some of the most astute investors around, but for you and me, we should stick where the probabilities favour us, i.e. indexing of long-term investment policy mix and sticking with it.

It is worth remembering the research finding highlighted in the Eye-opener section (Bogle, 2007) that in the USA, from 1970 to 2005, of the 355 US equity mutual funds around in 1970 only three (less than 1%) delivered statistically significant and consistent performance through to 2005. The chances of you or even your adviser picking these managers in advance are simply too low. Play the game that loses you the fewest points. Choose a good passive fund instead. As Bogle himself would say:

'Don't search for the needle, buy the haystack.'

4.7 Don't just take my word for it

So, having probably reached the conclusion that a passive index approach rather than an active approach makes most sense in terms of maximising your probability of long-term success, you are now with the minority of investors that think like you. The rest of the investors, both individuals and institutions, are still trying to pursue a points-winning strategy. However, you may be surprised by who has advocated the use of index investing as a sensible way to invest for most investors. Let me name a few, all of whom have made reputations for themselves as leading active managers or proponents of active management. You can rest assured that adopting a lose-the-fewest-points strategy is the only way for you to manage your own investing, or for your adviser to do so.

Warren Buffett (the Sage of Omaha), widely regarded as one of the greatest active investors of our time, has been described by John Bogle (Targett, 2001) as follows:

'He thinks like an index investor: he buys a few large stocks, holds them for a good holding period – forever – and it's worked quite brilliantly.'

In further support of index funds, Warren Buffett himself stated in one of the annual letters to shareholders (1998) of the investment firm Berkshire Hathaway that he and Charlie Munger run:

'Most investors, both institutional and individual, will find the best way to own common stocks is through an index fund that charges minimal fees. Those following this path are sure to beat the net results (after fees and expenses) delivered by the great majority of investment professionals.'

Peter Lynch, one-time manager of Fidelity Investment's Magellan Fund, the world's largest actively managed fund, and highly respected active manager states of most investors that (Anon, 1990):

'They'd be better off in an index fund.'

Charles Schwab, the pioneer of online brokerage in the USA, actively supports indexing as the core of an optimal long-term portfolio and states (Schwab, 1999):

'Most of the mutual fund investments I have are in index funds, approximately 75 per cent.'

David Swensen, CIO of the Yale Endowment and one of the most respected institutional investors, agrees:

'You should invest only in things that you understand. That should be the starting point and the finishing point. For most investors the practical application of this axiom is to invest in index funds (low-fee investments that aim to mirror the performance of a particular stock market index). The overwhelming number of investors, individual and institutional, should be completely in low-cost index funds because that's easy to understand.'

What better testimonials could you ask for than those? So, without any hesitation I suggest to you that you choose, as your default, index-replicating products to create your long-term investment policy portfolio. Avoid trying to add returns by moving your mix of investment around or trying to pick winning stocks or managers. The chances are slim that you will be able to do it consistently. I know it is tempting to get swayed by the supposed evidence of short-term performance of markets and managers but you will not be being rational if you are. Play the highest probability game. The rationale for adopting a passive approach to investing is made succinctly by Professor Keane (2000):

'The significance of the empirical evidence is not that passive investment will always outperform active investment, but that, at the time of decision-making, the balance of probabilities is always in favour of passive investment.'

Active fund management employees invest in passive funds

In a recent survery by Ignites[1], it interviewed 1,001 active management employees in the UK and discovered that two thirds of them have sizeable amounts invested in passive funds and 45 per cent who hold a 'significant' amount in them.

4.8 Your investment philosophy rules

1 Set an appropriate investment policy mix of assets and stick to it at all times.

2 Remember at all times the wise words of Charles Ellis:

'The ultimate outcome is determined by who can lose the fewest points not win them.'

3 A penny saved is a penny earned. Obsessively keep other people's hands out of your portfolio pie.

4 Active management is a tough game for all but the few most brilliant or lucky. You have a low chance of winning points and a high chance of losing points if you go this route.

5 Avoid trying to time markets and being tempted to jump between asset classes, countries, sectors or managers. Chasing returns is a road to wealth destruction.

6 Do not try to pick stocks. Too much evidence demonstrates that after all costs, fees and taxes are taken into account it is a game you will not win.

---

[1] As described in: Newlands, C., (2013), 'The fund emperors' new clothes', *Financial Times* June 30, 2013. Available at www.ft.com

7 You will lose if you try to pick a manager by their performance record. Be sensible and pick a fund that has a 60–80% chance of beating all active funds over the long run, i.e. an index tracker/passive fund.

8 However bright you think you are, or however confident you are, or how convincing a story, sales patter, brochure of performance record is, do not be tempted either to change your investment policy mix or become an active investor yourself.

9 Index all bond and equity market investments wherever possible.

10 Sticking with a passive buy-hold-rebalance index funds approach to investing provides you with a much more straightforward approach to investing at a number of levels, as you will see.

Anthony Bolton – the exception that proves the rule

In the introduction, I made an apology to the cohort, be it a small one, of fund managers who truly have something special – the ability consistently to beat the market over long periods of time, either through their exceptional individual skills, a unique investment process, or a combination of the two.

The insight below comes from the First Edition of *Smarter Investing*: Anthony Bolton was a fund manager at Fidelity, one of the world's largest and most respected active fund management firms. He is an exceptional manager: he has been managing his Special Situations fund for more than 25 years (few others can match his longevity); he is truly dedicated to making money for the investors who place their faith in him; and he is very much a contrarian at heart (unlike some), being prepared to manage his money in quite a different manner from most of his peers and the market benchmark. In his words (Davis, 2004):

> *'If you want to outperform other people, you have got to hold something different from other people. If you want to outperform the market, as everyone expects you to do, the one thing you mustn't hold is the market itself.'*

His UK-focused Special Situations fund has done just that; exhibiting a focus on smaller to medium-sized companies and value stocks, although that masks the flexibility of his approach to the companies he invests in; and his track record has been exceptional. With his retirement, he has firmly placed himself in the pantheon of active

▶

investment greats, alongside the likes of Warren Buffett and Peter Lynch, one of his former colleagues at Fidelity.

For investors who put £1,000 into his fund at its launch in 1979, their money in December 2004 would be worth about £90,000, whereas the market would only have made you just over £20,000. That is 6% every year, on average, better than the market and twice his nearest rival. One of his exceptional feats was to make a positive return of around 4% in the bear market of March 2000 to March 2003, when the market itself was down almost 40% – only a handful of other managers made positive returns in this period. This is a truly remarkable record.

Active management can really pay, if you get it right, because compounding outperformance over time makes a big difference to the money in your pocket. No one in this case would begrudge paying a 1.5% annual fee and all the other associated fund costs! I do not deny the fact; all I am trying to do is help you face the realities when you invest your money and try to make the best decisions you can to increase your chances of success. In that sense, and somewhat disappointingly, going the active route in search of the truly talented is a gamble – a low chance of a high payout, in this case an exceptionally high payout.

Ironically, Anthony Bolton's exceptional track record helps to highlight the very real challenge you are up against. Forgetting the notion that you can invest directly in the markets yourself successfully, finding true talent like Anthony Bolton is not easy and you need to ask yourself if you have the skills and the time to try to do so.

First of all, it is very hard to pick a manager in advance of the twenty to thirty years that you will need them to manage your money. Who in 1979 knew that Anthony Bolton would be one of the best fund managers yet? It is made no easier by the fact that managers hop from job to job so quickly. Bolton is one of only 17 managers who have managed their fund for more than 15 years, out of more than 300 funds.

Here is an illustration of the dilemma you face. Imagine you had £10,000 to invest at the start of 1989. You open the paper and see that his Special Situations fund has beaten the market by a remarkable 8% a year for nine years. You (rightly as it turns out, of course) decide that he is the man to look after your money. You invest. Three years later you find yourself a whopping 45% or so behind the market, turning your £10,000 into £9,700 against the market's £14,300. What do you do? Hold? Sell? The problem is that you simply do not know, at that point in 1991, if he is brilliant or whether his luck has just run out. Even Ned Johnson, the head of Fidelity, seemed to have his doubts, calling him in to talk about the fund's performance.

In 1996 you almost get back in line with the market but 1997 and 1998 see you drop back by about 20% against the market. Still going to hold? In fact, it would have taken you until 2000 to get back ahead of the market. Eleven years of uncertainty – would you really have had the stomach to see this through? I doubt it and I can understand why. If you had, though, you would have ended up with almost twice what the market delivered by the end of 2004! Very few investors have held the fund since inception and over half of today's 250,000 investors have invested in the five years to 2004.

That brings us back to the issue of needing to find a manager now who will be around for the period of time you need them, i.e. from today. New investors in this particular fund will not have Anthony Bolton managing their money. Do you believe his replacement will replicate his unique talent and insight? Who else out there is the next Anthony Bolton? And how can you pick them now, given that past performance is a weak indicator of future success in most cases? That's your dilemma. As a smarter investor you should accept that you may have to give up an outside chance of a very substantial upside of tomorrow's Anthony Bolton and simply accept that the market return, as near as possible, is a worthy ambition, if a somewhat boring one.

Congratulations to Mr Bolton, and to those other managers who in a few years' time we will look back on and say, 'Boy, they were good!' while secretly wishing we had found them today.

Fast forward to 2013 . . .

Well here is the next instalment to that story. In 2006, the fund was split into global and UK products. The global portion was managed by Jorma Korheren, who Anthony Bolton had groomed to be his successor. If anyone could pick a winning manager surely Bolton and the executives at Fidelity could. Well in 2012 Korheren exited the fund

▶

with its performance down more than 5% versus a rise in the MSCI AC World index of 19% over the period under his stewardship. Since then a new manager has come in . . .

Anthony Bolton himself has had no easier time as he moved to Hong Kong to try his arm at picking Chinese equities. His fund suffered an embarrassing start with a couple of material blow-ups, and has trailed its benchmark since inception. But this is a long-term game. Will he be a winner? Will he generate skill-based returns above the true benchmark of Chinese mid/small cap stocks that he invests in? Who knows? He has just given up and retired.

References

Ang, A., Goetzmann, W. and Schaefer, S. (AGS) (2009) *Evaluation of Active Management of the Norwegian Government Pension Fund.* Oslo, Norway: Ministry of Finance.

Anon (1990) 'Is there life after Babe Ruth? Peter Lynch talks about why he's quitting Magellan', *Barron's*, 2 April, p. 15.

Barber, B. M. and Odean, T. (1998) 'Trading is hazardous to your wealth: the common stock investment performance of individuals', *The Journal of Finance*, vol. LV, no. 2, 773–806.

Blake, D., Lehman, B. N. and Timmerman, A. (1999) 'Asset allocation dynamics and pension fund performance', *The Journal of Business*, vol. 72, no. 4, 429–61.

Bogle, J. C. (2003) 'The policy portfolio in an era of subdued returns', Bogle Financial Markets Research Center (http://www.vanguard.com).

Bogle, J. C. (2007) *The Little Book of Common Sense Investing.* New York: John Wiley & Sons.

Brinson, G. P., Hood, L. R. and Beebower G.L. (1986) 'Determinants of portfolio performance', *Financial Analysts Journal*, vol. 42, no. 4, 40–48.

Buffett, W. (1998) *Chairman's letter to shareholders 1997*, Berkshire Hathaway Inc.

Busse, J., Goyal, A. and Wahal, S. (2008) *Performance and Persistence in Institutional Investment Management* (www.ssrn.com).

Carhart, M. (1997) 'On persistence in Mutual Funds', *Journal of Finance*, no. 52, 57–82.

Chordia, T., Roll, R. and Subrahmanyan, A. (2003) 'Evidence on the speed of convergence to market efficiency', UCLA Working Paper, 3 November.

Cuthbertson, K., Nitzsche, D. and O'Sullivan, N. (2006) 'The Market Timing Ability of UK Equity Mutual Funds' (http://ssrn.com).

Cuthbertson, K., Nitzsche, D. and O'Sullivan, N. (2008) 'False Discoveries: Winners and Losers in Mutual Fund Performance' (http://ssrn.com/ abstract=1093624).

Davis, J. (2004) *Investing with Anthony Bolton*. UK: Harriman House, p. 18.

Ellis, C. D. (2002) *Winning the loser's game*, 4th edn. New York: McGraw Hill, pp. 3–7.

Fernandez, P. (2009) *Rentabilidad De Los Fondos de Inversion* (in Spanish). Javier del Compo. IESE Business School (www.iese.edu).

Keane, S. (2000) *Index funds in a bear market*, a monograph published by Glasgow University in association with Virgin Direct.

Laise, E. (2009) 'Best stock fund of the decade: CEM Focus', *Wall Street Journal*, 31 December (www.wsj.com).

LeBaron, D. Vaitlingam, R. and Pitchford, M. (1999) *The Ultimate Book of Investment Quotations*. Oxford: Capstone.

Malkiel, B. G. (1999) *A random walk down Wall Street*. New York: W. W. Norton.

Malkiel, B. G. (2000) 'Are markets efficient? Yes even if they make errors', *The Wall Street Journal*, 28 December, p. A10.

Rhodes, M. (2000) *Past imperfect? The performance of UK equity managed funds*. London: FSA, FSA Occasional Paper Series 9 (www.fas.gov.uk/pubs.occpapers/ op09.pdf).

Schwab, C. (1999) *Charles Schwab's guide to financial independence: simple solutions for busy people*. New York: Three Rivers Press, p. 90.

Sharpe, W. F. (1975) 'Are gains likely from market timing?', *The Financial Analysts Journal*, vol. 31, no. 2 (March/April), 60–69.

Sharpe, W. F. (1991) 'The arithmetic of active management', *The Financial Analysts Journal*, vol. 47, no. 1 (January/February), 7–9.

Sinquefield, R. (1995) Opening address: Schwab Institutional Conference, San Francisco, CA, 12 October.

Sparks, D. (1997) 'The Juggernaut who's flattening short-sellers', *Business Week*, 13 October (www.businessweek.com).

SPIVA (2012) S&P Indices Versus Active Funds Scorecard – Year end 2011 (www. spiva.com).

SPIVA (2013) S&P Indices Versus Active Funds Scorecard – Year end 2012 (www. spiva.com).

Targett, S. (2001) 'Survey – index-based investing: An industry enjoying life in the fast track', *Financial Times*, 18 July.

Vanguard (2012), 'The case for index fund investing for UK investors' (www. vanguard.co.uk).

Waring, M. B. and Siegel, L. B. (2003) 'The dimensions of active management', *The Journal of Portfolio Management*, vol. 29, no 3, 35–51.

5

Smarter investment behaviour

While we all like to think that we are capable of making rational decisions, it appears that when it comes to investing, a switch inside even the most sensible person seems to flick and rationality disappears in a cloud of emotion. It is impossible for me simply to tell you to be rational in the decisions that you face, but what I can do is point out the consequences of emotional behaviour on your wealth accumulation and some of the demons that drive it.

5.1 You are your own worst enemy

Being an investor is not easy. You have to contend not only with the erratic and unpredictable nature of markets but also the sometimes erratic and irrational way in which you will be tempted to think and behave. This book encourages you to do your best to make rational decisions and to make your head rule your heart in all matters relating to investing. Yet for most, while understanding that being rational makes sense, putting it into practice can be exceedingly difficult. Benjamin Graham, one of the great investment minds of the twentieth century, famously stated (Graham and Dodd, 1996):

'The investor's chief problem – and even his worst enemy – is likely to be himself.'

Irrational investing manifests itself in many different ways: chopping and changing your investment plan influenced by what has just happened to the markets; trading shares in an online brokerage account; trying to pick market turning points, i.e. when to be in or out of different markets; being tempted into buying flavour of the month investment ideas or products; or chasing performance. The list of irrational decision-making opportunities is long and distinguished. John Bogle summed this up perfectly in an address to the Investment Analysts Society of Chicago (2003):

'If I have learned anything in my 52 years in this marvellous field, it is that, for a given individual or institution, the emotions of investing have destroyed far more

potential investment returns than the economics of investing have ever dreamed of destroying.'

Reflect on this for a moment

Eye-opener 2 at the start of this book looked at the performance record of individual investors in the USA over the 20-year period to 2011. The staggering results of the study showed that because investors are all tempted by the media, their own research or their advisers, to chop and change their investment strategy and chase last year's returns, the average equity investor earned just 4% annually over this period compared to the market return of 10%. That is a bad result, even allowing for some possible flaws in methodology (Kitces, 2012), the fear and greed cycle of investors is undoubtedly a drag on investor performance.

The difference between the returns that a fund delivers are known as time-weighted returns. The return an investor in a fund actually receives is known as the money weighted return and will be impacted on cash flows into or out of the fund. Remember the CMG Focus Fund that delivered a return of 18% p.a. but investors received –11% p.a. due to their buying at the top and selling at the bottom. The difference between the two has been referred to as the 'behaviour gap'.

Some useful research (Phillips, 2011) provides some evidence that this behaviour gap is persistent across all broad fund sectors (see Table 5.1). In the US, Morningstar, where this data has been sourced, provides both time and money-weighted returns to investors – it is a shame that it is not available in the UK – what are we afraid of?

Table 5.1 **Investor behaviour penalises wealth**

Fund group by asset class	Investor return % (Dollar-weighted)	Total return % (Time weighted)	Behaviour gap %
US diversified funds	2.3	3.3	−1.0
US sector funds	3.9	6.1	−2.2
Balanced funds	4.0	5.1	−1.2
International diversified funds	4.9	6.0	−1.0
International regional funds	6.4	8.8	−2.4
Taxable bond funds	4.5	6.3	−1.8
Municipal bond funds	2.0	4.0	−2.0
Alternative	9.9	13.1	−3.1
All funds	3.4	4.7	−1.3

Source: Phillips (2011)

Get a grip on yourself

Unfortunately emotional demons affect the way in which you make your investment decisions. Understanding these demons may help you to identify how you can try to keep them in control. The times when most investors become irrational are generally periods of market trauma or market exuberance. As Warren Buffett said (2001):

'The line separating investment and speculation, which is never bright and clear, becomes blurred still further when most market participants have recently enjoyed triumphs. Nothing sedates rationality like large doses of effortless money.'

Buy high, sell low – a recipe for wealth destruction

Figure 5.1 shows how many people invest, allowing their emotions and lack of market knowledge to drive the type of wealth destruction that you saw in the research above. While most investors can understand the simple concept of buy low, sell high, the very nature of their behaviour results in exactly the opposite. Investors tend to be influenced by what is going on in the markets over the short term. This makes them vulnerable to what the industry refers to as being 'whip-sawed' as they move from last year's bad performing investment to this year's best performer.

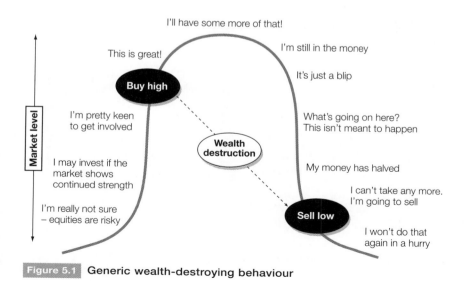

Figure 5.1 **Generic wealth-destroying behaviour**

Let us take a look at this behaviour in practice in the UK. Figure 5.2 shows the net retail sales by unit trusts and open-ended investment companies (OEICs) to UK investors. Rationally, you would expect that after the UK equity market had fallen by 40% or so in 2007–2008, new fund flows into equities would increase, as investors were getting better value for their money than at the start of 2007 when the market was at a high. The opposite was true – in 2008 there were net redemptions of over £1.2 billion. It is clear that fund sales are driven by short-term market sentiment, where investors become increasingly eager to enter the market when markets have performed well recently, i.e. when they are relatively expensive, and tend to cut back their investment when they fall, i.e. when they are cheaper. This is ironic given that in all other walks of life we have no trouble in being attracted to goods and services which are cheap, yet when it comes to investing we seem to lose not only our rational selves, but also a good deal of common sense.

As you can see from Figure 5.2, the level of sales of equity funds rises and falls almost exactly in line with the market. As equity markets fall, bond sales increase in proportion. Given that the vast majority of sales are made through advisers of some description, it begs the question as to just how valuable and costly this market-timing based advice really is. It appears to constitute selling last quarter's best performer, or am I being too sceptical? Decide for yourself. It is a good illustration of emotions taking over, and bad advice encouraging them.

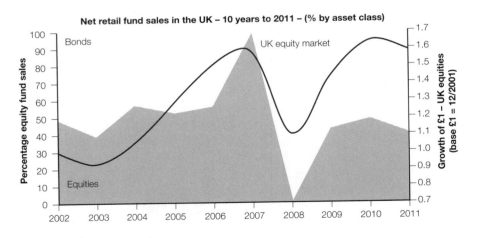

Figure 5.2 Buy high – sell low – the road to wealth destruction

Source: Data from IMA – Retail sales data from www.investmentfunds.org.uk

This is perverse and is best described by Warren Buffett, who has a habit of speaking common sense (1998). He poses a short quiz to his shareholders:

'If you plan to eat hamburgers throughout your life and are not a cattle producer, should you wish for higher or lower prices for beef? Likewise, if you are going to buy a car from time to time but are not an auto manufacturer, should you prefer higher or lower prices? These questions, of course, answer themselves.'

He follows on with the paradox of investors:

'But now for the final exam: if you expect to be a net saver during the next five years, should you hope for a higher or lower net stock market during that period? Many investors get this one wrong. Even though they are going to be net buyers of stocks for many years to come, they are elated when prices rise and are depressed when they fall. In effect, they rejoice because prices have risen for the 'hamburgers' they will soon be buying. This reaction makes no sense. Only those who will be sellers of equities in the near future should be happy at seeing stocks rise. Prospective purchasers should much prefer sinking prices.'

The problem is that these sentiments persuade some investors to change tack when market trauma events occur and often act precisely against their own best interest. To be a good investor at times is a bit like playing a game of poker with yourself, pitching your logical-self against your emotional-self and seeing who blinks first.

5.2 Challenges to decision-making

Many investors act irrationally, rather than rationally as economic theory demands; this irrational behaviour is a relatively new and interesting area of academic study. A whole industry has grown up in the past couple of decades studying it called 'behavioural finance'.

As Henry Ford once said:

'There is one principle a man must follow if he wishes to succeed, and that is to understand human nature'.

The next few pages are not meant to be a review of the psychology of investment decision-making as espoused by these academics, but a practical guide to how you can avoid being tempted into becoming irrational. If you understand a little more about who you are and importantly how, where and when you may be tempted into being irrational then you will have made some useful progress. It is based in part on the general ideas of behavioural economists, in large part on my experience of dealing with a wide number of investors over the past few years, and will probably seem to you like just a dose of common sense.

Addicted to bad behaviour

Do you remember the late 1990s? It was the era of tech stocks, of 'new paradigms' and day-trading, when sensible people gave up sensible jobs to try and make money trading on the stock market on a minute-by-minute basis? Today, with hindsight it seems to us like madness. However, new neurological research reveals that the neural activity of an investor who is making money on their investments is identical to that of a person who is on cocaine or morphine (Zweig, 2007). Perhaps we should have a little sympathy for those who lost everything.

With class 'A' drugs encouraging bad behaviour on the upside, and the part of the brain that responds to mortal danger processing losses on the downside, it is not hard to see the emotional perils that lie in wait for us all as investors.

Perhaps surprisingly, success in investing is not about deep investment knowledge or intelligence. After all, Sir Isaac Newton managed to lose all his money on the stock market when the South Sea Bubble collapsed, despite his ability to calculate the motion of heavenly bodies. It is about the ability to understand human nature, as suggested by Henry Ford, and to control the harmful decisions that it often drives. Warren Buffett too, concurs.

'Success in investing doesn't correlate with IQ once you're above the level of 100. Once you have ordinary intelligence, what you need is the temperament to control the urges that get other people into trouble in investing'.

Are we slaves to behavioural weaknesses?

Losing weight is usually easier said than done. In fact, in a wide range of instances in our lives, whilst we understand what we should be doing in order to improve our current and future well-being, for example, lose some weight, do more exercise, stop smoking, give more to charity, drink less, save more or buy low and sell high, we fail to control or even modify our behaviour, despite realising that we should. In fact many of the innate biases and traits that hinder our efforts to, for example, lose weight, are the same as those that hinder our ability to make good, rational investment decisions. To get you in the mood for our discussion of bad behaviour, here are a few facts to chew on that come from recent research (Wansink, 2009) on eating:

■ On average you will eat three times as many chocolates if they are right next to you than if they are two metres away (behavioural issues: proximity, familiarity, greed).

■ If you eat with one other person you will eat about one-third more than on your own.

■ If you dine with seven or more you will eat nearly twice as much as on your own (behavioural issue: going with the herd).

Quite quickly, you can see that some simple rules would help to negate these negative behaviours – have less food on your plate (by having smaller plates), put temptations out of sight and have fewer dinner parties!

What all this has to do with investing will hopefully become clear throughout this chapter. In short, by understanding that we all possess innate and unhelpful biases and a proclivity for using mental short-cuts to make decisions (known in the jargon as heuristics), we position ourselves to understand the true value of a disciplined investment programme that minimises our behavioural errors.

Investors – like moths to a flame

Have you ever wondered why moths are attracted to, and sometimes immolate themselves in, a flame? The reason is evolution. Moths appear to navigate using the moon as a reference point, keeping it at a specific angle to their direction of travel. In the past few thousand years, man has invented artificial light (moon proxies) in the form of torches, candles and electric bulbs that moths still respond to as if they were the real moon. In their efforts to keep the light source in the correct relative position, they end up circling in towards it. It is hard to overcome behaviours with several hundred million years of evolution behind them – some moths learn the hard way.

Likewise, to understand human nature we need to look at it in the context of our evolutionary past and the evolutionary process itself. Evolution occurs by a process of natural selection where the favorable heritable traits exhibited by an individual (defined by its genes) become more common in successive generations of a population. Physiological responses that made us run from shadows, avoid pain, devour sources of plenty in a greedy way would have been selected for. As Amos Tversky, one of the leading behavioural economists points out (Zweig, 2007):

'Sensitivity to losses was probably more [beneficial] than the appreciation of gains ... it would have been wonderful to be a species that was almost insensitive to pain and had the infinite capacity to appreciate pleasure. But you probably wouldn't have survived the evolutionary battle.'

It has been estimated (Kahneman and Tversky, 1979) that humans have a pain-to-gain ratio in investing of 2:1 i.e. losses hurt twice as much as gains – we are risk averse.

Lessons from *Star Trek*

Mr Spock, as you may remember from *Star Trek* days, is half-humanoid and half Vulcan. The extreme rationality of his Vulcan genes overpowers his emotional side, making him an extremely useful member of the team in times of crisis (and probably a good investor). Dr McCoy, on the other hand, is human and prone to all the emotional influences that affect his decision-making. We all have a bit of Mr Spock and Mr McCoy in us. The use of this analogy is borrowed from James Montier's excellent book on behavioural investing (Montier, 2010), which is well worth a read.

Our emotional side, and the one that makes intuitive decisions, is our X (or reflexive) system. It includes the amygdala, an old part of the brain in an evolutionary sense that is the centre focused on managing risk and fear, along with the nucleus accumbens that is integral to greed and our desire for reward. The latter is thought to be involved in drug addiction. Our X-system helps us to interface smoothly with the world, focusing us on our goals and avoiding trouble.

The C (or reflective) system, on the other hand, is the logical side of our brains, which kicks in when the more emotional side of our minds is floundering. It would appear though that our emotional decision-making has evolved to trump our logical thinking. For example, imagine you are in the big cat house at London Zoo. A lion you are looking at suddenly jumps at the bars you are standing by. Your immediate response is likely to be to jump away, despite the logical response being that there is no need to do so because it is safely behind a set of thick steel bars. In evolutionary terms, better a false positive than a false negative.

Individuals differ in the degree to which emotion and logic influence their decision-making. A number of simple quizzes can very quickly sort one person from another. For example, try to answer the following two questions as honestly as possible:

■ How much would you pay to eliminate a 1-in-1,000 chance of an immediate death?

■ How much would you need to be paid to willingly accept an extra 1-in-1,000 chance of an immediate death?

In fact, the two outcomes are the same. If you have more Vulcan genes in you, your answer, like Mr Spock's, would be 'the same amount'. If you are more emotionally driven you may well say that you would require more for the second than the first.

Human nature on the rampage

The problem we face is that we tend to use our intuitive decision-making process more often under a set of conditions that apply to the types of decisions we face as investors. These include complexity, incomplete and changing information, competing goals (e.g. preserving capital today by taking little risk, but risking failure to meet our long-term goals by not taking enough risk), when we are stressed and when we need to make decisions that involve other people in the process.

There are many ways in which human nature conspires to make our investment decision-making less than optimal and in most instances these are interlinked, compounding their negative effect. A few of the key behaviours are explored in a little more depth below.

Making investment decisions

As you make investment decisions, you go through a mental process of trying to evaluate the wealth outcomes that you can expect and trying to assess the likelihood that they will happen. You have a wide choice of options and you need to weigh up one against the other. It is hard trying to process all the information that is available in any ordered and value-added way and in the end you generate some sort of intuitive feel for what the answer is for you.

A lack of knowledge, combined with a number of illusions and biases can lead to errors in making decisions that may damage your chances of making the most from your money. These include: the likelihood that you take on an inappropriate and usually higher level of risk than you might have considered sensible if your assessment of the effect had been more realistic; the possibility that the outcome you get is not one you considered, but should have done; the greater likelihood that you will continue to make

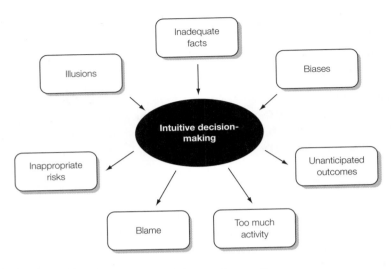

Figure 5.3 Intuitive decision-making can be costly

decisions rather than leaving your investments alone; and the common and sometimes ugly outcome of blaming your adviser or yourself when your luck runs out (Kahneman et al., 1998).

All in all, not being aware of and not curbing your inner biases and illusions is likely to be painful, upsetting, and from a wealth perspective grossly sub-optimal. Figure 5.3 summarises the decision-making process.

5.3 Key evolutionary blindspots

There are many ways in which human nature conspires to make our investment decision-making less than optimal and in most instances these are interlinked, compounding their negative effect. A few of the key behaviours are explored in a little more depth below. For those of you who wish to learn more, the books by Jason Zweig and James Montier are a good place to start (see the References at the end of this chapter).

I know that I am better than the other fools out there

The human being is, by and large, overconfident in his or her abilities. For example, out of 600 professional fund managers asked in a study (Montier, 2010), almost three-quarters said they were better than average (in the same way that 80% of us believe that we are better than average drivers). A number of studies have shown that overconfidence leads investors to overestimate their knowledge, underestimate the risks involved and increase their perception of their ability to control events. For example, many people will bet more on a coin that they flip themselves than on the outcome of a coin already flipped and hidden from view. The illusion of control grows with familiarity. Overconfidence is a dangerous state of mind, encouraging investors to believe that they have better insight into future events than the market, such as when to move into or out of equities.

> **Lesson**: Have some humility – plenty of clever people get spanked regularly by the markets.

There is a distinct pattern emerging here

An easy-to-understand example of this behaviour can be seen on the roulette tables of Las Vegas and Macao. A rational gambler knows that the probability of making a profit always lies in favour of the casino and he also knows that the chance of any number coming up has the same odds as any other number of coming up. Yet, a sequence of three red '9s' in a row or other similar 'pattern' can create quite a stir at the table. In investing, we often mistake random noise for what appears to be a non-random sequence.

> **Lesson**: The trend is not your friend – it is probably meaningless.

Problems with probability (and maths in general)

As humans, we seem to really struggle with working through probability calculations in a logical and mathematical manner. There are many examples of experiments, a bit like the Spock and McCoy quiz above, where individuals fail to make logical and rational decisions. For example, many people are willing to pay more for something that improves the probability of a specific outcome from, say, 95% to 99% than from 45% to 49%, yet the improved outcome is financially equivalent. In many cases, our own probability estimates are more likely to be wrong than right. We shy away from even the simplest maths, such as working out that all-in investment costs of 2% (not unusual for many active strategies) strips 40% of the expected upside of investing in equities that have returned around 5% above inflation over the long term. While that does not seem fair, not many investors seem to do much about it, or perhaps even know.

> **Lesson**: Do not ignore the maths. Sit down and spend a little time teasing out the numbers. (If you cannot, get your adviser to calculate the numbers in £-terms.)

The Monday morning quarter-back – hindsight delusion

With hindsight we often honestly think we could have predicted what has happened, such as a fall in the markets. Experiments have shown that two groups, presented with opposing series of events leading to the same stated outcome, will both believe that the outcome could have been predicted in advance, based on the information they hold. Interestingly, when these same scenarios are presented as educated guesses about future events, participants become very less certain about their own predictive abilities.

Renowned behavioural economist, Robert Shiller (1997), undertook some research relating to the Japanese market crash in 1989. Prior to the event 14% of those asked thought that the market was overvalued, but post-event 32% of those asked said they thought the market was overvalued. Hindsight delusion, combined with overconfidence and susceptibility to seeing trends where none exist is a recipe for wealth destruction.

> **Lesson**: Do not believe that you have predictive powers – you do not, I assure you.

I will throw my anchor out here thanks

The human mind really likes to use 'anchors' when forming opinions, which in many cases leads to extraordinarily inaccurate estimates of outcomes. As an example, experiments undertaken by two of the most respected behavioural economists, Amos Tversky and Daniel Kahneman, used a wheel-of-fortune with the numbers 1 to 100 on it. Before asking their subjects a number of difficult questions, such as how many African nations are in the United Nations, they span the wheel. They first asked if the number was higher or lower than the number on the wheel, and then asked for the participants' guesses. When the wheel stopped on 10 the median guess was 25, but when it stopped on 65 the median number was 45.

> **Lesson**: Do not get hooked on specific numbers, like what the FTSE 100 index has done and then compare your portfolio to it – in all likelihood you will own a different looking portfolio for specific and valid reasons and your returns will be different.

It is more familiar to me, and I get it

Humans tend towards making spontaneous generalisations, based on how they are influenced by recent events, press coverage or experiences, and the vividness with which a situation is portrayed. For example, most Americans believe that there are more murders in the USA than suicides, but this is not the case. The press make more of murders, night after night on the cable TV stations – suicides rarely get a mention. If we witness a bad car accident, we tend to drive more slowly and carefully for a while. During the residential property boom, many investors felt that buy-to-let property was a safe asset, with little risk, leveraging themselves up on the endless hype in the press and recent past experience. Add in the cocaine-like stimulation of rising investments and it is (with hindsight!) easy to see why they behaved like they did. As Massimo Piattelli-Palmarini (1994) says,

'The easier it is to imagine an event or a situation, and the more the occurrence impresses us emotionally, the more likely we are to think of it as also objectively frequent.'

Lesson: Do not get carried away by what is going on today – look to the future both for the up and the downsides.

I like a good story

No one likes a good story more than an investor with cash to invest, and few are better story-tellers than fund managers, product sales persons and the investment press. The danger is that a narrative of fictitious events that make for a plausible sounding script, with linked events (reducing probability in reality), tends to raise the probability of the outcome of the story happening in our minds. The 'plausible' story takes over from reality.

Shakespeare recognised this propensity in people and made it the central theme of *Othello*, where a jealous subordinate, Iago, builds a web of events and inferences to lead Othello into believing that his new, smitten bride, Desdemona, has been unfaithful to him. In his rage he kills her. Similar stories surround the reasons to invest in gold, commodities, vintage wine etc. etc.

Lesson: Be a sceptic – everything taken with a pinch of salt.

Obsessive portfolio monitoring

Many investors find it difficult to see the long-term wood for the short-term trees. Their focus tends to be on the effects of recent market conditions on their wealth and this affects their ability to make good decisions for the long-term success in meeting their lifetime purchasing power needs.

What the eye doesn't see …

The advent of online accounts and investment tracking software has made this a lot worse and too many investors now look at their investments too frequently, getting highly excited as the markets rise and desperately disappointed as they fall. On any day, the chance of seeing a loss on your equity investments is around 50:50 (Swedroe, 2002). Even once a year you have around a 30% chance or more that you will see a loss. Given the ratio of pain to gain, the longer the period between peeks the better!

> **Lesson**: Look at your cash everyday if you wish, your bonds every couple of years and your equities every ten years! Really, do not look at your performance more than once a year.

The consequences of our bad behaviour

The severe consequences of allowing our inner Mr McCoy to overcome the more rational Mr Spock in us, demonstrated that this probably equates to about 1–3% unnecessary wealth destruction every year, on average. This in turn compounds into significant differences in outcomes for Mr McCoy and Mr Spock's investment programmes. Destructive investment decisions, including trying to 'win' by chasing managers and jumping in and out of markets, often results in buying at the top and selling at the bottom.

5.4 Interesting research to mull over

Take a look at the research below. It provides a good insight into the behaviour that many investors portray, to their great cost.

Investor behaviour destroys wealth

Research undertaken by Brad Barber and Terrence Odean (2000), which looked at over 60,000 household accounts of a discount brokerage firm in the USA, from February 1991 to December 1996, analysed the investment performance for equities held by these individuals. It revealed some interesting facts: average turnover, i.e. the percentage of the portfolio value bought and sold, was very high at 80% a year and average net returns, after transaction costs, were 15.2% compared with 17.1% for the market, calculated on an annualised basis; most shockingly, the top 20% of households with the highest turnover, of approximately 10% per month, generated an annualised net return of only 10%, being a full 7% lower than the market.

The central message from this research is that trading is hazardous to your wealth, largely due to costs. Putting a monetary value on this is revealing. A $100,000 portfolio invested in an index (tracker) fund, assumed reasonably to return the benchmark less 0.5% costs, or 16.6% per year, would have grown to $250,000 during this period whereas the individuals with high turnover would have returned only $175,000. Being overconfident in their own perceived skills cost these people a staggering $75,000. A sobering thought.

Overconfidence destroys wealth

The same researchers also looked at 35,000 household accounts from a large brokerage firm from February 1991 to January 1997 (Barber and Odean, 2002). They found that, consistent with other research that shows that men tend to be more overconfident than women (although both are overconfident), men trade 45% more than women. This is reflected in risk-adjusted returns 1.4% a year lower than women. Looking at single women and men, single men trade 67% more than women and generate annual risk-adjusted net returns 2.3% less than single women. Given that by and large self-invested investors, i.e. those that buy and sell shares and other investments themselves through a brokerage account, underperform the markets, as we saw above, this is bad news for wealth accumulation for either sex.

5.5 Simple steps to control evolution

All is not lost. While barely doing justice to the growing literature on how and why investors behave so much to their detriment, this brief outline has hopefully alerted you to the dangers and some of the pitfalls of giving our emotions too much rein in our decision-making. What then is the solution?

Process, process, process

Investing using a well thought-out, evidence-based and systematic investment process helps to take much of the emotion out of investing. Its aim is to deliver investors with the highest probability of a successful investment outcome. That is what process provides (Table 5.2). It does not guarantee that the outcome will always be favourable – it cannot, given the uncertainty of the markets. What it does do is to help us to make strong, rational decisions and to avoid the silly mistakes that prove to be so costly, so often; particularly chasing markets and managers in search of 'market beating' returns and being sucked into the latest investment fad by recent trends, plausible marketing stories and press coverage. Bad process or a lack of process has an upside outcome that is really more luck than judgement.

Being aware of the fact that we all carry deep-seated behaviours that tend to result in us being susceptible to wealth-destroying decisions, allows us to understand and accept the value of investing using a disciplined and unemotional investment process executed in a systematic way. By reflecting on ourselves, we can take the first steps to becoming better investors.

Try to be rational about your investing, from planning how you will invest to how you will respond when times get tough, as they will at some point. It is hard when markets are painful. But the costs of being irrational are far higher, as we have seen. Here are a few pointers:

- Take time planning your investment strategy.

- Form an understanding of the chances you have of achieving the

Table 5.2   The importance of process

	Good outcome	Bad outcome
Good process	Deserved success	Bad break
Bad process	Dumb luck	Poetic justice

Source: Russo and Schoemaker (2002)

long-term outcome you want and the chances that you may not achieve it.

▦ Consider the range of returns that your portfolio will, in all likelihood, exhibit during the time you are investing, however unpalatable they may seem. Forewarned is forearmed.

▦ Put a plan in place, for when times get tough, that details how you should respond, based around: 'Don't panic, be brave, do nothing'! Perhaps even try using a 'Ulysses' contract with yourself that commits you to a predetermined commitment to put down in writing any emotional demand to change investment course (both on the up and downsides), when the market sirens sing. This forces the brain to switch from an emotional to a rational mode.

▦ Stick to your long-term plan unless personal circumstances unexpectedly change significantly and you need to reassess your goals. Never change a plan because of what markets are doing today, or how a fund you do not own has done.

▦ Do not look at your portfolio too often; it will only make you feel overly euphoric or miserable. Think long term.

▦ When you do, look at your whole portfolio and judge how it is doing relative to your long-term purchasing power goals. Do not get over-anxious about short-term weak performance in a single element, or even your portfolio as a whole. That is the markets for you.

▦ Do not believe that you can outsmart the market – you are probably being overconfident, seeing patterns where none exist, being over-optimistic, or have an unrealistic hindsight view of events.

▦ Do not therefore try to own individual stocks yourself through a brokerage account. There are far better ways of doing things.

▦ Avoid the temptation of gambles and insurance, however tempting they may be. These products play on your emotions and you often pay usurious costs that are hidden in the structure (unless you understand the Black & Scholes option pricing model – No? Then avoid these products).

▦ Maintain a healthy level of scepticism about all products and advice.

▦ Systematically rebalance your portfolio (i.e. return it to its original strategy) as you need to keep the portfolio at an appropriate level of risk based on your willingness, ability and need to take on risk. Serendipitously, such a process forces you to take money out of assets that have performed well and to reinvest them in less well performing assets in a disciplined, non-forecast-based manner. This avoids emotive decisions about the 'value' of markets, and may potentially result in a rebalancing bonus over time.

■ Be prepared for the emotional impact of the portfolio you own. Get to know it. Understand just how big its potential falls may be. Desensitise yourself to future shocks as much as you can.

5.6 Wise words to leave you with

Perhaps reflect a while on these wise words written by Charles D. Ellis in his excellent book *Winning the Loser's Game* (Ellis, 2002):

'The hardest work in investing is not intellectual, it's emotional. Being rational in an emotional environment is not easy. The hardest work is not figuring out the optimal investment policy; it's sustaining a long-term focus at market highs or market lows and staying committed to a sound investment policy. Holding on to sound investment policy at market highs and market lows in notoriously hard and important work, particularly when Mr Market always tries to trick you into making changes.'

He shares more wisdom with us:

'Don't trust your emotions. When you feel euphoric you're probably in for a bruising. When you feel down, remember that it's darkest just before dawn and take no action. Activity in investing is almost always in surplus.'

References

Barber, B. M. and Odean, T. (2000) 'Trading is hazardous to your wealth: the common stock investment performance of individuals', *The Journal of Finance*, vol. LV, no. 2 (April), 773–806.

Barber, B. M. and Odean, T. (2002) 'Boys will be boys: Gender, overconfidence, and common stock investment', *Quarterly Journal of Economics*, vol. 116, no. 1 (February), 261–92.

Bogle, J. C. (2003) 'The policy portfolio in an era of subdued returns', Bogle Financial Markets Research Center (www.vanguard.com).

Buffett, W. (1998) *Chairman's letter to shareholders 1997*. Berkshire Hathaway Inc.

Buffett, W. (2001) *Chairman's letter to shareholders 2000*. Berkshire Hathaway Inc.

Ellis, C. D. (2002) *Winning the loser's game*, 4th edn. New York: McGraw Hill.

Graham, B. and Dodd, D. (1996) *Security analysis: The classic 1934 edition*. New York: McGraw Hill.

Kahneman, D. and Tversky, A. (1979) 'Prospect Theory: An analysis of decision under risk', *Econometrica*, 47, 263–91.

Kahneman, D., Higgens, E. and Riepe, W. (1998) 'Aspects of investor psychology', *Journal of Portfolio Management*, vol. 24, no. 4, 52–65.

Kitces, M. (2012) 'Does the Dalbar Study grossly overstate the Behaviour Gap' (www.kitces.com).

Montier, J. (2010) *The Little Book of Behavioral Investing*. Hoboken, NJ: Wiley & Sons.

Phillips, D. (2011) 'Reflections on Fund Management: Five Lessons from 25 Years' (www.morningstar.com).

Piattelli-Palmarini, M. (1994) *Inevitable illusions: How mistakes of reason rule our minds*: Hoboken: NJ: John Wiley.

Russo, J. E. and Schoemaker, P. J. H. (2002) *Winning Decisions*. New York: Doubleday.

Shiller, R. (1997) *The Wall Street Journal*, 13 June. As quoted on: www.investorhome.com/psych.htm. See also: www.econ.yale.edu/~shiller.

Swedroe, L. (2002) *Frequent monitoring of your portfolio can be injurious to your financial health* (www.indexfunds.com).

Zweig, J. (2007) *Your Money and Your Brain*. Simon & Schuster.

Smarter portfolios

Now that you are a convert to the lose-the-fewest-points philosophy and you have your emotions in control, we can begin the process of building a portfolio that makes sense for you, providing you with a reasonable chance of success and survivability – about as much as you can ask for as an investor.

Chapter 6: Smarter risk insight

The reality of being an investor is that you have to take on some risks. While lending your money out in the short term to the government or to a good bank (by placing a deposit) may feel safe, it is rare that the returns on offer are sufficient to allow you to meet your financial goals, particularly when inflation and tax are taken into account. Stepping away from this risk-free world takes courage. This chapter shows you that it is not that difficult to do once you have a sensible framework in place for assessing the risks you face. We will build a short, yet robust menu of investments that will form the core of your portfolio.

Chapter 7: Smarter portfolio construction

The challenge and ultimate goal of smarter portfolio construction is to create a robust and stable *'portfolio for all seasons'* that is likely to do a reasonable job of weathering the storms that the markets will inevitably test you with over your investment lifetime. This chapter builds some sensible portfolios – from low risk to high risk – from the short, yet robust, menu of risks/assets identified in Chapters 6.

Chapter 8: Smarter portfolio choices

Having established the structure of six portfolios along the risk spectrum, which should cater for most investors – from 100% defensive to 100% growth-oriented – it is important to explore the characteristics of each. In this chapter each portfolio is explored in depth and linked to an investor's emotional risk tolerance and his or her financial need to take portfolio risk and their capacity to suffer losses without jeopardising their unique goals. Appendices 1 and 2 help you to define what these are for you, given your own unique circumstances.

6

Smarter risk insight

'Risk surrounds and envelops us. Without understanding it, we risk everything and without capitalising on it, we gain nothing.'

Breakwell and Barnett (2007)

6.1 Making sensible risk decisions

Before we get ahead of ourselves, it probably makes sense to stop and think about what risk actually is. At its very basic level risk can be defined as: the *probability* of an *adverse* event (*hazard*) happening and the *effect* of this exposure due to a specific hazard *on you*. The words in italics are critical, particularly as each is often open to interpretation or estimation. In short, risk is the product of the probability of a hazard occurring and the impact it will have.

Everyday we are faced with 'risk' choices, from crossing the road or using a chainsaw, to the long-term health risk of that tempting doughnut, cigarette or final glass of wine. Often we make these risk decisions instantaneously, perhaps intuitively, often naively or sometimes with reckless disregard for, or understanding of, the outcome. This applies to investment risk decisions too.

We sometimes struggle to make good risk decisions. The problem is that our emotional decision-making process tends to kick in when problems are badly structured and complex; when we have effects or goals that are ill-defined; when we feel we have too little, or poor, information; and when we feel under pressure. Well, that nicely sums up the types of decisions we face as investors!

6.2 Risk is good, when handled well

We have grown used to thinking of risk as a bad thing, but we need to change our mindset and embrace risk in an intellectually robust and controlled way. The quote that opens this chapter sums it all up with the words *'Without understanding it, we risk everything and without capitalising on it, we gain nothing'*. As investors, we need to follow this sound advice making sure that we fully understand the broad gamut of risks that we face and capitalise on the 'good' risks that we identify and avoid the 'bad' risks as best we can. That is what a robust investing process is about – it is not about chasing returns. If we can get the risk inputs right then the right outputs – returns that help deliver our financial goals that do not scare us to death – will most likely follow. Without a systematic process for managing risk we are simply gamblers, not investors.

Lessons from Olympic cycling

The phenomenal success of the British Olympic cycling team did not happen by chance, nor did Bradley Wiggins' amazing victory in the 2012 Tour de France or Chris Froome's in 2013 with the Team Sky outfit. How it was achieved provides us with a very useful lesson in designing and running a successful investment plan. The performance director of the team, David Brailsford, adopted a success programme focused on the *'aggregation of marginal gains'* to use Brailsford's own words.

When asked before the Olympics how many gold medals the team would win, he explained that they did not really think in those terms as they had no control over whether the Australians or Germans would turn up with their own Sir Chris Hoy. What they could do though was make sure that all the detail was right for each and every input into the cycling programme. This included things like: bike – weight and aerodynamics; clothing – new skin suit technology, helmet shape; time in the wind tunnel to get the right position on the bike; diet and nutritional input; rest time and physiotherapy etc. Gold medals are the possible outcome from a programme of tightly managed inputs.

Parallels in investing

The issue is similar as we build our own success programme for investing. We cannot ultimately control what the markets do, but if we select and manage the input decisions really tightly, and measure, monitor and control them along the journey, we give ourselves every chance of success (Figure 6.1).

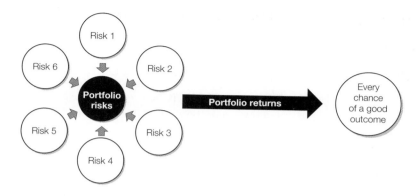

Figure 6.1 Get the risk inputs right and the returns should follow

Avoiding bad risk choices is a key part of the process. Whatever you may think about Donald Trump, his words of advice when it comes to investing are worth noting:

'Sometimes your best investments are the ones that you don't make'

The process of investing is thus one of risk selection and management. A plethora of risks exist from market (bond, equity, currency) to liquidity, complexity, product, counterparty and manager risks, to name a few. Risk decisions fall into four decision outcomes: take, avoid, reduce or transfer.

At its simplest, investing is about deciding which outcome category each risk falls into. These decisions can only be made with insight and reference to the theory and empirical evidence that exists. Only risks that are adequately rewarded should be taken on in portfolios. We will dip deeper into this a little later, when we will attempt to categorise a broad number of risks under each of these four outcomes (see Table 6.3).

In practice, there are three main categories of risk that an investor has to contend with:

■ **Market risk:** this is risk associated with being an owner of equities or bonds, and if you invest overseas, the risk of currency exposure on your investments.

■ **Implementation risk:** this relates to putting your strategy into practice, including liquidity issues, manager performance challenges, product structural risks, counterparty risks etc.

■ **Goal risk:** this is the risk associated with the achievement of the goals that you set for your portfolio.

6.3 Our starting point – risk-free assets

Until recently – before they stopped being issued – the nearest thing to a risk-free asset that a UK investor could own was a National Savings index-linked certificate, which in effect was a promise by the UK government to repay you your capital, indexed up by the rate of inflation to protect your purchasing power, plus a little bit extra. Sometimes lending to the government on a short-term basis (e.g. one month) or placing a deposit below £85,000 with a high quality bank and backed by the government guarantee (although recent events in Cyprus show that nothing is truly risk-free) is considered to be risk-free. But as soon as you step away from these types of investments, you enter the realm of market risk either by branching out into bonds, or becoming an owner by way of equities.

Stepping away from risk-free assets

Imagine that you decide that you need to generate a higher return on your assets than just the risk-free rate (low risk = low return). You could go out and buy the shares of just one company. Most people would consider that to be pretty risky and they would be right. The risks associated with that one company would be high, with its share price and fortunes gyrating wildly over time (think about BP's journey over the past few years). You could decide to own the shares of two companies instead, picking the second from a different industry sector, such as Marks and Spencer. You would reduce your risk, as the shares would behave differently to one another being in two different sectors with different economic drivers. If one went bust, the other probably would not. You could get on a roll and decide to divide your investment amongst ten companies, then twenty companies and you would reduce your risk further. Eventually you would reach a point between thirty and fifty stocks where the risk of your equity investments is similar to that of the market – market risk – as exhibited by, say, the FTSE All-Share index. Adding another fifty companies to your portfolio would make little difference from a risk perspective.

6.4 Market risk – the theoretical framework

In a seminal piece of work by Professor William Sharpe (1964), for which he won a Nobel Prize, he put forward the idea that only market risk – that is

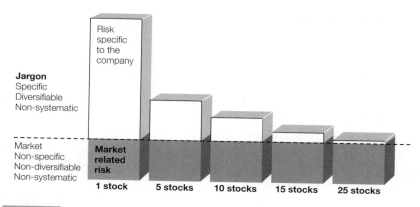

Figure 6.2 Company-specific risk is quickly eliminated

the risk that remains after all the risks associated with a specific company is diversified away – is rewarded. The only way to gain higher returns is to take on more market risk. In terms of terminology that you might come across, market risk is sometimes referred to as 'systematic' or 'non-specific' risk. Issuer specific (e.g. company or government) risk is also known as 'non-systematic' risk.

The model that he created is known as the Capital Asset Pricing Model (CAPM) and sits at the heart of modern finance (despite its critics). The underlying messages remain central to investment success: (a) avoid taking company-specific risks as they are not rewarded, and (b) market risk and return are related – more market risk = higher return (see Figure 6.2).

Market returns – the flip side of the risk story

However, the same is not true for achieving a market level of return. In reality a small number of stocks account for a high proportion of the return delivered by the market. As William Bernstein (2000) a leading thinker, practitioner and author states, when talking about capturing the market return:

'You can eliminate non-systematic portfolio risk, as defined by Modern Portfolio Theory, with a relatively few stocks. It's just that non-systematic risk is only a small part of the puzzle. Fifteen stocks is not enough. Thirty is not enough. Even 200 is not enough. The only way to truly minimize the risks of stock ownership is by owning the whole market.'

Recent research (Vanguard, 2012) supports this view. It looked at the dispersion of the performance of individual stocks in the Russell 1000 Index (a US large company index, a bit like the FTSE 100). It showed that in every year over the past five years (2007–2011) at least two-thirds of the stocks in the index exceeded or trailed the index return by more than 10 percentage points. This ranged from between about 65% to 80%. This research underlines just how important very broad diversification is, when trying to capture market returns.

6.5 Five key investment risk factors

The CAPM model was refined by Professors Eugene Fama and Kenneth French, two renowned academics in the USA, who developed the idea based on empirical data that three main risk factors define the characteristics of equity risk more effectively (they explain around 95% of a portfolio's risk) compared to Sharpe's single market risk factor (explaining around 75% of a portfolio's risk). They also noted that two risk factors define the broad characteristics of bonds (Figure 6.3). Their theory is commonly known as the 'Multi-factor Model' (Fama and French, 1993).

What does this mean for the practical investor?

Quite simply, it defines the five market risk decisions that we need to make when constructing portfolios. Stepping beyond risk-free lending adds risks. These riskier investments should deliver higher rates of return, over the longer term. We need to understand what each of these risks mean and whether we want to include them in our portfolios. Let us explore these five factors in turn.

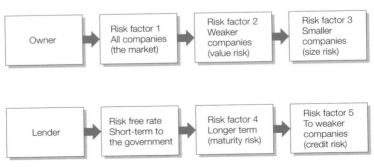

Figure 6.3 The five factors that describe equity and bond risk

6.6 Understanding equity risk

By buying equities you take on the risks associated with being an owner of a business. In the heady days when markets appear to go mad, it seems that people tend to forget that the stock market is not simply the electronic trading of pieces of e-paper, but the mechanism for valuing the future benefits of ownership in real companies run by real people with real products, reflected in the price of its shares. The level of your future wealth is inextricably linked to the fortunes of companies in which you are a part owner. Those fortunes depend on the ability of each company to employ their capital effectively, establish and execute a profitable business strategy, adapt to the uncertain forces that impact on the profitability of their industry and reap the benefit of the sheer hard work of those who work there.

In 1934, Benjamin Graham, one of the founding fathers of today's investment management industry, stated (Graham and Dodd, 1996):

'In the short run the market is a voting machine; in the long run, it is a weighing machine.'

In the longer term, the rewards that you receive are the cash dividends that the company pays and the rise in its share price attributable to the growth in earnings that the company can generate.

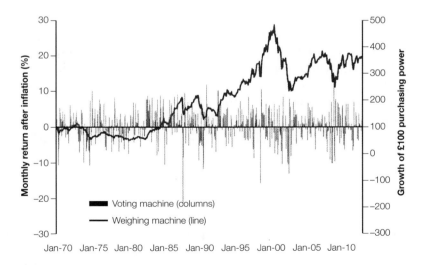

Figure 6.4 **The voting versus the weighing machine**

In the shorter term, these earnings can change, as can sentiment as to how much an investor should pay for these earnings. Share prices go up and down based on the market's collective interpretation of the latest information available. Bad earnings figures and negative sentiment can result in share price falls. In extremis companies can go bust and as a shareholder you can lose all your money.

It is the market's reaction to new news that moves share prices as the perceived prospects for earnings absorbed by the market. These minute-by-minute, week-by-week movements in share prices are the 'voting machine' that Benjamin Graham was referring to.

Over the longer term the returns for an equity investor weigh up the true value of ownership being the cash dividends received and the real growth in earnings that the company has delivered. This is the weighing machine. This longer-term return for taking on the voting machine risks of being an owner, above the risk-free rate, is known as the equity risk premium (see Figure 6.4).

Smaller company (size) and value risks

The Fama and French research referred to above, breaks down the risk that an investor receives into three key components:

- **Equity market risk:** being in the equity market as a whole, as opposed to simply holding 'safe' cash, for which you receive the equity risk premium, or ERP for short.

- **Size risk:** which is the risk of owning more risky smaller companies rather than larger companies, for which you would expect to receive an incremental premium – the size premium – relative to the market premium to compensate for these additional risks.

- **Value risk:** being the incremental risk of owning less healthy companies for which you would expect to receive an incremental premium – the value premium – relative to the market premium to compensate for these additional risks (Figure 6.5).

Investors need to evaluate whether or not they believe that these incremental risks, relative to those of simply owning broad exposure to developed markets and picking up the equity market risk premium, are likely to deliver adequate compensation for doing so. We will explore the research in the next chapter, when we construct the portfolios.

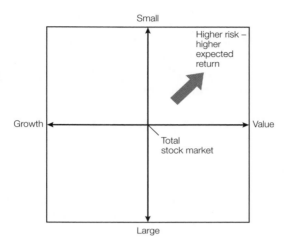

Figure 6.5 **Small and value stocks add risk, but also higher expected returns**

Considerable debate rages around these incremental risk premia, but with a bit of thought and common sense you can decide whether they should be part of your portfolio – the old saying 'all things in moderation' applies particularly well to risk choices in portfolios.

Note: As an aside you can imagine that this could be a useful tool in testing active manager skill as many managers simply have styles with long-term biases towards these return-enhancing factors that they sell and charge for as skill. Comparing their risk-factor-biased portfolios against broad market benchmarks is not a fair comparison. As we discovered earlier, the managers of the Norwegian fund delivered low market beating returns that were entirely attributable to the portfolio's exposure to these two factors – that is not manager skill, but systematic exposure to risks that, over time, are expected to deliver higher returns than the market.

6.7 Understanding bond risk

Simply put, bonds are IOUs issued by companies and governments to investors, which pay a fixed rate of interest to the lender, known as its coupon, and promises them that their principal will be returned at a set date in the future, known as its maturity date. Simple – well almost!

The relationship between yield and price

The coupon that the bond will pay will need to be attractive and reward you for the various risks that you are taking on, which may relate to the market as a whole or may be specific to the issuer and structure of the bond. Bonds are generally issued at a price of 100 referred to as 'Par'. At the maturity date of the bond, if you had invested £100 when a bond was first issued, you would receive back £100 at maturity. In the interim, though, the price of the bond, and thus the value of your capital invested, may move either up or down as yields change. Let us see why this happens.

Over time, after the bond is issued, the market's perception of the risks a bondholder is bearing is likely to change and the yield – the compensation that investors require for taking these risks – will change too. Examples could be yield rises on account of a new, higher expectation for inflation, or perhaps the weakening financial state of the issuer. As the coupon (rate of interest) is fixed throughout the bond's life, the only way in which a change in yield can be delivered is through a change to the bond's price. If yields rise, bond prices fall. If yields fall, bond prices rise. This is sometimes referred to as the bond see-saw, with yields at one end and prices at the other (Figure 6.6).

The components of a bond's yield

At its simplest, the yield on a bond can be broken down into six components, some of which relate to all bonds (the risk-free rate) and some of which relate to the specific circumstances of the issuer of the bond and the characteristics of the bond. Let us start by looking at a risk-free investment i.e. lending on a short-term basis (say for one month) to a government with an AAA credit rating (the highest there is). The risk of not receiving the

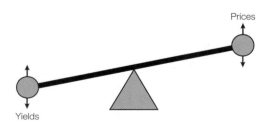

Figure 6.6 **The bond see-saw**

interest due and your money back is negligible. The rate of return you will receive will be made up of two things:

■ **Real yield:** the real (after inflation) return that you expect to be paid – the real yield – in compensation for supplying your capital to the government as opposed to utilising it elsewhere to your benefit. There is obviously some uncertainty in this return and investors expect a small risk premium to compensate for it.

■ **Inflation expectation:** the market's expectation for future inflation needs to be included to make sure that you receive the real return you are due. Because this estimate for inflation has some uncertainty in it, investors expect a small premium for taking it on.

As you move away from this risk-free position, the yield on the bond is going to rise for two major reasons. These are the two risk factors mentioned above:

■ **Credit (default) risk:** this is the risk of not being paid the coupon on the bond and receiving the par value of the bond at its maturity date. The lower the credit quality of the bond's issuer, the higher the yield must be to compensate for higher levels of default. Credit risk is sometimes referred to as default risk. Credit rating is explored in more depth below.

■ **Maturity (interest rate) risk:** this is the risk to the price of your bond that relates to changes in future interest rates. The longer you

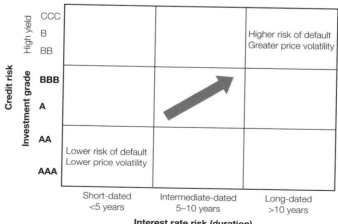

Figure 6.7 Credit risk and maturity risk choices

lend your money for, the greater the impact a change in market yields (in response to changing risks) will have on the price of the bond. This is explored in a little more depth below (Figure 6.7).

Other factors that relate to the specific bond include:

- **Liquidity risk:** depending upon how much of the bond has been issued, how it has been issued and who holds it will impact on how liquid it is, i.e. how easy it is to sell at a fair price. The less liquid the bond, the higher the compensation an investor will demand for holding it.

- **Structural risk:** certain structural features that may be more attractive to the borrower than to the investor, for which the investor needs to be compensated.

Credit (default) risk in practice

Rating agencies assign credit quality ratings to companies and governments who issue bonds. You will have heard the term 'Triple-A rated', which refers to the strongest issuer and is often used in everyday conversation. UK government debt has recently been downgraded from AAA to AA by one of the rating agencies. Ratings from AAA to BBB are known as *investment grade* and BB and below are known as *sub-investment grade, high yield* or *junk*. Table 6.1 provides some broad insight into the credit rating system. As you slide down the alphabet through the Bs and the Cs, the cost of capital rises as does the expected return, reflected in the increased yield an investor receives for lending money to them. In other words, as the risk of default rises, investors will demand additional compensation.

The question that needs to be answered is whether or not this credit or 'default' risk is adequately compensated. In short, high credit quality is preferred (AA and above on average) as the lower the credit risk, the less robust i.e. defensive they are when equity markets crash. More on that in Chapter 7.

Tips: Always look out for the 'average credit quality' for any bond fund that you are interested in. Check out what the minimum average credit quality constraint is and review the distribution of the credit ratings of the holdings of the fund.

| Table 6.1 | An insight into what credit ratings mean |

Moody	S&P	Fitch	Broad definitions (derived from S&P)
Investment grade			
Aaa	AAA	AAA	Extremely strong capacity to meet obligations
Aa1	AA+	AA+	
Aa2	AA	AA	Very strong capacity to meet obligations
Aa3	AA-	AA-	
A1	A+	A+	
A2	A	A	Strong capacity to meet obligations but some vulnerability
A3	A-	A-	
Baa1	BBB+	BBB+	Adequate capacity to meet obligations but some vulnerabilities
Baa2	BBB	BBB	
Baa3	BBB-	BBB-	Lowest investment-grade rating
Non-investment grade (high yield)			
Ba1	BB+	BB+	Not immediately vulnerable, but could be
Ba2	BB	BB	
Ba3	BB-	BB-	
B1	B+	B+	More vulnerable to adverse conditions
B2	B	B	
B3	B-	B-	
Caa1	CCC+	CCC	Currently vulnerable
Caa2	CCC		
Caa3	CCC-		
Ca	CC		Currently highly vulnerable
	C		A bankruptcy petition has been filed
C	D	DDD	In default
/		DD	
/		D	

Maturity (interest rate) risk in practice

If you leave money in your current account, where you have instant access to your funds, you do not generally expect to get paid much interest. However, if you placed a deposit for two years (leaving aside the credit risk issue above) you would expect to receive a higher rate of interest for tying up your money. That is because (a) your money can erode in spending power terms through the effects of inflation; (b) you have an opportunity cost of tying up your money which the borrower needs to compensate you for; (c) you have the risk of not knowing what return you will be able to reinvest the interest payments at. This is known as the time value of money.

The flip side of the increased expected return from owning a bond that matures further into the future is that its price, which moves to reflect the market's ever-changing yield requirement, will be more sensitive to movements in yields.

The bond see-saw above explains the generic relationship between yields and prices but it only tells us that as yields rise, bond prices fall and vice versa. The sensitivity of a bond's price to a change in yields is known as its *duration* and is a measure described in years. It describes how far out along the bond see-saw you are sitting. Think of it this way: a bond represents a series of cash flows being the regular coupon payments you receive and your principal back at maturity. Duration is the measure of the average maturity of these cash flows payments, discounted into today's money, where each payment is weighted by its value. Put simply, it is the average time in which a bondholder is paid back.

Rule of thumb to calculate gains or losses

There is some complicated mathematics to do to calculate a bond's duration, but don't worry, you will never have to do it! What you do need to know is how sensitive prices are to movements in yields for bonds with different durations. A very useful rule of thumb exists that allows you to understand the impact of a change in yields on the price of a bond (or fund made up of many bonds).

Duration × Rise (fall) in yield = Capital loss (gain)

Remember to add the coupon you receive into your calculation to see whether your total return is a gain or a loss. In Table 6.2 you can see very clearly that the longer the duration of a bond, or a portfolio of bonds, the greater the change in price for a given movement in yields. This is important to understand.

Table 6.2   **The longer the duration, the more volatile the price**

Price change			Duration			
Yield rise	1 year	2 years	3 years	4 years	5 years	10 years
1%	−1%	−2%	−3%	−4%	−5%	−10%
2%	−2%	−4%	−6%	−8%	−10%	−20%
3%	−3%	−6%	−9%	−12%	−15%	−30%

The question that needs to be answered is whether or not this 'maturity' or 'interest rate risk' is adequately compensated. In short the answer is not adequately enough – shorter-dated bonds are preferred as they are less volatile, as you can see below. More on that in Chapter 7.

> **Tip**: Always find out what the *weighted average duration* of any bond fund product is. Duration figures should be readily available on the fund's fact sheet and if they are not then ask for them from the fund provider. Once you know the fund's duration you can work out how much its price will fall for a given rise in bond yields. Never buy any form of bond investment without knowing its duration.

6.8 Risk choices are limited

As you can see, when you strip investing bare, it is pretty uncomplicated. There are two main ways in which you can generate returns: by being an owner or by being a lender. Getting the right mix between these is the key step. These returns can be enhanced by taking on credit and maturity risk as a lender and equity market risk, size and value risks as an owner, but,

Table 6.3   The risks we face and how we will deal with them

Market risk	Take	Avoid	Reduce	Transfer
Equity risk – broad market	X			
Equity risk – size (smaller companies)	X			
Equity risk – value (less healthy companies)	X			
Bond risk – credit AA and above	X			
Bond risk – < AA average		X		
Bond risk – short duration	X			
Bond risk – long duration		X		
Currency risk – non-GBP equity	X			
Currency risk – non-GBP bonds				X
Implementation risk	**Take**	**Avoid**	**Reduce**	**Transfer**
Company specific risk			X	
Sector specific risk			X	
Country specific risk			X	
Liquidity risk		X		
Active manager underperformance risk		X		
Counterparty risk			X	
Inflation risk			X	
Deflation risk			X	
Fraud risk			X	

again, only if as an investor you feel that you are adequately compensated for doing so. Table 6.3 provides a summary of the risks we face and sorts them into the four key outcomes: take the risk, avoid the risk, reduce the risk or transfer it.

The decisions that it conveys are based on my own assessment of the evidence, which is summarised at various points in Chapter 7 for those asset classes that we seek to use.

6.9 Risk choices in the real world

While the framework above defines what risks we do or do not want to take in portfolios, and provide a good steer for us, we now face the task of looking at real world investments and deciding, against some straight-forward criterion, how specific asset classes and investment strategies that we see and hear about, stack up. In practice, risk choices are not always clear cut and we need to look at each asset class in turn, and make a judgement as to whether or not they should be included on your menu, given the tools we have at our disposal (historical data, economic and investment theory and a good dose of common sense).

Practical criteria for including building blocks

The criteria for inclusion fall into two main categories: those relating to the investment characteristics of the asset class and those that concern the ability of the asset class (i.e. the risks you want to take) to be replicated effectively. Let us look at the first category.

Criterion 1: Market-based returns

The returns of the asset class should rely on market-based returns and not manager skill. This comes back to the active versus passive debate that we hopefully settled in Chapter 4. You want to make sure that you understand and that you know where the returns are coming from (i.e. the economic rewards of being an owner and/or a lender). You do not want your returns to be based on the transient moment of luck or judgement of individuals – back capitalism every time, not individual skill! If you cannot explain to yourself where returns come from, perhaps think about not using this building block.

Criterion 2: Useful history

The return history should provide adequate insight into the characteristics that the building block exhibits. Some investment opportunities come backed almost only with a good story and the air of hope (often sprayed around by the marketing department). Others come with short and flawed track records (such as hedge fund industry performance where very significant biases offer a misleading picture). We want to base our decisions on data that at least provides adequate insight into the ups and downs over preferably longer periods of time. Look hard at the numbers presented to you. Do you understand their limitations? What are they telling you?

Criterion 3: Positive contribution

The functional attributes that the asset class possesses should make a meaningful contribution at the portfolio level. When an asset class is added to a portfolio mix, it needs to bring something positive to the table. It should deliver one of a number of contributions: provide an equity-like return, such as those derived from the UK equity market; it should offer the opportunity for higher equity returns than the broad market; or it should do a good job of reducing equity market risk. Remember that the risk of owning an asset class needs to be adequately compensated. Additionally, some asset classes do a better job at protecting wealth in different situations, such as unanticipated inflation, deflation or simply when the world is running scared (e.g. during the Credit Crisis).

The second category set relates to the practical implementation of the portfolio strategy that you decide upon.

Criterion 4: Return capture

Products that cleanly replicate these characteristics should be available given the level of your assets and circumstances. There is little point pursuing an asset class or investment strategy that you cannot access effectively either because the minimum economic investment is too high or access to the assets is based upon private transactions – private equity being a case in point for most individual investors. You may also not want to get involved in products that introduce non-market risks, such as counterparty risk.

Criterion 5: Liquid

Any products should have sufficient liquidity to allow you to rebalance your portfolio efficiently, when it drifts away from its long-term strategy, as it will. A good and recent example is the use of bricks and mortar commercial property funds that directly purchased real estate on behalf of the fund. In 2008 redemptions were high in a falling market and emergency redemption clauses were invoked, tying in clients for several months in some cases. The ability of clients to adjust their own portfolios, just at the time they need to, is an important attribute.

Criterion 6: Low costs

Products have low all-in costs that eat up as little of the market returns on offer as is possible. This is important because expensive products may take a significant proportion of the market return, to the benefit of all those involved in its management and distribution, while you take 100% of the market risks. Costs really matter in this game, as you will see when we explore this point in more depth later.

Filtering out the good from the bad

In Table 6.4, you will see a summary of how different asset classes stack up against these criteria. Many investment professionals, advisers and

Table 6.4   Defining the asset class menu

Criteria	1	2	3	4	5	6
Asset class/Strategy	Market return	Data history	Contri-bution	Replicable	Liquid	Low cost
Developed market equity (market)	✓	✓	✓	✓	✓	✓
Developed market equity (small)	✓	✓	✓	✓	✓	✓
Developed market equity (value)	✓	✓	✓	✓	✓	✓
Emerging market equity (market)	✓	✓	✓	✓	✓	✓
Emerging market equity (small)	✓	✓	✓	✓	✓	✓
Emerging market equity (value)	✓	✓	✓	✓	✓	✓
Global real estate	✓	✓	✓	✓	✓	✓
Commodity futures	X	X	✓	X	✓	✓
Fund of hedge funds	X	X	X	X	X	X
Private equity investment	✓	X	X	X	X	X
Structured products	✓	X	X	✓	X	X
Gold and other precious metals	X	✓	X	✓	✓	✓
High yield (<BBB) bonds	✓	✓	X	X	X	X
Cash	✓	✓	X	✓	✓	✓
Shorter-dated (AA min) bonds*	✓	✓	✓	✓	✓	✓
Longer-dated <(AA min) bonds*	✓	✓	X	✓	✓	✓
Shorter-dated inflation linked bonds*	✓	✓	✓	✓	✓	✓
Longer-dated inflation linked (AA min) bonds*	✓	✓	X	✓	✓	✓

Excluded assets =

* If non-GBP then fully hedged back to GBP at the fund level

individual investors, perhaps including you, may disagree. You need to have strong and defensible reasons for doing so and evidence to back up your case. The evidence used is explored in the individual asset class summaries and discussion later in the book.

Asset class assumptions

Tables 6.5 and 6.6 provide a reasonable set of forward looking assumptions for the building blocks that are included on the menu. The underlying rationale is covered in Part 5 of the book where we dig a little deeper into each asset class. Note that these are useful as they form the basis for the

Table 6.5   On-menu asset class assumptions – return and risk

Building block	Expected real return	Premium	Risk
Growth-oriented, risky assets			
Developed equity markets	5% p.a.		20%
Emerging equity markets	7% p.a.	+2% p.a.	30%
Value (less healthy) equities	7% p.a.	+2% p.a.	25%
Smaller company equities	7% p.a.	+2% p.a.	25%
Global real estate	4% p.a.		15%
Defensive assets			
Shorter-dated bonds (AA min)	1%		5%
Shorter-dated inflation linked bonds (AA min)	0.5%		8%

Table 6.6   Correlations between asset classes

Asset class		Asset 1	Asset 2	Asset 3	Asset 4	Asset 5	Asset 6	Asset 7	Asset 8
UK equity	Asset 1	1.0							
UK value equity	Asset 2	1.0	1.0						
UK small cap equity	Asset 3	0.8	0.7	1.0					
World ex-UK equity	Asset 4	0.8	0.8	0.7	1.0				
World ex-UK value equity	Asset 5	0.8	0.8	0.7	1.0	1.0			
World ex-UK small cap equity	Asset 6	0.7	0.6	0.7	0.8	0.8	1.0		
Emerging markets equity	Asset 7	0.7	0.6	0.7	0.8	0.8	0.7	1.0	
Global commercial real estate	Asset 8	0.5	0.5	0.5	0.6	0.7	0.7	0.6	1.0

1.0–0.8   = marginal benefit   0.7–0.4   = reasonable benefit   <0.4   = strong benefit

return and risk that the portfolios we come up with may exhibit. These are simply reasonable guesses and you should probably model in some more disappointing outcomes into your plans.

References

Bernstein, W. J. (2000) 'The 15-Stock Diversification Myth' (www.efficientfrontier.com).

Breakwell, G. and Barnett, J. (2007) *The Psychology of Risk: An Introduction.* Cambridge University Press, p. 1.

Fama, E. F. and French, K. R. (1993) 'Common risk factors in the returns on stocks and bonds', *Journal of Financial Economics*, 33, 3–56.

Graham, B. and Dodd, D. (1996) *Security Analysis: The Classic 1934 Edition.* New York: McGraw Hill.

Sharp, W. F. (1964) 'Capital asset prices: a theory of market equilibrium under conditons of risk', *Journal of Finance*, 19(3), 425–42.

Vanguard (2012) 'Dispersion! Not correlation!' (www.vanguard.com; https://institutional.vanguard.com/VGApp/iip/site/institutional/researchcommentary/article/InvResDispersionCorrelation)

7

Smarter portfolio construction

Building a sensible and robust portfolio is not as complicated or as difficult as people make out. For some investors, simply owning a broad exposure to global equities, for example using an index tracker fund and holding cash in the right proportions, is sufficient. This is a sort of 90/10 portfolio, with 90% of the value for only 10% of the hassle. Such a strategy would put most private client fund managers and stockbrokers out of business!

Beyond this simple yet effective structure, the decisions that are made are simply refinements. At the end of the day, the various decisions we are going to consider making are trying to improve (a) just owning global equities and (b) simply owning cash. That does not mean that these incremental decisions are not of value, they are – just like the time and effort David Brailsford spends with his helmet design and wind tunnel tests.

It makes good sense to try to construct more robust and better diversified portfolios based on the evidence we have to hand, a bit of hard thinking and a good dose of common sense. What does not make sense is getting caught up in overcomplicated software models, taking on risks that are not adequately rewarded or the myriad of faddish sectors and market 'opportunities' peddled by those who think that complexity justifies their fees.

As you will see, the smarter investing approach is to keep things robust, transparent and simple, resulting in effective and survivable portfolios. We have already selected a sensible menu of asset classes to use, in the previous chapter.

7.1 The past is eventful, the future is uncertain

You only need to look back at the past thirty years or so to register just what might be thrown at you and your portfolio. We have had oil crises, war, terrorism, rampant inflation, low inflation, three major equity market crashes, irrational exuberance in the dot.com world and the housing market, the credit crisis and the recent spectre of deflation, to name just a few. It does not seem unreasonable to think that it makes sense to cover a few of these bases. You have the opportunity to build a portfolio for all seasons. As ever, in investing there is no right or wrong answer, just answers that probably give you a better chance of surviving with your investment programme intact and your goals achieved. It is worth bearing in mind the wise words of John Bogle:

'Asset allocation [your mix of building blocks] is not a panacea. It is a reasoned – if imperfect – approach to the inevitable uncertainty of the financial markets.'

And as William Bernstein succinctly agrees:

'Since the future cannot be predicted, it is impossible to specify in advance what the best asset allocation will be. Rather, our job is to find an allocation that will do reasonably well under a wide range of circumstances.'

7.2 Building a portfolio for all seasons

It is impossible to tell what lies ahead, but history does provide us with some insight into the magnitudes and frequencies of both sides of the coin. If we accept that we face such uncertainty, the only protection that we have is

Table 7.1 Make use of the roles that different asset classes play

Asset class contribution	Key portfolio role			Environment			
	Return	Return +	Diversifier	Inflation	Unanticipated Inflation	Deflation	Crisis
Equity-oriented assets							
Developed markets	X				X		
Emerging markets		X			X		
Value companies		X			X		
Smaller companies		X			X		
Global real estate (REITs)	X		X		X		
Bond/defensive assets							
Shorter-dated (AA min) bonds*				X	X	X	X
Shorter-dated inflation linked bonds*				X	X	X	X

* If non-GBP then fully hedged back to GBP at the fund level

to try to own a well-diversified mix of assets that have the potential within their structure, and the process through which they generate economic returns, to mitigate some of the risks that we, as investors, face and to deliver the returns we need. Table 7.1 summarises the different roles that our 'on-menu' asset classes (risk factors) that we selected in Chapter 6 can play.

A clear understanding and acceptance of what each asset class building block brings to the table, i.e. the key role it plays and the risks that it mitigates, will allow you to view your portfolio as a whole and not as its constituent parts. This is vitally important because at any point one asset class is likely to be doing better than another. Looked at in isolation the temptation is to chase the market. Looking at it holistically encourages us to remember that each asset has its role and its time.

In summary, the goal when constructing portfolios is to create a basket of risks that is:

■ Broadly diversified across securities, markets and asset classes (e.g. equities, bonds).

■ Offers a robust and attractive ('efficient' to use the industry jargon) relationship between risk and reward.

■ Exhibits a range and pattern of returns that is appropriate to you.

7.3 The construction approach

I have seen many approaches to constructing portfolios, from the seemingly sophisticated asset allocation models run by investment banks to the exceptionally simple two-building-block (bonds and equities) approach outlined above. Better practitioners will end up in approximately the right place, whatever process they adopt, and one cannot say that any answer is wrong if the split between growth and defensive assets takes into account the client's emotional tolerance for risk, their need to take it and their financial capacity to absorb losses. You should be in the right ball park. The approach adopted here is based on solid investment theory and has a certain clear logic that makes great sense to most people. To put in into context, it might help to review quickly the investment theory on which it is based.

Not so modern, Modern Portfolio Theory

The beneficial effect of combining asset classes whose return patterns are not exactly similar (i.e. they are imperfectly correlated) is to increase the return of a portfolio without increasing its bumpiness of returns, or alternatively to keep the same level of return and decrease the bumpiness of returns. This phenomena of diversification was first explored in depth and mathematically described by Harry Markowitz in the 1950s and is generally referred to as Modern Portfolio Theory (Markowitz, 1952). He won the Nobel Prize for it. Simply put, and without doing down Markowitz's achievement, you can smooth portfolio returns by owning blocks that are zigging, while other blocks you own are zagging, without giving up return. The more they zig and zag without relationship to each other the more the relationship between return and risk is improved. Modern Portfolio Theory still lies at the centre of much investment industry thinking today, despite its critics (Bernstein, 1996). Portfolios that display the best trade-off between risk and return are said in the lingo of the investment world to be 'efficient'. A rational investor might be expected to select the appropriate efficient portfolio to invest in.

As an interesting aside, it is perhaps ironic that Markowitz himself confessed that he did not use his Nobel Prize-winning equation when it came down to investing his own money! He simply states:

'I visualized my grief if the stock market went way up and I wasn't in it — or if it went way down and I was completely in it. So I split my contributions 50/50 between stocks and bonds.' (Zweig, 2007)

As another aside, means-variance optimisation (MVO) software, which is derived from the quadratic equation that Markowitz developed, is still widely used in the investment industry, but is rarely used with much common sense or insight. What it attempts to do is to identify portfolio structures at every point along the risk spectrum where the trade-off between return and risk is most favourable. The result is a graph that usually looks like a banana, referred to as the 'efficient frontier', but is of less practical use. Unconstrained optimisation tends to generate unintuitive portfolio structures, due to estimation error maximisation (Michaud, 1989). Outcomes are extremely sensitive to small changes in the return/risk relationship, and return in particular. Reflect on this comment if you are tempted by the sexiness and seemingly sophisticated nature of optimisation software, and advisers that use it:

'Despite the mysticism many perceive in these tools, understand that all these tools do is to solve a mathematical equation. They do not know what you are inputting into them and will calculate whatever you ask them to. These tools don't even know they are solving financial problems (or creating them).' (Loeper, 2003)

In accordance with Modern Portfolio Theory (MPT) a rational investor should seek to own an efficient portfolio. Another piece of seminal academic work provides us with an insight into how we can tackle the portfolio construction problem.

Whisky and water – keeping it simple

James Tobin's Separation Theorem (Tobin, 1957) suggests that the most efficient portfolio available is the 'market portfolio', i.e. the market cap weighted global asset mix (i.e. all the bonds and equities in the world). No portfolio has a theoretically better set of risk/return characteristics as this equilibrium portfolio. Thus, in a theoretical world, investors should own this market portfolio and simply add risk-free assets to it to create lower risk/lower reward portfolios, or leverage it if they wish to increase the risk of the portfolio beyond that of the market portfolio.

Our approach is a sort of common sense derivation, based around creating a reasonably efficient and effective pool of risky assets, taking the market risks we want to take and then diluting this risky pool by adding defensive, less risky assets to it to a level that is appropriate. I was talking this approach through with one of my clients, BoulterBowen WealthCare, one day and they coined it the 'whisky and water' approach – a great word picture, for which I thank them. Let us follow this simple analogy through. From hereon in we will talk about the 'whisky' element as the Return Engine and the 'water' component as the Defensive Mix.

Blending scotch

Considerable care is taken in the creation of a blended malt whisky to create a distinctive flavour from a number of single malts that is robust and will remain consistent over time. That is our risky mix of growth/return oriented asset classes that meet our selection criteria. Whilst some will drink their Scotch neat, others, depending on their palate and desire to avoid ill effects, will dilute it with water to a flavour and strength that is right for them. That is the addition of our defensive assets that water down the strength of the pool of risky assets.

The first step then is to create our blended portfolio of investment assets; the second is to identify what goes into the defensive, less risky mix; and the final step is to mix the two together to create suitable portfolio choices (see Figure 7.1).

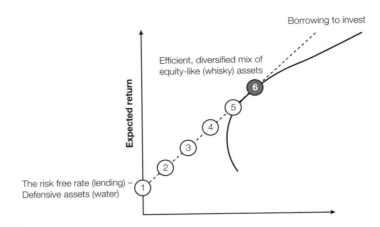

Figure 7.1 A simple yet effective approach

7.4 Ground rules for the Return Engine

The goal in creating the growth-oriented (whisky) mix is to create a diversified portfolio that will deliver strong, equity-like above inflation returns over the long term. Hopefully, through diversification, this mix will deliver returns at least in line with a broad alternative of UK or global developed market equities over the long term, but at lower risk. In order to create an orderly construction of your portfolio, five key issues need to be addressed:

- Issue 1: how globally diversified should your portfolio be?

- Issue 2: what allocation will you make to higher risk emerging markets?

- Issue 3: Will you overweight your exposure to smaller and value (less healthy) companies across all markets to increase your expected returns?

- Issue 4: Will you include other asset classes to diversify equity market risk, such as commercial property? (Note that this is distinct from adding defensive assets to this risk basket.)

- Issue 5: Should you take on non-GBP (or other base currency) currency exposure?

Issue 1: Global diversification

For many investors, when they think of equity risk, they think about UK equities and the FTSE 100 index (the 'Footsie'). This is their natural reference point, despite the fact that it only covers the top 100 companies out of approximately 15,000 (or more) eligible global companies that they could be invested in. This liking for one's own market is known as home bias and is very common and pronounced across both institutional and individual investors. Yet, the UK market only accounts for around 10% of global equity market capitalisation and its Gross Domestic Product or GDP (a gauge of economic output) is less than 5% of the global economy. You can see the immediate flaw in being wholly invested in the UK.

Talk to an investment purist and they would say that the most effective starting point is fully backing capitalism across the globe and owning a share of more or less every listed company in the world, based on their market capitalisation. Not a bad idea in my mind.

The reaction of many investors, when they look through a global equity fund to the country allocation, is a reluctance to trade a home bias in the UK for what appears to be a bias to the USA. But remember that the USA accounts for around one-quarter of global GDP and around 35% of global equity market capitalisation in both developed and emerging markets. When it comes to structuring the growth-oriented Return Engine mix, options at both ends of the spectrum (100% home bias to a market cap weighted global portfolio) are provided, along with a compromise balance between the two (see Figure 7.2).

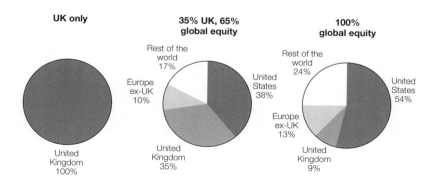

Figure 7.2 **Developed market equity allocation options**

Source: Data from Global Equity – MSCI World Equity Index

The central risk of UK equities performing poorly over short and longer periods of time should make it obvious that owning a more diversified exposure to companies around the world makes good sense. The salutary lesson of the Japanese market that languished 60% below its peak almost twenty years later is one reason why you need to diversify globally.

Why does 'home bias' occur?

There are a number of suggested reasons why home bias occurs, such as avoiding non-domestic risks, the costs of investing overseas, information asymmetries – where investors know more about domestic stocks (or at least think they do), corporate governance differences and behavioural biases. It is likely that it is a mix of all of these to some extent, and will vary by investor. On the behavioural side of the equation, some investors appear to have a distaste for, or fear of, foreign stock (Huberman, 2001). Others tend to suffer regret when they own a portfolio that behaves differently from that of their home market (Solnick, 2008). Familiarity, patriotism and overconfidence, for example in names like Marks & Spencer or BP, sometimes makes investors feel that they are investing in something less risky, or with better prospects than an unknown name. In reality this is unlikely to be the case. Less sophisticated and experienced investors also seem to exhibit higher levels of home bias in their portfolios (Kimball et al., 2010).

Looking a bit deeper at the issue

A paper on globalisation (Russell Investments, 2010) posed three simple questions with thought-provoking answers. They are worth repeating at the start of this brief insight into 'home bias' – the phenomenon (and puzzle) as to why investors, both individual and institutional, tend to have a far higher allocation to equities listed on their home markets, than to international markets. Investment theory and logic would suggest that home bias is neither entirely rational nor optimal. The questions posed were as follows:

Q1: What is the largest bank in the world, by market capitalisation (i.e. the value of its shares)? *Answer: ICBC of China.*

Q2: Where is General Electric's largest research & development facility located? *Answer: Bangalore, India.*

Q3: How many of the top return-generating companies over the past three years were in the US? *Answer: one in the top 201.*

Ever more global – a few interesting insights

The rate of globalisation has been dramatic over the past three decades, driven by free trade organisations such as NAFTA and the World Trade Organization, lower tariffs on imported goods around the world, the global expansion of the supply chains and operations of multinational companies, and the internet. Take McDonalds for example: twenty-five years ago, the Big Mac was available in 6,000 restaurants in the USA and 1,000 overseas. Today there are now more than 18,000 franchised outlets worldwide representing more than 50% of the corporation's profits. In fact, global trade has risen since 1970 from under 20% of global GDP to around 60% of GDP.

Distinguishing between markets is not easy

Take, for example, the FTSE 100 index (the top 100 listed UK companies by capitalisation); around 70% of its constituent companies' earnings come from overseas, of which an absolute 20% comes from emerging markets. Standard Chartered Bank (sponsors of Liverpool Football Club, who have a very large following in Asia), derives most of its revenues from the emerging markets. Vodafone is another example of a company where the majority of its revenues are generated outside the UK (mainly the USA). In the USA, constituent companies of the S&P 500 Index derive in excess of 40% of earnings from outside the USA, like McDonalds. In fact approximately 70% of world equity market capitalisation is dominated by multinational companies (Brinson, 2005).

Samsung Electronics, a Korean company, is one of the largest stocks in the MSCI Emerging Markets Index, and generates somewhere in the region of 40% of its revenues from Europe and the Americas (Staverman, 2011). The web of cross-border corporate earnings is extremely complex.

It is tempting to think that perhaps one could be sufficiently globally diversified by staying at home, safely investing in familiar companies like HSBC – the Hong Kong & Shanghai Banking Corporation to give it its full name. While that may be feasible, particularly if the home market is large and diverse enough such as the USA, the solution is likely to be sub-optimal in the UK. It can also lead to biases in the sectors that an investor is exposed to such as mining, oil and banks in the UK.

For most, global diversification makes good sense

Modern Portfolio Theory, the foundation stone of sensible investing, suggests that diversification – placing eggs in multiple baskets – can and should help to deliver a better relationship between the risk taken and the return received. On that basis, investors should consider spreading a majority of their equity eggs into baskets outside of their home market.

The paradox, as investors strive for diversification, is that globalisation appears to have increased the correlation between markets. During the credit crisis all equity markets fell together (although high quality bonds did a sterling job). Yet to dismiss diversification as a spent force risks throwing the baby out with the bath water. For long-term investors, well spread portfolios have the likelihood, although not the guarantee, that they will deliver a better investment journey.

Research (Asness, 2010) indicates clearly that global diversification makes sense. Using market data from 1950 to 2009 demonstrated that broad diversification made a material difference to wealth protection on the downside over one, five and ten years time horizons across the majority of investor home bases reviewed. The paper concluded that in the short term, market panic and global contagion tend to result in markets falling together, but in the medium to long term (which should concern investors more) the underlying basket of economic growth provides protection from one economy performing poorly. That is a pretty good summary (see Table 7.2).

Perhaps as importantly, one of the principal aims of the Return Engine element of the portfolio is to capture the wealth creation delivered by the dynamism of global capitalism. Remember that in 2012, the global economy actually grew by around 3–4% after inflation, despite the sluggish, after-inflation growth of Western economies. In order to capture this wealth creation potential, over time, investors must own global capitalism in a far

Table 7.2   Global diversification reduces downside risks

	Worst 1-year (%)		Worst 5-years (%)		Worst 10-years (%)	
	Domestic	Global	Domestic	Global	Domestic	Global
Japan	−47	−51	−47	−48	−54	**−41**
Germany	−54	**−39**	−53	**−47**	−45	**−30**
UK	−61	**−47**	−67	**−36**	−61	**−21**
France	−53	**−43**	−53	**−45**	−58	**−25**
US	−48	**−47**	−45	**−32**	−40	**−16**
Australia	−48	**−44**	−60	**−44**	−34	**−21**
Average	−51	**−45**	−54	**−42**	−49	**−26**

Bold = *improved outcome*

Source: Asness (2010)

broader manner than is on offer by simply investing in FTSE companies, despite their overseas earnings exposure. Missing out on 90% of what you could own makes little sense.

Diversification within developed markets (e.g. USA, Germany, France, Japan etc.) is all about risk reduction, not better returns. The cost of raising capital, in aggregate, by companies in one market is expected to be broadly similar across developed markets, over time.

> **Note**: It is important to make sure that you do not continually judge your robust, globally diversified Return Engine, once it is constructed, against a home-based benchmark that is familiar to you, such as the 'Footsie' (FTSE 100). Torturing yourself over short-term market noise is a recipe for an unhappy investment experience. Try to remember the longer-term reasons why your portfolio is structured as it is – as a portfolio for all seasons – and learn to take comfort in its robustness.

Issue 2: Emerging market exposure

While many glibly talk about emerging markets, we rarely stop to think what this really means, getting caught up in the now too familiar story that they are the future and the west is in terminal decline. Believe that one at your peril. Emerging markets are still risky to invest in, and not just because they are volatile.

Companies in emerging markets have a considerably higher cost of capital, in aggregate. The flip side of the coin is that the expected return for providing capital (owning equities or bonds) is higher than that of developed markets. Many investors seem to forget that these risks are quite considerable and need to be taken in a controlled manner and in moderation; they include corruption, political instability, the lack of an established rule of law, limited freedom of the press, weak corporate governance and the sudden imposition of foreign exchange restrictions (remember Malaysia in 1997), to name a few. As we stated in Chapter 6 and cover further in Chapter 12, sensible expectations for higher expected returns are probably in the region of 1% to 2% above developed market equities over the longer term.

How much should you allocate to emerging markets?

We already know that many companies listed in developed markets have high exposure to emerging economies and we know that owning local companies may well be a riskier proposition. As such allocations of between 10% and 20% of the growth part of the portfolio would be reasonable.

Much less and they make little difference, much more and the risk is that it begins to overpower the structure based around developed market equities. A weighting based on global market capitalisation would be in the region of 15%.

Issue 3: Overweighting smaller and value companies

An opportunity exists to try to raise the expected return from the Return Engine of the portfolio by adding incremental slices of smaller companies and value (less healthy) companies to the portfolio pie. These two incremental risks were covered in Chapter 6 and are explored more deeply in Chapter 12. The incremental expected return, over and above the return from a broad market exposure may well be in the region of 1% to 2%, which is a valuable contributor to portfolio returns.

Inevitably, while attempting to capture these longer-term risk premia, periods will exist in the shorter and possibly longer term where these tilts may not pay off against the broader market (Figure 7.3). The chances of a positive premium (which adds valuable returns to your portfolio) and the chances of a negative premium was explored in recent research (Fama and French, 2012).

The authors concluded:

'In a nutshell, the message ... is that long time periods are required to be reasonably sure that the average equity premium, the average size premium, or the average value premium will be positive ... Indeed, no matter how long the investment period, one can never be perfectly certain that the realized average premium will be positive. Such is the nature of risk and return!'

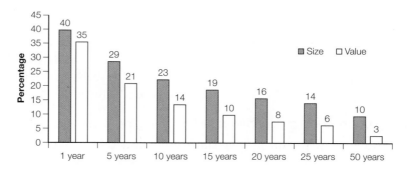

Figure 7.3 Chances of a negative risk premium

Source: Data from Fama and French (2012)

Reasonable allocations

As such, allocations of between 10% and 20% (to each of value and smaller companies) of the Return Engine would be reasonable. Much less and they make little difference, much more and the risk is that short-term underperformance of the broad market makes you tempted to bail out of the strategy. The more confident that you are in the efficacy of these premia, the more you could allocate to them. My advice is to use them, but do not bet the farm.

Issue 4: Decide on your equity market diversifiers

The bulk of the 2000s have been a salutary lesson in the fact that equity markets do not always go up or quickly bounce back, which was the delusion carried over from the raging bull market of the 1980s and 1990s. The UK market went nowhere from 2000 to 2008 (via an up and down ride). The spectre of Japan should sit in the back of any investor's mind. As Laurence Siegel of the Ford Foundation so encouragingly once stated (Siegel, 1997):

'Risk is not short-term volatility, for the long-term investor can afford to ignore that. Rather, because there is no predestined rate of return, only an expected one that may not be realised, the risk is that, in the long-run, stock returns will be terrible.'

Growth-oriented equity market diversifiers, such as global commercial property, may help to smooth shorter-term equity market falls, as well as providing some comfort over the long-term, if Siegel's warning comes true over your investing lifetime.

You need to decide if you want to include these asset classes or if you wish to ignore them, sticking with equities and simply reducing the risk you take by diluting your equity exposure with defensive assets. Read up about each in Chapter 12 and make your own mind up.

The degree to which each asset class helps to smooth the portfolio returns, i.e. how effective their diversification benefit is, depends on how highly correlated their returns are. If you could find four uncorrelated asset classes with equity-like returns, you could halve the risk of the portfolio without giving up any return. The problem lies in finding them! Global commercial real estate provides useful potential diversification benefits.

Making sensible allocations

Again, any allocation should be material enough to make a difference, but not too large as you will be forgoing the higher expected returns from equities which you are having to shed to accommodate the diversifying asset class. An allocation in the region of 10% is not unreasonable. Anything less than 5% risks fiddling around the edges.

Issue 5: Non-GBP currency exposure

As an extension to the home bias issue above, owning assets outside your home market, i.e. non-UK assets for a UK sterling-based investor, exposes you to currency risk. To keep things simple, let us consider an investment in the US equity market. You in fact own two assets: the underlying ownership in a number of US companies and the US dollar. Imagine that US equities rise by 10%. For a US dollar-based investor, their return is that 10%. For a UK investor, they will receive the 10% plus the change in value of these assets depending on whether pound sterling has strengthened or weakened against the dollar. Imagine you originally bought £1,000 worth of US shares at US$2 to each £1. At the end of the year, the equity market remains unchanged, but the exchange rate is now US$1 per £1. Your shares are worth US$2,200 in dollar terms, but when you translate that back into pound sterling terms at the new rate they are worth £2,200! Currency may be either beneficial or detrimental to your portfolio: beneficial when sterling weakens, as it did dramatically in 2008, and detrimental when sterling appreciates, as Figure 7.4 illustrates.

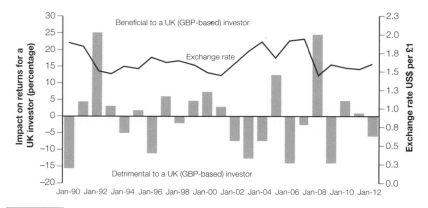

Figure 7.4 **Sometimes you win, sometimes you lose**

Source: Data from S&P 500 Index – Morningstar EnCorr. All rights reserved. Exchange rate – Bank of England

There are several properties of currency worth considering. First, it is a rate of exchange and in itself has no economic return-generating mechanism like being an owner or a lender. Second, over the long run the exchange rate should be in line with the purchasing power parity between two countries. This principal is succinctly explained by the *Economist* and their well-known Big Mac Index:

'Burgernomics is based on the theory of purchasing-power parity, the notion that a dollar should buy the same amount in all countries. Thus in the long run, the exchange rate between two countries should move towards the rate that equalises the prices of an identical basket of goods and services in each country. Our 'basket' is a McDonald's Big Mac, which is produced in about 120 countries. The Big Mac PPP is the exchange rate that would mean hamburgers cost the same in America as abroad.'

Third, currencies tend to be uncorrelated to equities in particular and thus provide some potential diversification benefit in an equity-oriented portfolio. They also tend to have low correlations between each other. Finally, currency movements have volatility more akin to equities than bonds.

How do you handle currency risk? The easy starting point is to avoid currency exposure in your defensive asset classes by owning GBP-denominated bond assets, e.g. index-linked gilts. If you happen to own any global bond exposure, this should be fully hedged (this should be done at the fund level by the fund manager). You want to avoid the equity-like volatility of currency being mixed in with your low-volatility assets.

Table 7.3   **To hedge or not to hedge? – that is the question**

Currency base	MSCI ACWI unhedged return %	MSCI ACWI hedged return %	Frequency of better returns with hedging			
			1 year	3 years	5 years	10 years
British Pound	10.9%	10.8%	53%	52%	60%	63%
US Dollar	9.7%	9.1%	42%	38%	34%	41%
Japanese Yen	5.8%	6.7%	56%	50%	50%	52%
Canadian Dollar	9.7%	9.1%	42%	38%	34%	41%
Deutsche Mark/Euro	7.3%	8.6%	56%	64%	65%	54%
Swiss Franc	5.7%	6.9%	53%	57%	53%	34%

Source: MSCI (2011) (www.msci.com)

When it comes to your equity exposure (and other risky assets) you could, like many institutional investors, take on the currency risk as a means of diversifying the portfolio. Countless papers have been written on the optimal level of hedging currency exposure, but at the end of the day it comes down to a practical issue. Virtually all global and country equity funds are unhedged, i.e. you will suffer the full impact of any currency movements, which could be in your favour or against you. The long-term investor can afford to take the view that these will even out over time. The empirical research (MSCI, 2011) would appear to back the assertion that it is a wash – sometimes you would be better off hedging and at other times you would be worse off (Table 7.3).

And finally . . .

The other important piece of guidance that you should take on board is that the allocations you make should reflect your confidence in the underlying evidence and arguments put forward. For example, if two asset classes have the same premia, but the evidence and argument support one case more than the other, you would not employ an equal weighting in your portfolio. You may decide on balance to exclude several asset classes, simply because you do not feel comfortable with them. My advice is do not own anything that you do not understand and feel comfortable with.

7.5 The Return Engine in practice

Figure 7.5 summarises the resultant structure of the Return Engine.

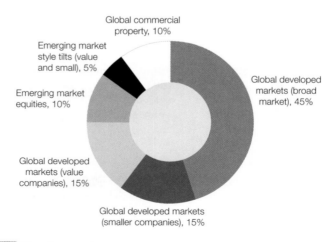

Figure 7.5 The Return Engine (whisky) component

Table 7.4 Alternative Return Engine structures

Return Engine (whisky) assets	Home bias				Global			
	UK	Broad	Diversified	Tilted	Simple	Broad	Diversified	Tilted
UK – market	100%	25%	25%	15%				
UK – value				5%				
UK – smaller companies				5%				
Developed World ex-UK market		60%	50%	30%				
Developed World ex-UK – value				10%				
Developed World ex-UK – smaller co's				10%				
Global – market (developed)					100%	85%	75%	45%
Global – value (developed)								15%
Global – smaller companies (developed)								15%
Emerging markets – market		15%	15%	10%		15%	15%	10%
Emerging markets – value and small				5%				5%
Global commercial real estate (REIT)			10%	10%			10%	10%
Total allocation	**100%**	**100%**	**100%**	**100%**	**100%**	**100%**	**100%**	**100%**

Alternative structures

Other possible Return Engine structures are set out in Table 7.4. It probably makes sense, as a minimum, to adopt the basic global structure to make sure that you have both the comfort of knowing that you are not wholly reliant on UK listed companies for your equity returns over your investing lifetime and that you have a moderate long-term allocation to faster-growing, higher-risk economies in the emerging nations. The global style tilts option is for those who feel comfortable with the evidence and arguments and are able (either directly or through a capable adviser) to manage this on an ongoing basis. In Part 4, possible implementation products are suggested for each of these allocations.

The important thing to remember is that none of these are wrong, and complex does not necessarily mean better for you. Diversification does, however, make good sense, even if it does not work on every occasion. You should vary your own mix around these broad guidelines.

7.6 How effective is this construction?

There are three main levels to answering this question.

Level 1: It is built with sensible components

The first is that the logic of the building blocks used makes sense: we have combined blocks that generate a strong core return with some higher risk blocks that should help to enhance returns and others that should provide some protection to equity market risk. It is a well diversified and sensible core structure.

Level 2: Its historical track record stacks up

At the next level we can take a look back at how this portfolio would have performed over a given period of time. In Table 7.5 there is a comparison between the UK equity market, global equity markets and the global style tilts portfolio (as in Table 7.4 above) over the period from July 1989 to December 2012. The start date is the common data start point for the assets included. It is a pretty brutal starting point for global equities as it is the moment the precipitous fall of the Japanese equity market began. Even so the numbers tell a positive story.

Table 7.5 Comparing the Return Engine to Global and UK equities			
Period: 7/1989 to 12/2012	Return Engine	UK equities	Global equities
Annualised real return %	4.8%	4.9%	2.6%
Growth of £100	£297	£306	£182
Risk %	16%	15%	16%
Return per unit of risk	0.30	0.33	0.16
Real return – past 10 years (annualised)	7.2%	5.3%	4.0%
Real return – past 5 years (annualised)	0.9%	–0.7%	–0.2%
Peak to trough (1/00 to 1/03)	–33%	–46%	–48%
Peak to trough (11/07 to 2/09)	–40%	–42%	–34%
Worst 1 year	–36%	–37%	–39%
Worst 3 years	–13%	–17%	–20%
Worst 5 years	–3.5%	–8.6%	–8.4%
Worst 10 years	0.7%	–3.2%	–3.9%

Source: Data from Morningstar EnCorr and Dimensional Fund Advisers. All rights reserved. Data used for simulation of the Return Engine is provided in Appendix 3.

During two particularly tough periods for investors: 2000–2002 (the Tech Wreck) and 2007–2009 (the Credit Crunch) – as you can see, diversification helped to reduce the cumulative losses incurred over this period. While this illustrates that diversification is an important decision, in periods like the early 1990s, when property fell substantially and global markets fared worse than the UK, it did not pay off; but that does not make it invalid. Investing is an imperfect science.

What is interesting to note is that while the risk has been the same, when measured by volatility, it appears that the downside impact of the worst-case periods has been reduced by the diversification into other asset classes. Returns have stood up well. Diversification is a tool worth using. Smarter investing requires that you simply stack the odds of success in your favour by making sensible decisions along the way.

Level 3: Given our expected return and risk assumptions

Finally, we can estimate, based on the long-term asset class assumptions that we make about each asset class going forward, (a) its return (i.e. the equity market return from developed markets plus any premia for emerging markets, less healthy (value) companies and smaller companies); (b) the risk of the portfolio, given that the imperfect return correlation between

Table 7.6	Expected characteristics of the Return Engine		
	Return %	Risk %	Return/risk
Smarter Portfolios: Global Style Tilt Portfolio	6.3%	21%	29%
UK equity (FTSE All Share)	5.0%	20%	25%

building blocks should help to reduce the portfolio risk below the sum of its parts. The underlying assumptions used are summarised in Chapter 6. The portfolio parameters have been calculated using Harry Markowitz's equation and represent a portfolio of assets that have been rebalanced back to their original allocation percentages at the start of each year. No costs have been deducted. The result is illustrated in Table 7.6.

In conclusion

By taking a wide range of asset classes and combining them together in a thoughtful manner, some of which are in themselves pretty risky, you can create a portfolio such as the Return Engine – the whisky element – that has an expected efficiency higher than that of the UK/developed markets, the basic starting point of portfolio construction. Remember too that it provides protection from the risk that the UK equity market simply fails to perform over our own investment lives.

7.7 Building a robust Defensive Mix (water)

Having created a sensible and robust growth-oriented portfolio, which should deliver equity-like returns over the longer term, we need to turn our attention towards the defensive assets mix. These assets will be used to water down the growth-oriented mix to a level that is consistent with your financial need to take risk, your emotional tolerance for it and your financial capacity to suffer losses (see Appendices 1 and 2).

This is an area that quite a few investors get confused about, and make basic, avoidable mistakes with. One problem is that many investors feel that, having taken on bond exposure at the expense of equity exposure, they should try to get as much juice out of the Defensive Mix as possible. Alternatively, they own some fixed income in order to generate an income to live off and again try to squeeze as much income as they can. This has material consequences.

Cautious investor

Concerns:
Volatility of capital and inflation

Risk-tolerant investor

Concerns:
Equity market crash

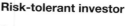

Emotional tolerance for risk increasing

Allocation to risky assets increasing

Role of defensive assets:
Low volatility
Protection from inflation

Solution:
UK index-linked gilts (shorter dated)
National Savings Certificates

Role of defensive assets:
Defence against
equity market extremes

Solution:
High quality bonds
e.g.UK gilts

Figure 7.6 The role of bonds depends on what kind of investor you are

James Tobin and the 'whisky and water' approach would simply suggest that you take all the risk in the growth-oriented portfolio and simply add the risk-free water to it. As such the Defensive Mix needs to be just that – it is there to protect your wealth. Theoretically that sounds both rational and simple to do. In practice it needs a little thought.

In order to try to make sense of creating our defensive asset mix, we need to take a step back and ask ourselves what the bond (fixed income) part of the portfolio is there for. This is summarised in Figure 7.6.

The cautious long-term investor

Imagine that you are an investor that finds the whole concept of investment worrying and the loss of capital scares you. As a long-term investor of this ilk, there is one thing that you must protect against and that is inflation. Even at what seem relatively low levels of inflation, your spending power in retirement could be significantly eroded.

> **Tip:** The Rule of 72 is a useful one: divide 72 by the rate of inflation to see how quickly the price of goods will double. For example, with inflation of 3% the price of goods will double in 24 years (72/3 = 24). That is likely to be a risk that you simply cannot afford to take.

Many very cautious investors simply put their cash on deposit. Take a look at Table 7.7 and ask yourself if holding cash is a low-risk strategy, when inflation is taken into account (leaving aside the credit risk issue of whether

Table 7.7   Cash returns after inflation 1955–2012

Holding period	1 Year	3 Years	5 Years	10 Years	20 Years
Worst return % p.a.	–12.9%	–7.1%	–5.4%	–3.6%	–1.0%
Worst – effect on £100	£87	£80	£76	£69	£82

Source: Data from the Bank of England

the bank the deposit is placed with is sound – after the Cyprus bailout in 2012, who knows what is safe?). The risk of a period of high and unanticipated inflation is a major risk to the long-term cautious investor.

To mitigate the risk of inflation effectively, investors should own assets that naturally protect against inflation. That points you towards inflation-linked securities such as those issued by the UK government. Your choice is between UK index-linked gilts (bonds) or index-linked National Savings Certificates (although at the moment they are not being issued), or globally issued inflation linked bonds (but these should be high credit quality and all non-GBP currency hedged back to GBP by the fund manager of the fund).

These structures pay you an income and return of capital that is protected from inflation, based on the Retail Price Index for gilts and NS&I products, when issued. In practice they do a reasonably good job of protecting you against inflation. Note that global inflation linked bonds hedged to GBP provide only a proxy for UK inflation, but that is better than nothing.

In contrast, conventional bonds perform very poorly at times of unanticipated rises in inflation: yields must rise to compensate investors for the new level of inflation and prices, as a consequence, fall. An example of such a time was the 1970s. If inflation comes in as anticipated, then conventional bonds (i.e. those not inflation-linked) should deliver inflation like returns, plus a little bit.

Ideally, you would own shorter-dated inflation-linked bonds and shorter dated conventional bonds, again hedged back to sterling if you go global (e.g. five years) as they have lower price sensitivity to changes in yields and therefore have a low level of volatility and thus short-term risk to capital.

In practice your implementation options are somewhat limited by availability of suitable products, although that is slowly changing. This is discussed in more detail in Chapter 11.

The more risk tolerant long-term investor

At the other end of the risk spectrum, imagine that you are a pretty risk tolerant investor comfortable with suffering interim losses in pursuit of more aggressive goals. As a consequence you own a pretty high allocation of equities/risky assets, let us say 80%. Unlike the cautious investor, you are protected reasonably well from inflation by owning equities and global commercial property in your growth-oriented mix. You are not too worried by volatility, as reflected in your risky asset mix, unlike the cautious investor. What you really want to do is to own the best diversifier when the equity market crashes, but giving up as little equity exposure as you can.

UK gilts are a potentially strong diversifier of equity market risk. Despite their normally positive correlations to equities, at times of equity market trauma high-quality bonds (gilts) have the potential, although not the certainty, to act as havens of safety and liquidity, with commensurate positive consequences for yields (down) and prices (up) as investors flood into this asset class. David Swensen of the Yale University endowment fund makes this point clearly.

'Only high quality, long-term bonds perform well in times of severe stress, allowing investors to view the opportunity costs of holding bonds as an insurance premium incurred to insulate portfolios from extreme positions.' (David Swensen, CIO Yale Endowment)

This seems to make logical sense and the empirical evidence seems to support the case reasonably well. As ever, in investing you will be able to find occasions when this did not work. It is a question of balance. Simply owning lower volatility, shorter-dated, high credit quality bonds works as a reasonable alternative. Note that this exposure could be gained by owning non-GBP denominated bonds, but with all currency hedged back to Sterling by the fund manager.

Avoid lower credit quality and 'high yield' bonds

So far we have ignored lower quality investment grade bonds (those with credit ratings of BBB and above, but below an arbitrary cut-off of AA), along with high yield bonds (less than BBB). Their superficial appeal is that they generate higher levels of yield, but at a price. For cautious investors the price is that the lower you go on credit quality the more they act like equities, which could generate material losses. For more risk tolerant investors, the problem is that they act more like equities, just at the time you need them to be standing fast, i.e. when equity markets crash. Take

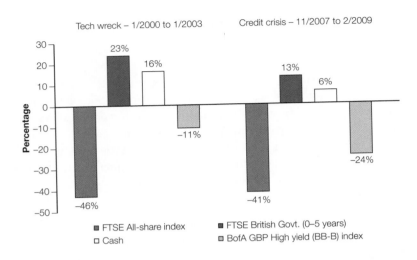

Figure 7.7 **Stick with high quality bonds for good defensive properties**

a look at the evidence in Figure 7.7, covering a couple of periods in the turbulent 2000s when equity markets crashed and see which type of bonds you would have preferred.

At the end of the day it comes down to a balance of evidence, logic and practicalities. For the investor seeking to avoid complexity they could hold shorter-dated index-linked gilts, gilts or non-GBP denominated bonds (AA and above), but with all currency hedged back to Sterling by the fund manager.

Suggested structures for the defensive assets mix

In light of the arguments and evidence above, it becomes clearer what a well-structured defensive portfolio could look like (see Table 7.8). Ideally, shorter-dated inflation-linked bonds would be combined with short-dated bonds for cautious investors, possibly in equal measure. You will need to decide for yourself, but aiming to play in the shorter-dated, high quality space is a pretty good starting point. Table 7.8 provides some basic Defensive Mix Allocations.

Figure 7.8 provides an insight into how a very simple portfolio of 50% 0–5 year UK index linked gilts and 50% shorter dated UK gilts (0–5 years) would have performed, compared to cash. Certainly this is a better structure than just holding cash.

Table 7.8 Sensibly structured defensive mix options	Smarter Portfolios					
Defensive assets mix	0	20	40	60	80	100
Basic						
UK cash	100%	80%	60%	40%	20%	0%
Risk mitigation based						
Inflation linked bonds (AA, short-dated 0–5 years)[1]	50%	40%	30%	20%	10%	0%
Bonds (AA, short-dated 0–5 years)[1]	50%	40%	30%	20%	10%	0%
In the absence of shorter-dated inflation linked bonds						
Inflation linked bonds (AA, Intermediate 5–15 years)[1]	25%	20%	15%	10%	5%	0%
Bonds (AA, 0–5 years)[1]	75%	60%	45%	30%	15%	0%

(1) Government or corporate issuers. If global then all non-GBP currency should be hedged back to GBP

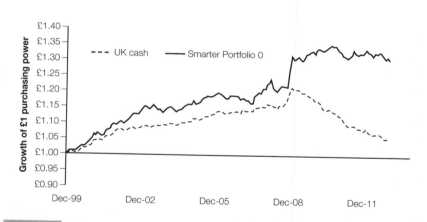

Figure 7.8 **A better combination than just using cash – 2000 to 2012**

7.8 Combining the whisky and the water

Now that we have our growth-oriented Return Engine (whisky) and Defensive (water) asset mixes sorted out, we can combine these together to offer different choices along the risk spectrum. These are set out in Table 7.9. As you can see, these are defined by incremental steps in growth-oriented assets of 20%. Much below this and the portfolios are too similar to be able to distinguish any real difference between them and one risks levels of spurious accuracy in dividing up the risk spectrum much further.

Table 7.9   Portfolio choices at sensible positions along the risk spectrum

Global style tilts	Cash	Smarter Portfolios					
		0	20	40	60	80	100
Growth assets mix							
Global – market (developed)			9%	18%	27%	36%	45%
Global – value (developed)			3%	6%	9%	12%	15%
Global – smaller companies (developed)			3%	6%	9%	12%	15%
Emerging markets – market			2%	4%	6%	8%	10%
Emerging markets – value and small			1%	2%	3%	4%	5%
Global commercial real estate (REIT)			2%	4%	6%	8%	10%
Defensive assets mix(1)							
Bonds (AA short-dated 0–5 years)(2)		50%	40%	30%	20%	10%	
Inflation linked bonds (AA short-dated 0–5 years)(2)		50%	40%	30%	20%	10%	
Cash	100%						
Total allocation	100%	100%	100%	100%	100%	100%	100%
Portfolio parameters(3)		0	20	40	60	80	100
Expected after inflation (geometric) return %	0.0%	0.8%	2.2%	3.5%	4.6%	5.5%	6.3%
Expected risk %	2%	5%	6%	9%	13%	17%	21%

(1) A basic alternative is to hold cash, but with the associated inflation and credit risk.
(2) Government or corporate issuers. If global then all non-GBP currency should be hedged back to GBP.
(3) Based on the asset class assumptions made – see Chapter 6.
Source: Data from Morningstar EnCorr and Dimensional Fund Advisers. All rights reserved.

But do so, if you wish to! Remember that there are no right or wrong answers, just some that are probably better than others.

These portfolios are explored in more depth in the next chapter.

References

Asness, C. S. (2010) 'International diversification works (eventually)', *Financial Analysts Journal*, vol. 67.

Bernstein, P. (1996) *Against the Gods*. New York: John Wiley.

Brinson, G. (2005) 'The future of investment management', *Financial Analysts Journal* (www.ssrn.com).

Fama, E. F. and French, K. R. (2012) 'Volatility & Premiums in US Equity Returns' (www.dfaeurope.com;http://www.dfaus.com/pdf/Volatility_and_Premiums.pdf).

Huberman, G. (2001) 'Familiarity breeds investment', *Review of Financial Studies*, 14(3).

Kimball, M. S. and Shumway, T. (2010) 'Investor sophistication and the home bias, diversifiation and employer stock puzzles', 29 January (http://ssrn.com/abstract1572866; http://dx.doi.org/10.2139/ssrn.1572866)

Loeper, D. B. (2003) 'The alternative to alternative classes', Wealthcare Capital Management.

Markowitz, H. M. (1952) 'Portfolio selection', *The Journal of Finance*, 7(1; March), 77–91 (www.jstor.org).

Michaud, R. O. (1989) 'The Markowitz Optimization Enigma: Is Optimized Optimal?', *Financial Analysts Journal*, 45(1) (January/February): pp. 31–42.

MSCI Index Research (2011) 'Global investing: the importance of currency returns and currency hedging', April (www.msci_bara.com).

Russell Investments (2010) 'Globalization, equity markets and the perils of home-country bias', *Viewpoint* (September).

Siegel, L. (1997) 'Are stocks risky? Two lessons', *Journal of Portfolio Management*, Spring, 29–34.

Solnik, B. (2008) 'Equity home bias and regret: an international equilibrium model', 1 January (http://ssrn.com/abstract828405; http://doi.org/10.2139/ssrn.828405).

Staverman, B. (2011) 'The many ways into emerging markets' (www.bloomberg.com).

Swensen, D. (2000) *Pioneering portfolio management*. New York: Free Press.

Tobin, J. (1957) 'Liquidity preference as behaviour towards risk', *The Review of Economic Studies*, no. 67.

Zweig, J. (2007) *Your money and your brain*. London: Souvenir Press, p. 4.

8

Smarter portfolio choices

8.1 Deciding on a sensible portfolio

The next step is to decide which portfolio makes sense for you. You have six portfolios to choose from. This needs a bit of careful thought and Appendices 1 and 2 provide some guidance. In short, you need to identify the following three parameters (see Figure 8.1).

Your risk profile or emotional tolerance for losses

Every investor has an emotional point beyond which it becomes too painful to stay invested. Your risk tolerance is a relatively stable psychometric trait irrespective of market conditions. It can be tested for using a psychometric risk profiling questionnaire – e.g. FinaMetrica (see Appendix 1). Your 'best fit' risk score provides insight into where you should feel most emotionally comfortable in terms of the level of growth-oriented Return Engine assets that you should include in your portfolio.

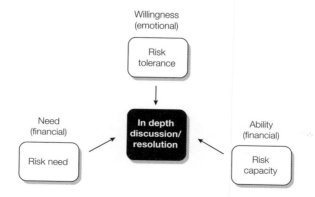

Figure 8.1 **You need to consider three aspects**

Your financial need to take risk

This relates to the returns you need to achieve to meet your lifestyle goals, which will depend on the assets you have, the expenditure goals you have set, and your contributions to your investment pool. How hard you have to make your portfolio work is a product of these elements (see Appendix 2 for how to work out some of the numbers and the rate of return you need to achieve to deliver your goals). The higher the level of return you need to achieve, the more risk you will need to take. More risk (measured in terms of losses) implies a higher level of 'growth' assets.

Your financial capacity for losses

This describes the amount of money that you can afford to lose before you begin to jeopardise your financial goals.You will have a unique set of goals – some may be more critical than others. Your portfolio could suffer losses; how much can you lose, before you endanger your critical goals? Longer investment horizons, and high levels of wealth to liabilities, may increase risk capacity. How much flexibility you have in your life/plan will also influence your capacity for losses (e.g. working longer, contributing more). Only you will know.

8.2 Portfolio insights – summary matrix

The summary matrix in Table 8.1 provides some useful insights into both the up and the downsides of these portfolios and provides a start to establishing which portfolio is most appropriate for you.

Investment horizon

Think carefully about how long your money is really going to be invested for. In the case of a university fees pot, that may be a precise number of years, whereas in retirement that could be up to 30 or even 40 years. If your time horizon is short, then you need to think about owning a less risky portfolio.

Risk tolerance score – FinaMetrica

You should read Appendix 1 to find out more about your risk tolerance. I would encourage you to take the questionnaire referred to, to give you a fair gauge of where you fit. The score ranges detailed here provide a good link to the type of portfolio that fits your emotional tolerance for risk most effectively. It is only a starting point for your thinking, not a portfolio picking tool!

Understanding the numbers on the upside

Return numbers are provided in three formats: long-term (113 year) outcomes using UK cash and UK equities from the Barclays Equity Gilt Study; outcomes since 1980, a reasonable starting date for the asset classes we have selected (note that bond returns have been far higher than history and expectation); and expected returns based on the return assumptions made in Chapter 6.

Understanding the numbers on the downside

The risk percentage number provided is – in industry jargon – the annualised standard deviation of returns, which is what the fund management industry often refers to as 'risk'. Despite its rather statistical description, what it describes is actually quite useful, i.e., what percentage of returns fall within a certain range either side of the average return.

As a rule of thumb, if you add the risk percentage to either side of the average annual return, this will roughly define the range within which two out of three annual returns is likely to fall. So, for Smarter Portfolio 6, above, this would give an approximate range of [+27% to −15% (i.e. 6.3% +/−21%)]. Nineteen out of twenty returns should fall roughly within +48% to −36% (i.e. 6.3% +/−2 × 21%). So, despite the jargon, this is a useful measure.

Note: for the more statistically minded, we should use the arithmetic mean rather than the geometric mean – but for gauging the quantum of the ranges the latter will do just fine – let us avoid spurious accuracy!

Remember that outliers are likely to occur in real life, perhaps more frequently than the statistics suggest. Some of the downsides experienced by these hypothetical portfolios in terms of worst outcomes over different investment horizons, and also at the time of two major market falls – the Tech Wreck (2000–2002) and the Credit Crisis (2007–2009) – help to get a handle on your emotional and financial capacity for losses. Forewarned is forearmed.

Table 8.1 Summary matrix for Smarter Portfolios 0 to 100

SMARTER PORTFOLIO	0	20	40	60	80	100
Return Engine assets	0%	20%	40%	60%	80%	100%
Defensive assets	100%	80%	60%	40%	20%	0%

Emotional risk profile (FinaMetrica 2.0)						
Best fit score (version 1.5)	0–16	17–38	39–53	54–68	69–88	89–100
Best fit score (version 2.0)	0–25	26–42	43–55	56–67	68–87	88–100

Minimum horizon (years)	>5	>10	>10	>15	>20	>20

Return insights						
After inflation return p.a.						
1900–2012[1]	0.9%	2.0%	2.9%	3.7%	4.4%	5.0%
1/1980–4/2013[2]	3.5%	4.6%	5.6%	6.5%	7.2%	7.7%
Expected long-term return[3]	1%	2%	3%	4%	5%	6%
Years to double your money	72	36	24	18	14	12

Risk insights						
Risk (%)						
1900–2011	6%	7%	10%	13%	16%	20%
1/1980–4/2013	4%	5%	7%	10%	13%	16%
Expected risk	5%	6%	9%	13%	17%	21%
Worst falls (peak to trough) – 1/1980 to 4/2013						
Number of falls > 2%	18	18	22	23	26	23
Number of falls > 5%	6	5	9	13	16	16
Number of falls > 10%	0	1	3	7	9	10
Number of falls > 20%	0	0	0	3	4	5
Worst decline %	–8%	–11%	–17%	–24%	–32%	–40%
Worst decline % – months falling	8	13	9	9	16	16
Worst decline % – months to recover	7	12	25	26	13	22
Compared to UK equity market crashes[4]						
Tech wreck (UK equities down 46%)	11%	1%	–9%	–18%	–26%	–34%
Credit crisis (UK equity down 42%)	8%	–3%	–13%	–23%	–32%	–40%
Worst decline of £100 purchasing power – 1/1980 to 4/2013						
Worst 1 year	£94	£91	£84	£77	£71	£64
Worst 3 years	£98	£94	£89	£80	£72	£65
Worst 5 years	£104	£105	£103	£95	£87	£79
Worst 10 years	£117	£120	£120	£115	£108	£100
Approximate chance of loss[5]						
Chance of loss over 5 years	1-in-3	1-in-4	1-in-5	1-in-4	1-in-4	1-in-
Chance of loss over 10 years	1-in-4	1-in-8	1-in-8	1-in-6	1-in-6	1-in-
Chance of loss over 20 years	1-in-5	1-in-15	1-in-15	1-in-12	1-in-10	1-in-

Estimated costs of funds used (p.a.%)[6]	0.35%	0.40%	0.45%	0.50%	0.55%	0.60

(1) Barclays Equity Gilt Study – cash combined with UK equities
(2) Simulated portfolio returns after estimated fund costs
(3) Expected return derived from asset class assumptions using MVOPlus software (rounded) – no guarantee.
(4) Tech wreck – 1/2000 to 1/2003, credit crisis – 11/2007 to 2/2009
(5) Uses expected risk and return figures in a Monte Carlo simulation (10,000 lives) – before costs and charges
(6) For simulated returns 1/1980 to 4/201. This is on the higher side – downward pressure on costs is likely. Some current options are chea

Notes to the table

The dataset used to create these numbers is detailed in Appendix 3. The portfolio returns have been shown after the effects of inflation, but before other costs. They have also been rebalanced (i.e. their asset class weightings have been returned to their original allocation) once a year. Again no transaction costs have been deducted.

8.3 Smarter Portfolio insights

On the next six pages you will find a more detailed look at the six Smarter Portfolios 0 to 100 (see Figures 8.2–8.7). Once you have narrowed down your likely suitable portfolio using the portfolio matrix, you can then use the relevant figure to look more closely at the characteristics of this portfolio. Compare and contrast different Smarter Portfolios to work out where you feel most comfortable.

SMARTER PORTFOLIO 0	
Return engine assets	0%
Defensive assets	100%
FinaMetrica 'Best fit' range	
Best fit score (version 1.5)	0-16
Best fit score (version 2.0)	0-25
Maximum horizon (yrs)	>5yrs

Return insights – after inflation	
1900-2012[1]	0.9%
1/1980-4/2013[2]	3.5%
Expected long-term return[3]	1%
Years to double money	72

Risk - Risk%	
1900-2011	6%
1/1980-4/2013	4%
Expected risk	5%

Risk - market falls	
Number of falls > 2%	18
Number of falls > 5%	6
Number of falls >10%	0
Number of falls > 20%	0

Risk - UK market crashes	
Tech wreck (UK eq. down 46%)	11%
Credit crisis (UK eq. down 42%)	8%

Risk-effect on £100 purchasing power	
Worst 1 year	£94
Worst 3 years	£98
Worst 5 years	£104
Worst 10 years	£117

Risk-chance of loss	
Chance of loss over 5 yrs	1 in 3
Chance of loss over 10 yrs	1 in 4
Chance of loss over 20 yrs	1 in 5

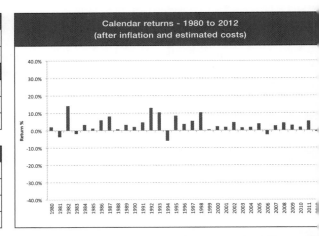

Calendar returns - 1980 to 2012
(after inflation and estimated costs)

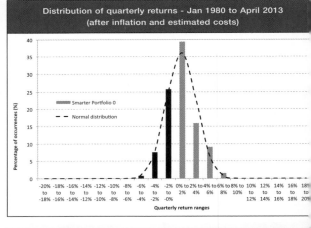

Distribution of quarterly returns - Jan 1980 to April 2013
(after inflation and estimated costs)

Decline	Peak rate	Trough rate	Recovery date	Decline (mths)	Recovery (mths)
−8%	Aug-89	Aug-90	Nov-90	8	7
−8%	Jan-94	May-94	Nov-95	4	18
−7%	Feb-83	Jul-84	Nov-84	17	4
−6%	Jan-06	Jun-07	Jan-08	17	7
−6%	Mar-08	Nov-08	Dec-08	8	1
−5%	Mar-81	Oct-81	Mar-82	7	5
−3%	Jun-03	Oct-03	Nov-04	4	13
−3%	Aug-86	Nov-86	Feb-87	3	3
−3%	Feb-85	Apr-85	Aug-85	2	4

Figure 8.2   Detailed insight: Smarter Portfolio 0

MARTER PORTFOLIO 20	
eturn engine assets	20%
efensive assets	80%

inaMetrica 'Best fit' range	
est fit score (version 1.5)	17-38
est fit score (version 2.0)	26-42
laximum horizon (yrs)	>10yrs

eturn insights – after inflation	
900-2012[1]	2.0%
1980-4/2013[2]	4.6%
xpected long-term return[3]	2%
ears to double money	36

isk - Risk%	
900-2011	7%
1980-4/2013	5%
xpected risk	6%

isk - market falls	
umber of falls > 2%	18
umber of falls > 5%	5
umber of falls >10%	1
umber of falls > 20%	0

isk - UK market crashes	
ch wreck (UK eq. down 46%)	1%
redit crisis (UK eq. down 42%)	−3%

isk-effect on £100 purchasing power	
orst 1 year	£91
orst 3 years	£94
orst 5 years	£105
orst 10 years	£120

isk-chance of loss	
hance of loss over 5 yrs	1 in 4
hance of loss over 10 yrs	1 in 8
hance of loss over 20 yrs	1 in 15

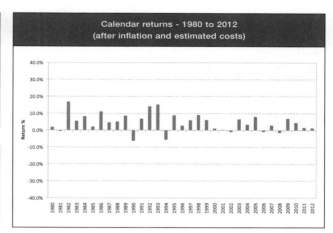

Decline	Peak rate	Trough rate	Recovery date	Decline (mths)	Recovery (mths)
−11%	Aug-89	Sep-90	Sep-91	13	12
−10%	Mar-08	Nov-08	Apr-09	8	5
−8%	Jan-94	Jun-94	Nov-95	5	17
−5%	Jan-01	Sep-01	May-03	8	20
−5%	Feb-85	Jun-85	Feb-86	4	8
−5%	Jul-87	Oct-87	Feb-88	3	4
−5%	Jan-84	Jul-84	Sep-84	6	2
−4%	Feb-92	Aug-92	Sep-92	6	1
−4%	Dec-79	Apr-80	Sep-80	4	5

gure 8.3   Detailed insight: Smarter Portfolio 20

SMARTER PORTFOLIO 40	
Return engine assets	40%
Defensive assets	60%
FinaMetrica 'Best fit' range	
Best fit score (version 1.5)	39-53
Best fit score (version 2.0)	43-55
Maximum horizon (yrs)	>10yrs

Return insights – after inflation	
1900-2012[1]	2.9%
1/1980-4/2013[2]	5.6%
Expected long-term return[3]	3%
Years to double money	24

Risk - Risk%	
1900-2011	10%
1/1980-4/2013	7%
Expected risk	9%

Risk - market falls	
Number of falls > 2%	22
Number of falls > 5%	9
Number of falls >10%	3
Number of falls > 20%	0

Risk - UK market crashes	
Tech wreck (UK eq. down 46%)	−9%
Credit crisis (UK eq. down 42%)	−13%

Risk-effect on £100 purchasing power	
Worst 1 year	£84
Worst 3 years	£89
Worst 5 years	£103
Worst 10 years	£120

Risk-chance of loss	
Chance of loss over 5 yrs	1 in 5
Chance of loss over 10 yrs	1 in 8
Chance of loss over 20 yrs	1 in 15

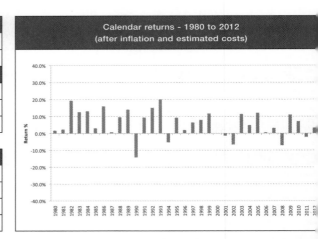

Calendar returns - 1980 to 2012
(after inflation and estimated costs)

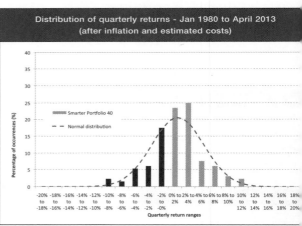

Distribution of quarterly returns - Jan 1980 to April 2013
(after inflation and estimated costs)

Decline	Peak rate	Trough rate	Recovery date	Decline (mths)	Recover (mths)
−17%	Dec-89	Sep-90	Oct-92	9	25
−16%	Oct-07	Nov-08	Sep-09	13	10
−13%	Aug-00	Sep-02	Mar-04	25	18
−9%	Aug-87	Nov-87	Jun-88	3	7
−9%	Jan-94	Feb-95	Nov-95	13	9
−8%	Feb-85	Jul-85	Feb-86	5	7
−7%	Mar-98	Aug-98	Nov-98	5	3
−6%	Jan-80	Apr-80	Sep-80	3	5
−6%	Dec-10	Sep-11	Jan-12	9	4

Figure 8.4   Detailed insight: Smarter Portfolio 40

MARTER PORTFOLIO 60	
eturn engine assets	60%
efensive assets	40%
inaMetrica 'Best fit' range	
est fit score (version 1.5)	54-68
est fit score (version 2.0)	56-67
laximum horizon (yrs)	>15yrs

eturn insights – after inflation	
900-2012[1]	3.7%
/1980-4/2013[2]	6.5%
xpected long-term return[3]	4%
ears to double money	18

isk - Risk%	
900-2011	13%
/1980-4/2013	10%
xpected risk	13%

isk - market falls	
umber of falls > 2%	23
umber of falls > 5%	13
umber of falls >10%	7
umber of falls > 20%	3

isk - UK market crashes	
ech wreck (UK eq. down 46%)	−18%
redit crisis (UK eq. down 42%)	−23%

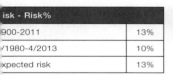

isk-effect on £100 purchasing power	
/orst 1 year	£77
/orst 3 years	£80
/orst 5 years	£95
/orst 10 years	£115

isk-chance of loss	
hance of loss over 5 yrs	1 in 4
hance of loss over 10 yrs	1 in 6
hance of loss over 20 yrs	1 in 12

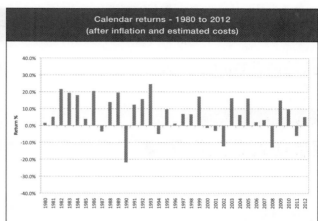

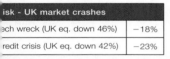

Decline	Peak rate	Trough rate	Recovery date	Decline (mths)	Recovery (mths)
−24%	Dec-89	Sep-90	Nov-92	9	26
−23%	Oct-07	Feb-09	Feb-10	16	12
−22%	Aug-00	Sep-02	May-05	25	32
−16%	Aug-87	Nov-87	Jan-89	3	14
−11%	Mar-98	Aug-98	Dec-98	5	4
−11%	Feb-85	Jul-85	Feb-86	5	7
−10%	Jan-94	Jan-95	Nov-95	12	10
−10%	Dec-10	Sep-11	Jan-13	9	16
−8%	Jan-80	Apr-80	Nov-80	3	7

Figure 8.5   Detailed insight: Smarter Portfolio 60

SMARTER PORTFOLIO 80	
Return engine assets	80%
Defensive assets	20%
FinaMetrica 'Best fit' range	
Best fit score (version 1.5)	69-88
Best fit score (version 2.0)	68-87
Maximum horizon (yrs)	>20yrs

Return insights – after inflation	
1900-2012[1]	4.4%
1/1980-4/2013[2]	7.2%
Expected long-term return[3]	5%
Years to double money	14

Risk - Risk%	
1900-2011	16%
1/1980-4/2013	13%
Expected risk	17%

Risk - market falls	
Number of falls > 2%	26
Number of falls > 5%	16
Number of falls >10%	9
Number of falls > 20%	4

Risk - UK market crashes	
Tech wreck (UK eq. down 46%)	−26%
Credit crisis (UK eq. down 42%)	−32%

Risk-effect on £100 purchasing power	
Worst 1 year	£71
Worst 3 years	£72
Worst 5 years	£87
Worst 10 years	£108

Risk-chance of loss	
Chance of loss over 5 yrs	1 in 4
Chance of loss over 10 yrs	1 in 6
Chance of loss over 20 yrs	1 in 10

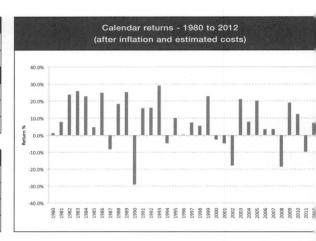

Calendar returns - 1980 to 2012
(after inflation and estimated costs)

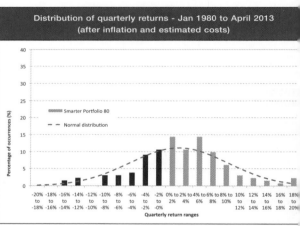

Distribution of quarterly returns - Jan 1980 to April 2013
(after inflation and estimated costs)

Decline	Peak rate	Trough rate	Recovery date	Decline (mths)	Recovery (mths)
−32%	Oct-07	Feb-09	Mar-10	16	13
−31%	Aug-00	Sep-02	Jul-05	25	34
−31%	Dec-89	Sep-90	Feb-93	9	29
−23%	Aug-87	Nov-87	Mar-89	3	16
−16%	Mar-98	Aug-98	Mar-99	5	7
−14%	Dec-10	Sep-11	Jan-13	9	16
−14%	Feb-85	Jul-85	Feb-86	5	7
−12%	Jan-94	Jan-95	Dec-95	12	11
−10%	Jul-81	Jul-82	Oct-82	12	3

Figure 8.6   Detailed insight: Smarter Portfolio 80

SMARTER PORTFOLIO 100	
Return engine assets	100%
Defensive assets	0%
FinaMetrica 'Best fit' range	
Best fit score (version 1.5)	89-100
Best fit score (version 2.0)	88-100
Maximum horizon (yrs)	>20yrs

Return insights – after inflation	
1900-2012[1]	5.0%
1/1980-4/2013[2]	7.7%
Expected long-term return[3]	6%
Years to double money	12

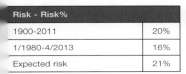

Risk - Risk%	
1900-2011	20%
1/1980-4/2013	16%
Expected risk	21%

Risk - market falls	
Number of falls > 2%	23
Number of falls > 5%	16
Number of falls >10%	10
Number of falls > 20%	5

Risk - UK market crashes	
Tech wreck (UK eq. down 46%)	−34%
Credit crisis (UK eq. down 42%)	−40%

Risk-effect on £100 purchasing power	
Worst 1 year	£64
Worst 3 years	£65
Worst 5 years	£79
Worst 10 years	£100

Risk-chance of loss	
Chance of loss over 5 yrs	1 in 4
Chance of loss over 10 yrs	1 in 6
Chance of loss over 20 yrs	1 in 10

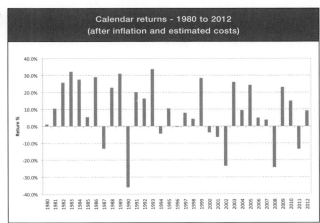

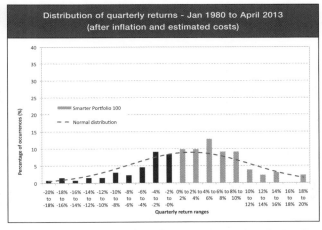

Decline	Peak rate	Trough rate	Recovery date	Decline (mths)	Recovery (mths)
−40%	Oct-07	Feb-09	Dec-10	16	22
−39%	Aug-00	Sep-02	Sep-05	25	36
−37%	Dec-89	Nov-09	May-93	11	30
−29%	Aug-87	Nov-87	Apr-89	3	17
−21%	Jul-97	Aug-98	Mar-99	13	7
−19%	Dec-10	Sep-11	Jan-13	9	16
−17%	Feb-85	Jul-85	Feb-86	5	7
−14%	Jul-81	Jul-82	Oct-82	12	3
−13%	Jan-94	Jan-95	Dec-95	12	11

Figure 8.7   Detailed insight: Smarter Portfolio 100

4

Smarter implementation

Hopefully at this point you have a good idea of what your portfolio strategy is going to be and the building blocks that you are going to use. Now, you need to turn this plan into reality. Unfortunately, many investors fail to follow through, blinded and confused by the plethora of product choice. This section provides some guidance on pulling the trigger.

Chapter 9: Smarter product choices

Here you will find guidance on selecting the best passive (index) products in the marketplace. Simple selection criteria are provided, along with a few ideas of some of the asset class implementation products that you could take a look at. This is a very rapidly expanding universe and you need continually to be alert to new products being launched. Even if you employ an adviser, you need to be able to scrutinise the choices that they are making on your behalf.

Chapter 10: Smarter advice – DIY or hire an adviser?

This is an important step. You need to decide whether you want to take on the full responsibility for implementing your portfolio strategy and its ongoing management, or whether you want to appoint an adviser to do this for you and act as your guide and mentor over time. This chapter is designed to help you to decide which course of action is right for you. It also provides some good tips on finding the right sort of adviser.

Smarter product choices

Now is the time to pull the trigger and turn your thinking into reality. It is not too hard with a bit of guidance.

At this point you will have selected your Smarter Portfolio and chosen the level of home bias, asset class diversification and return tilts that you feel most comfortable with. Now you need to decide how you can best replicate the risk factors that you want exposure to in your portfolio. That process requires the establishment of some selection criteria, which we will review below.

Even if you decide that you are going to use an adviser to help you (see Chapter 10), this chapter is important because it will provide you with a framework to analyse the product selection choices that they make and to question them about their choices. It is your money and you need to be comfortable that you are invested in the best products available.

Fortunately the products available to passive investors are improving rapidly in both depth, quality and structure.

9.1 The serendipity of index-fund investing

As Warren Buffett is reported to have said (Bogle, 2002):

'When the dumb investor realizes how dumb he is and invests in an index fund, he becomes smarter than the smartest investor.'

Play the game with the highest probability of success and invest in passively managed index products wherever possible. Choose the lose-the-fewest-points approach. The Dilbert cartoon by Scott Adams, shown overleaf, sums up the situation perfectly. For those of you in the UK, a mutual fund is the equivalent of a unit trust or OEIC.

Going down the market-replicating route, you will achieve a number of

really critical practical, as well as investment, benefits. These are consistent with your philosophy of losing the fewest points:

- You are likely to beat the majority of actively managed funds over the long run, even if over short periods some active managers outperform the market.

- If you choose a good fund you will probably never have to change managers during your investing lifetime, saving yourself a lot of angst, tax and transaction charges.

- You do not have to worry about whether your fund manager is destroying your investment strategy with bad decisions or drifting away from the risks you wish to take.

- You immediately and dramatically reduce the number of providers and products that you need to consider. This makes your selection process simpler and improves the chances of selecting the best product.

Take some time undertaking the selection process properly. Just because a fund or ETF is passively managed does not mean that it necessarily holds the investing moral high ground. There are some shockingly structured and costly index products out there and you need to be wary of which you choose. Fortunately the selection criteria and process is pretty simple to pick the good from the bad. Here is how you can go about that process.

9.2 Choosing your market benchmark/proxy

For each asset class exposure in your Smarter Portfolio, you have to decide what benchmark most effectively captures the risks (and rewards) that you are seeking to capture. You then need to find a product that replicates this benchmark, such as the way in which the FTSE All-Share index provides access to the broad UK equity market. It also provides the basis for reviewing how well each of your chosen products (funds or ETFs) is doing in capturing these characteristics. In most cases this benchmark will be a published market index, such as the FTSE All-Share index, which covers a specified group of securities tracked in accordance with some clear and consistent rules. There are many indices to choose from and picking the right one is important. Below are some pointers for doing so.

Building-block benchmark choices

The benchmarks that you could use for the various asset classes are set out in Table 9.1. In some cases you can see that for a couple of building blocks, more than one suggestion has been made.

You should always seek to use total return indices where the income, in the form of dividends from equities and coupons from bonds, is reinvested in the market, as opposed to price indices where it is not, as a significant proportion of your long-term returns come from reinvesting income. Whether the share class accumulates and reinvests dividends, or distributes income in cash, is a secondary decision.

When you select a fund, such as an index (tracker) fund, it is imperative to make sure that you are selecting a product that tracks the index you want it to track. That may sound obvious, but be careful. Just because a fund is called a UK Index Tracker, it does not mean it is tracking the FTSE All-Share index, in fact many replicate the FTSE 100, thereby missing out the medium-sized and smaller companies. The same applies to exchange-traded funds; make sure you know what they are replicating.

Table 9.1   Asset class benchmarks

RETURN ENGINE ASSETS	MARKET PROXY BENCHMARK
Broad market exposure	
UK equity market	FTSE All Share Index (not the FTSE 100)
World ex-UK equities (developed)	FTSE World ex-UK Index MSCI World ex-UK Index
World equity (developed)	MSCI World Index FTSE All World Developed ex-UK
Emerging market equities	MSCI Emerging Markets Index (includes S. Korea)
World (developed & emerging)	FTSE All World Index MSCI All Country World Index (ACWI)
Risk factor tilts	
UK value equities	FTSE 350 Value Index FTSE UK Dividend Plus Index
UK smaller company equities	MSCI UK Small Cap Index FTSE 250 Index
World ex-UK value equities (developed)	MSCI World ex-UK Index Value
World ex-UK smaller co's equities (developed)	FTSE Global Small Cap ex-UK Index MSCI World ex-UK Index Small Cap
Global value equity	FTSE World Index Value Index MSCI World Index Value
Global smaller companies equity	FTSE Global Equity Index Series Small Cap Index MSCI World Small Cap Index
Non-equity asset classes	
Global commercial real estate	FTSE EPRA/NAREIT Global Real Estate Series Developed Index FTSE EPRA/NAREIT Global Dividend Plus Index

RETURN ENGINE ASSETS	MARKET PROXY BENCHMARK
UK Index-linked gilts (short-dated)	FTSE British Government Index Linked Gilt 0–5 years
UK Index-linked gilts (intermediate-dated)	Barclays UK Government InflationLinked 5–15 Yr Bond Index
Global inflation linked (short-dated, hedged to GBP)	Barclays World Govt. Inflation Linked 1–10 Yrs Index
UK Gilts (short-dated) Sterling investment grade corporates (short-dated) Global bonds (short-dated, hedged to GBP)	FTSE British Government Index (up to 5 years) Markit iBoxx £ Corporates 1–5 Index Citi WGBI 1–5 Yr Hdg GBP Barclays Global Aggregate Float Adjusted Bond Index Hdg GBP

Source: Vanguard (2012).

9.3 Product structures

When you come to selecting a product, you are presented with two main structures in the UK. That of investing via a unit trust or Open Ended Investment Company (OEIC) which are fund structures that you co-invest in with other investors, and exchange-traded funds that act like shares and are listed on the stock exchange. It is important to understand the differences between the two. Investment trusts are also covered although they are very limited in number when it comes to index replication.

Unit trusts and OEICs

In the UK, funds are known as unit trusts or Open Ended Investment Companies (OEICs), and in the USA they are referred to as mutual funds. In a fund, your money is pooled with other investors' money, but it is ring-fenced from the fund managements company's balance sheet, unlike when you make a deposit with a bank, or if you take out a with-profits policy with an insurance company. The assets are held by an independent custodian bank (ring-fenced from their balance sheet too). An independent board of trustees is charged with looking after the interests of investors in the fund. They appoint the custodian and fund managers. For your protection, the manager simply has a management contract to execute trades on the custodial account.

OEICs are a simple way to gain diversification across the whole market, which would be difficult for you to achieve cost-effectively on your own. You own units or shares in the fund, which are priced daily. Diversification of the manager risk is far less important than the diversification of the assets held in and across the funds you own.

While investing via funds has been a very effective way for individuals and institutions to gain access to broad company ownership or lending opportunities, one structural drawback is that you are exposed to the whims, to some extent, of the other investors in the fund. Large investments into or out of the fund will result in large transaction costs which are charged against the fund's performance. Even if you are a long-term buy-and-hold investor you will pay your share of their costs. Depending on what fund you own, this may range from the negligible to the significant. Bigger is generally better from this perspective. Some more forward thinking fund management firms have introduced dilution levies on entry and exit that force each investor to bear their own costs, which no one can really argue with. It is no more expensive this way – just fairer.

A well-structured fund with a wide number of investors and large in size, still provides a very worthy structure for the individual investor. In the UK passively managed index funds are often referred to as 'trackers'.

Lifestyle, risk-managed OEICs and target date funds

It is worth noting that there is a small but growing trend towards passive/ index lifestyle or risk-managed funds. These are funds where the fund manager establishes an asset allocation e.g. 40% in high quality bonds and 60% in developed and emerging market equities using a fund-of-funds approach (e.g. Vanguard). They handle all the decisions and rebalancing, back to the original mix. Some include tilts to value and small cap exposures too (e.g. Dimensional Fund Advisers). This can be a very cheap, efficient, simple and hassle-free way to build your real-life portfolio. They are well worth a look and are listed later in this chapter (Table 9.3).

Target date funds are usually offered as part of money-purchase pension schemes. A target date in the future – usually the date that you are going to retire and perhaps buy an annuity with your pension pot – is set for the fund e.g. the ABC 2030 Fund. The manager changes the allocation – usually into less risky assets such as bonds, as the end date of the fund approaches. This can be useful for some people in some circumstances.

Exchange-traded funds (ETFs)

These should be considered alongside index funds as worthy vehicles for a rational investor to use. Exchange-traded funds are similar to index funds but are shares listed on a stock exchange. Physically replicated ETFs hold (near enough) the basket of securities that constitute a chosen index. It should be noted that some ETFs are derivative backed and this exposes the investor to both basis risk (i.e. the risk that the derivate contract does not deliver the index return) and counterparty risk, i.e. the risk of default of the other side of the derivative contract. However, the UCITS III directives (adopted on an EU-wide basis that set certain guidelines on products and the sale of funds across borders) help to ensure that this exposure is limited to around 10% of the ETFs net asset value. The funds and ETFs that you buy should be UCITS III approved. The assets of an ETF are ring-fenced and in the event of the collapse of the product provider, investors have recourse to the ring-fenced assets.

Many of the world's major institutional investors use ETFs to help position their portfolios. ETFs tend to have low total expense ratios. One point to note is that many of them pay dividends, which you will need to reinvest yourself. Another is that depending upon how you intend to buy and sell your investments, e.g. when you rebalance occasionally back to your original mix, or when you add new monies, ETFs are likely to incur a transaction charge whereas funds may or may not.

Investment trusts

Investment trusts share many of the properties of funds but are companies listed on the stock exchange and are, in some ways, like ETFs. Investment trusts are usually actively managed, but a very small number, if any, replicate specific indices like an index fund. They can be bought through brokers. A quirk of investment trusts is that they trade at either a premium or a discount to their net asset value or NAV (effectively the liquidation value of selling all the stocks). These arise through supply and demand mismatches and also the perception of the management of the investment trust and perhaps the leverage (borrowing) they are able to use. Somewhat surprisingly, index-replicating trusts also seem to trade at discounts and premiums to the NAV. Costs can be lower than for OEICs and unit trusts. Some investors look to take advantage of the changes in discounts, but that is a secondary and difficult game. They may be worth a look, but your best bet lies in the OEIC and ETF universe.

9.4 Selecting good passive products

One of the great advantages of taking the index route, apart from giving yourself the best chance of achieving your goals, is that selecting a product is straightforward. Over the past couple of years, the choice and quality of index funds and ETFs have improved markedly, as Table 9.2 illustrates. The selection process, despite the rise in the number of products available, is relatively straightforward.

Tracking error is your critical selection criteria

The ultimate goal of using an index tracker fund, or ETF, is to gather as much of the market return as you can. The degree to which returns differ from the chosen index is known as tracking error (i.e. the standard deviation of returns relative to the index). This can be caused by a number of factors, which we will look at below. Tracking error of 2% is the outer limit of what is acceptable and the lower the better. Remember that even small differences can mount up over time due to the effects of compounding.

Table 9.2   Guidelines for selecting index funds

HIGH LEVEL CRITERIA	TARGET PARAMETERS
Index tracked (if applicable)	Check index – total return only
Geographic exposure	Check underlying exposure (benchmark)
Currency hedging	Hedged, partially hedged, fully hedged
Risk factors (equity)	Check factor exposure using Morningstar – market, small, value for equity
Risk factors (bonds)	Check weighted average credit risk, min credit grade Check weighted average duration
Tracking error to index	As low as possible, if relevant Check past record of tracking error At miminum eye-ball charts and compare index vs. fund*
Total expense ratio (TER)	<20 basis points – UK equity <40 basis points – developed equity <25 basis points – fixed income <75 basis points – value, small, property equity <75 basis points – emerging market equity
TER trend	Downward
Fund size and age	Preferably >£100 million Preferably >5 years
Fund turnover	<5% for major markets
Implementation	Physical stock (preferred) Derivative use SWAPs – avoid wherever possible Does it make sense for the fund?
Trading strategy	Establish flexibility/value of the trading strategy
Manager experience	Always look for a team that has done a good job across all funds
Commitment	This is a scale game – do they have the scale to compete? – Check groups passive funds assets under management

* Make sure you are comparing the funds benchmark against the fund

An established fund will be able to prove what its tracking error has been, demonstrate the consistency of its replication process and make you feel comfortable that it will be able to reproduce its strong results in the future. Some funds publish tracking error. If for some reason they do not, just compare the returns on a year-by-year and cumulative basis against the index (eye-balling charts is a good approach – the line of the fund should overlap the index as closely as possible), or ask their customer service team for the data. If the differences are large, on the upside as well as the downside, the fund is not well managed, or is replicating a different index from the one you think it is. There is no reason to choose a new index fund, which is unproven in its ability successfully to track the index. Here are some of the ways in which tracking error occurs.

Replication methods affect tracking error

The way in which the investment manager chooses to copy the index is important. There are three common methods that are used.

- **Full replication:** As its name suggests, each company in the index is purchased by the fund. This would give you zero tracking error in a world where transaction costs are zero, but it is not the world we live in. Inevitably, transaction costs will create some tracking error. In addition, smaller funds may suffer from having to buy odd lots of stock that cannot be split as the amount being purchased is too small. Corporate actions and dividend payments also create activity that may generate tracking error.

- **Sampling (or partial replication):** In this case, the manager takes the view that the cost of creating and maintaining a portfolio with all the securities in the index is greater than the tracking error risk of holding only some of the securities. The manager will use some form of optimisation model to put together a sample of securities that mimics the index as closely as possible.

- **Derivatives:** This method is less common and places most of the funds in cash and enters into SWAP instruments or derivatives. Sometimes funds use both sampling and derivatives. Generally avoid non-physical based methodologies – there is good enough product choice out there not to have to go down this route.

You should always check to see what type of process is used and ask why it makes sense for this kind of index. Take a look and see what other providers are doing.

Fees and costs contribute to tracking error

Fees always go a long way towards explaining tracking error, as not all index funds are made equal. Some charge very low fees of a few basis points

(100ths of 1%) and others as high as 1% for domestic retail products. Better still, find out what the total expense ratio (TER) or Ongoing Charge of the fund is – you can get this from the fund fact sheet or the Key Investor Information Document (KIID) which they are obliged to provide. Never pay an initial fee for an index fund. Some index funds are taking the 'mickey' with high upfront fees and high ongoing charges. Vote with your wallet and avoid them. I just want to reiterate the quote that I used earlier in the book from Morningstar, the world's pre-eminent fund research tool and database:

'If there's anything in the whole world of mutual funds that you can take to the bank, it's that expense ratios help you make a better decision. In every single time period and data point tested, low-cost funds beat high-cost funds.'

Size may contribute to tracking error

This is important due to lot sizes, explained above. It may affect the decision as to how the fund is replicated, which may not be the most effective method to use. Being in a small fund may expose you to additional tracking error if a large investor suddenly withdraws. Size may also imply limited manager experience.

Turnover may contribute to tracking error

In some jurisdictions, such as the USA, turnover is very important to the taxable investor and should be avoided as much as possible. Some funds may perform as well as other funds and have similar tracking error but after-tax returns may be lower as a result of portfolio turnover. In the UK, a unit trust or an OEIC does not pay capital gains tax, so turnover is less important, at least from a tax perspective. It does matter though from a transaction cost perspective.

Manager experience will affect tracking error

Index investing is not just a 'plug it into the computer and sit back' process. Skilled index managers are aware of each of the elements of their process where tracking error can occur and they manage them very tightly. There is no substitute for experience and success.

There are enough high-quality index funds and ETFs for you not to have to stray outside these parameters for your core building blocks, but 'tilt' asset classes are still an issue. Currently, index bond funds and ETFs are a bit limited in the UK. Over time, index fund fees are expected to fall and more managers will enter the market. It is likely that your choice of asset classes/ risk factors will also increase. Getting it right upfront is very important as you do not want to have to switch later on, particularly if you are a taxable investor. It is worth remembering that although there are limited funds to choose from, you only need one excellent fund for each asset class to build your portfolio with.

9.5 Passive fund providers

There are several dominant providers of passive products in the UK, whom you may wish to contact to get hold of some literature and prospectuses to review. There is also a wide range of smaller providers, whom you may want to seek out too. This is not a definitive list or in any way a recommendation – it just helps to steer you to some of the longer-established firms with the widest choice of building blocks. Some are omitted, not by implication but for the sake of simplicity. The onus is on you to work out which is most suitable for you.

Passive index fund providers

For UK investors the choice of passive providers and they product ranges that they offer have risen rapidly since the second edition of this book. The most notable new entrant into the market has been Vanguard (www. vanguard.co.uk) who are the pioneers of low-cost, passive investing. They immediately forced a step change in the pricing of passive funds offering a UK FTSE All-Share Index fund at 0.15% (15 basis points) per annum. They are also highly skilled at capturing market returns. Take a look at Table 9.3 on page 172. Their highly efficient trading and low cost approach is highly beneficial to investors. It is interesting to note that Vanguard is a mutual company.

Dimensional Fund Advisors (DFA), is perhaps best described as a passive risk factor fund provider. It focuses specifically on creating efficient portfolios that deliver pure risk factor exposures (i.e. value and small cap exposures) across global developed and emerging markets, rather than trying to replicate specific and common market indices. It manages them carefully to try to avoid some of the attritional costs that are associated with traditional index fund replication. They are only available to individual investors through selected advisers around the globe, including a growing number in the UK. If you use an adviser you should perhaps ask the question.

Other prominent passive fund providers in the UK include: Legal & General (www.legalandgeneral.co.uk), Blackrock (www.blackrock.co.uk), AVIVA, which was formerly called Norwich Union (www.aviva.co.uk), Fidelity (www.fidelity.co.uk), and HSBC (www.hsbc.com). There are quite a few others too and just because they are not listed does not mean that they are not worth a look.

The quickest way to get a list is to use the Investing in Funds website (www.investinginfunds.org/funds-and-sectors/fund-directory.html) and click on the 'index funds' search criteria. Once you have a list of names look on a platform such as Sippdeal which provides access to the Morningstar database of funds and see what is available. Platforms may provide you with access to better pricing (i.e. more favourably priced share classes). There is no point paying more for the same fund – ever!

Exchange-traded fund providers

When selecting an exchange-traded fund (ETF), a similar focus exists: check the total expense ratio and see how closely the ETF tracks its chosen index. See how much money is invested in the ETF you are looking at – bigger is generally better. Start with the bigger providers such as 'iShares' (www.ishares.co.uk). It is worth noting that iShares ETFs are predominantly backed by an underlying basket of securities. My preference would be to own a basket of actual securities – it seems cleaner and more transparent. However, you may need to make some compromises on this as you may not be able to find appropriate products. Certainly try to fill your core allocations using ETFs backed by a basket of securities or by using OEICs.

Keep a look out for new products. Be prepared to reinvest dividends.

In terms of monitoring your portfolio, index returns for each building block should be provided online by the provider. If not, ask the product provider for them. You have a right to know. Most ETF and OEIC providers supply quite detailed information on the tracking error of their products.

Morningstar: www.morningstar.co.uk

This is a global group that provides information on the universe of funds available to UK investors and provides a rating system for funds based on stars. This is a widely used service in the USA and increasingly in the UK. Some investors use the rating system as some sort of endorsement of future market-beating performance for higher-rated funds, which it is not.

On the website, go to the 'OEIC/Unit Trust' of 'ETF' tab on the home page and choose the 'Fund Screener' menu option in the 'Investment Tools' section. You can then use the screening process to narrow your search. You could screen by Morningstar style box (click on the box you are looking for funds in), costs (max Total Expense Ratio – use the target criteria) and fund size, perhaps. Alternatively look up the funds of the fund companies you have identified. It will only take a few minutes before you will get to grips with how it works.

If you use Morningstar via a platform like Sippdeal (they provide it free even before you sign up), you will be able to see what minimum investment levels you have access to for each share class if you use their platform – something you will not see on the Morningstar website itself.

Table 9.3 Asset class funds/ETFs – summary table to get you started.

ASSETS CLASS	STRUCTURE	CODE	IDEA – STARTING POINT	ONGOING CHARGES	KID SCORE
UK equity (market)	OEIC	V1	Vanguard UK Equity Index	0.15%	6
	OEIC	L1	Legal and General UK Index Trust	0.23%	6
	OEIC	H1	HSBC FTSE All Share Index Retail	0.28%	6
	OEIC	F1	Fidelity Money Builder UK Index	0.30%	6
	OEIC	D1	Dimensional United Kingdom Core Equity Fund	0.36%	6
UK equity (value)	OEIC	D2	Dimensional United Kingdom Value Fund	0.54%	7
	ETF	I2	iShares FTSE UK Dividend Plus	0.40%	6
UK equity (smaller companies)	OEIC	D3	Dimensional UK Small Companies Fund	0.66%	6
	ETF	I3	iShares FTSE 250	0.40%	6
	OEIC	H3	HSBC FTSE 250 Index	0.19%	6
International equity (market)	OEIC	V4	Vanguard FTSE Developed World ex-UK Equity Index Fund	0.30%	6
	OEIC	A4	Aviva Investor International Index Tracking SC2	0.28%	6
	ETF	I4	iShares FTSE Developed World ex-UK	0.50%	6
	OEIC	D4	Dimensional International Core Equity Fund	0.46%	6
International equity (value)	OEIC	D5	Dimensional International Value Fund	0.59%	7
International equity (smaller companies)			NONE (USE GLOBAL FUNDS INSTEAD)		
Global developed equity (market)	ETF	I6	iShares MSCI World	0.50%	6
	OEIC	D6	Dimensional Global Core Fund	0.43%	6
Global developed and emerging (market)	ETF	V7	Vanguard FTSE All World	0.25%	6
	ETF	I7	iShares MSCI ACWI (All Countries World Index)	0.60%	7
Global developed equity (value)	ETF	L8	Legal & General Global 100 Index Trust	0.31%	6

Global developed equity (smaller companies)	OEIC	D9	Dimensional Global Small Companies Fund	0.60%	6
	OEIC	V9	Vanguard Global Small Cap Index Fund	0.40%	6
Global developed equity style tilts (value & smaller co's.)	OEIC	D10	Dimensional Global Targeted Value Fund	0.66%	6
Emerging markets (market)	OEIC	V11	Vanguard Emerging Markets Stock Index	0.55%	7
	ETF	V11B	Vanguard FTSE Emerging Markets ETF	0.45%	7
	ETF	I11	iShares MSCI Emerging Markets	0.75%	7
	OEIC	D11	Dimensional Emerging Markets Core Fund	0.78%	6
Emerging markets style tilts (value & smaller co's.)	OEIC	D12	Dimensional Emerging Market Targeted Value Fund	0.95%	6
	ETF	I12	iShares Emerging Markets SmallCap	0.74%	7
Global commercial property	OEIC	B13	BlackRock Global Property Securities Equity Tracker	0.28%	7
	ETF	I13	iShares FTSE EPRA/NAREIT Developed Markets Property Yield	0.59%	7
UK short-dated high quality bonds	ETF	I14	iShares FTSE Gilts 0–5 ETF	0.20%	3
	ETF	I14B	iShares iBoxx £ Corporate Bond 1–5	0.20%	3
Global short-dated high quality bonds (hedged)	OEIC	D15	Dimensional Global Short-Dated Bond Fund	0.34%	3
	OEIC	V15	Vanguard Global Bond Index Fund	0.25%	3
UK index linked gilts (5–15)	OEIC	D16	Dimensional Sterling Intermediate Inflation-Linked Fund	0.25%	4
Global short-dated inflation linked bonds (hedged)	OEIC	F16	Fidelity Global Inflation Linked Bond Fund (actively managed)	0.75%	4

PORTFOLIO STRUCTURE	STRUCTURE	CODE	IDEA – STARTING POINT	ONGOING CHARGES	KIID SCORE
80% bonds/20% equities – home bias, no tilts, no property	OEIC	V-L1	Vanguard LifeStrategy 20% Equity Fund	0.29%	4
60% bonds/40% equities – home bias, no tilts, no property	OEIC	V-L2	Vanguard LifeStrategy 40% Equity Fund	0.30%	4
40% bonds/60% equities – home bias, no tilts, no property	OEIC	V-L3	Vanguard LifeStrategy 60% Equity Fund	0.31%	5
20% bonds/80% equities – home bias, no tilts, no property	OEIC	V-L4	Vanguard LifeStrategy 80% Equity Fund	0.32%	6
100% equities – home bias, no tilts, no property	OEIC	V-L5	Vanguard LifeStrategy 100% Equity Fund	0.33%	6
60% bonds/40% equities – no home bias, with tilts, no property	OEIC	D-MF1	Dimensional Multi-Factor Conservative Fund	0.50%	4
40% bonds/60% equities – no home bias, with tilts, no property	OEIC	DMF2	Dimensional Multi-Factor Balanced Fund	0.55%	5
0% bonds/100% equities – no home bias, with tilts, no property	OEIC	D-MF3	Dimensional Multi-Factor Equity Fund	0.62%	6

9.6 A possible shortlist – *caveat emptor*!

Table 9.3 provides a few product names to start your search with. Broadly, you can find pretty reasonable passive products that provide you with exposure to the risks that you are seeking to take on in the more core elements of your portfolio (UK, global and emerging equity, global real estate and short-dated bonds). Tilts to value and small cap stocks are a little less well covered, if you are trying to invest on a DIY basis. If you are using an adviser, then you may want to see if they use the Dimensional Fund Advisors' (DFA) range or other institutionally accessible products. Remember that you may have to balance the wish to gain exposure to a specific type of risk, with less than perfect product solutions. If you do not think the product is robust enough then perhaps you should consider reallocating that part of the portfolio and waiting until new products arrive on the market.

I make no recommendations here, but Vanguard, Dimensional and iShares are three major, skilled and reputable firms with a deep experience of delivering high quality market risk based funds. You will need to decide for yourself.

Mapping funds to Smarter Portfolios

Again, the process of mapping specific funds to the various Smarter Portfolios is not provided as any sort of recommendation but to provide some insight into how these various portfolios could be constructed using different 'real-life' products (see Tables 9.4 and 9.5). There is often more than one way to skin the cat. For example, say you want exposure to developed and emerging market equities, you could hold two funds – one covering developed markets, the other covering emerging markets – or you could hold one fund that incorporates both. Lifestyle funds/risk-managed funds could cover most of the asset classes you need or you may prefer to hold single asset class funds. It is worth remembering too that you can create a global exposure using a combination of UK and world-ex UK funds/ international funds (UK + International = Global).

The choice, as they say, is yours.

Table 9.4   Smarter Portfolios: Home bias

ASSET CLASS PRODUCT IDEAS	HOME BIAS							
	Simple (UK only)		Broad market		Diversified		Tilted	
Return Engine (whisky) asset classes	OEIC/ETF ideas	%	OEIC/ETF ideas	%	OEIC/ETF ideas	%	OEIC/ETF ideas	%
UK – market	V1, F1, L1, H1	100%	V1, F1, L1, H1, (VL1–5)*	25%	V1, F1, L1, H1, (VL1–5)*	25%	V1, F1, L1, H1, (D1), (VL1–5)*	15%
UK – value							(D1), D2, I2	5%
UK – smaller companies							(D1), D3, I3, H3, (D9), (V9)	5%
Developed World ex-UK market			V4, A4, I4 (VL1–5)*	60%	V4, A4, I4, (VL1–5)*	50%	V4, A4, I4, (D4), (VL1–5)*	30%
Developed World ex-UK – value							D5, (D4)	10%
Developed World ex-UK – smaller companies							(V9),(D9), (D4)	10%
Emerging markets – market			V11, V11B, I11 (VL1–5)*	15%	V11, V11B, I11, (VL1–5)*	15%	V11, V11B, I11, (D11), (VL1–5)*	10%
Emerging markets – value and small							(D11), D12, I12	5%
Global commercial real estate (REIT)					B13, I13	10%	B13, I13	10%

Defensive (water) asset classes	OEIC/ETF ideas	%	OEIC/ETF ideas	%	OEIC/ETF ideas	%	OEIC/ETF ideas	%
Short-dated, high quality bonds*	I14, I14B, D15, V15 (VL1–5)*	50%	I14, I14B, D15, V15, (VL1–5)*	50%	I14, I14B, D15, V15, (VL1–5)*	50%	I14, I14B, D15, V15, (VL1–5)*	50%
Short-dated, high quality, inflation-linked bonds*	D16, F16 (VL1–5)*	50%	D16, F16, (VL1–5)*	50%	D16, F16, (VL1–5)*	50%	D16, F16, (VL1–5)*	50%

Note: ( ) = joint allocation that covers all asset classes where this fund is designated. For example, (D1) is the Dimensional UK Core Fund that includes market and moderate value and small cap exposures, or (V9) which is the Vanguard Global Small Cap Index Fund which includes UK and non-UK exposure to smaller companies.

Table 9.5 Smarter Portfolios: Global (no home bias)

ASSET CLASS PRODUCT IDEAS	HOME BIAS					
	Broad market		Diversified		Tilted	
	OEIC/ETF ideas	%	OEIC/ETF ideas	%	OEIC/ETF ideas	%
Return Engine (whisky) asset classes						
Global – market (developed)	I6, (V1+V4), (V7), (I7)	85%	I6, (V1+V4)	75%	I6, (D6), (V1+V4), (V7), (I7), (D-MF1-3)*	45%
Global – value (developed)					(D6), L8, (D10), (D-MF1-3)*	15%
Global – smaller companies (developed)					D9, V9, (D6), (D10), (D-MF1-3)*	15%
Emerging markets – market	V11, V11B, I11, (V7), (I7)	15%	V11, V11B, I11, (V7), (I7)	15%	V11, V11B, I11, (V7), (I7), (D11), (D-MF1-3)*	10%
Emerging markets – value and small					(D11), D12, I12, (D-MF1-3)*	5%
Global commercial real estate (REIT)	B13, I13		B13, I13	10%	B13, I13	10%

Defensive (water) asset classes	OEIC/ETF ideas	%	OEIC/ETF ideas	%	OEIC/ETF ideas	%
Short-dated, high quality bonds*	I14, I14B, D15, V15	50%	I14, I14B, D15, V15	50%	I14, I14B, D15, V15, (D-MF1-3)*	50%
Short-dated, high quality, inflation-linked bonds*	D16, F16	50%	D16, F16	50%	D16, F16, (D-MF1-3)*	50%

Note: ( ) = joint allocation that covers all asset classes where this fund is designated. (V1+V4) = you could combine UK + International = you could combine UK + International = Global based on market cap weight – approx 10% UK, 90% international.

Note: * the risk-managed fund that you use will depend on the portfolio structure you have selected.

In conclusion

When selecting products to implement your Smarter Portfolio:

- Choose a sensible broad market index for each risk factor you are seeking to replicate.

- Start with the main providers of funds and ETFs – write a shortlist.

- Screen possible solutions against the criteria provided using Morningstar.

- Consider the risk exposure replication method carefully – physically replicated is preferred.

- If no or very weak products (for tilts) exist, consider reallocating exposure.

- Monitor on an ongoing basis.

- Keep an eye out for new products – they will be emerging rapidly.

References

Bogle, J. C. (2002) 'The investment dilemma of the philanthropic investor' (www.vanguard.com).

10

Smarter advice – DIY or hire an adviser?

The choice to run your own Smarter Portfolio or to hand over its implementation and ongoing management to an adviser is a big decision that you need to think carefully about. The choice depends on a number of issues, which we will explore below.

The key point that I want to make is that good advice and ongoing guidance over your lifelong investment journey from a leading adviser is worth its weight in gold. Poor advice and implementation could, on the other hand, have a seriously detrimental effect on your wealth, which in turn will impact on the aspirations that you have for your future lifestyle.

We will look at both options in turn, which will hopefully help you make the decision that is right for you. We will then look at how you go about selecting a leading adviser or a good platform for running your DIY portfolio on. Neither route is better than the other in any absolute sense, but one will be the better option for you.

10.1 Hiring an adviser

There is no straightforward method for deciding whether hiring an adviser is right for you. But you will probably have a gut feeling as to whether you feel comfortable with establishing your own financial and investment plan and implementing and managing it over time. If you do then you may want to manage it yourself. If not, you will need to look for a strong adviser.

As a starting point it may depend on how much money you have and what it represents. The ideas in this book apply to anyone investing; from someone putting £50 into their portfolio every month to build a nest-egg to someone looking to invest £10 million. If the money you are investing represents a small nest-egg that is never likely to be the core of your future financial well-being, you may think that it should be reasonably simple to invest yourself. It may be that this money is part of a money purchase pension plan run by your company and that you need to direct the monthly contributions you make in a sensible manner into the investment funds available on the plan menu. Again a DIY approach may make sense.

However, as wealth increases and as it becomes a central part of your future financial security and desired lifestyle, so the decisions that you make become more critical and complex. Worries such as running out of money, knowing that you are still on track despite recent markets, handling the paperwork and dealing with all the other issues that wealth brings are common. The lack of time in people's lives to think about and handle these issues compounds the stresses that can accompany wealth.

Table 10.1 Hire an adviser or adopt a DIY approach?

	Adviser	DIY
Your investments:		
Simple investment affairs?	No	Yes
Critical to your financial security and lifestyle?	Yes	No
Investment of pension plan contributions only?	No	Yes
Annual ISA allowance only?	No	Yes
You have wider wealth issues?	Yes	No
Your skills, interest and time:		
Uncertain what to do, despite reading the book?	Yes	No
Disinterested in investment matters?	Yes	No
Time poor?	Yes	No
Dislike paperwork?	Yes	No
Want ongoing guidance and handholding?	Yes	No
Want someone else to take care of it all?	Yes	No
You feel you can handle these administrative tasks:		
Selecting best-in-class products?	No	Yes
Raising cash regularly, if needed?	No	Yes
Rebalancing your portfolio when it gets out of line?	No	Yes
Managing the tax consequences of rebalancing?	No	Yes
Aggregating your wealth position for review?	No	Yes
Monitoring your progress toward your goals?	No	Yes
Happy to pay around 1% p.a. to an adviser?	**Yes**	**No**

Table 10.1 may help you decide between the two. Ring the answers that apply to you and see where you come out. Totally unscientific but it should get you thinking!

Only you can decide, but I am sure that you will have a pretty good feel for where you come out.

10.2 Picking a leading adviser

You can obviously see from the Table 10.1 that an adviser plays a number of key roles. Perhaps the most valuable thing that an excellent adviser can deliver is helping you to relax about your wealth, confident in the knowledge that your lifetime plan is robust, that your assets are invested in an appropriate and effective way and that you will be kept informed of the progress you are making towards your goals. That to many will be money well spent. The added bonus is that you can throw all the administration their way too! Key attributes that an adviser will have are described in the following paragraphs.

A focus on financial planning, which is essential in establishing why you want to invest in the first place and how these goals can be quantified into a sensible financial plan and investment strategy is crucial. Cash flow modelling will sit at the core of this approach. You may well also have a number of financial products that you will have collected over time that may need sorting out too.

Again, a decent adviser will have developed and will be able to explain clearly what their investment philosophy and process is. The way in which they arrive at your asset allocation should at least match the ideas set out in this book, and you should challenge them to explain to you why their approach differs, if it does. If they are truly evidence based, then they should have reached the conclusion that passive implementation, to capture the bulk of the market rewards on offer, is in your best interests and be prepared to concede on that point. If they do not then that surely raises questions! Some like to act like fund managers and others may simply enjoy being entertained by active managers trying to sell their wares (a form of legalised bribery known as marketing budgets). I go to a national adviser conference each year where product providers set out their stalls. Active managers have all the fun games – even a simulated drive in the cockpit of an F1 car last time around. Visit the passive fund providers' stalls and you are lucky to get even a small packet of mints! Costs matter!

Table 10.2	**Adviser checklist**

Their credentials	
Registered with the Financial Conduct Authority, ww.fca.gov.uk	✓
They are fee-based charging a percentage of your investable assets p.a.	✓
They take no other income from you of any kind, or from anyone else	✓
They offer a passive investment solution	✓
They offer some form of lifetime cashflow modelling	✓
Likely to be a Member of the Institute of Financial Planning	✓
Individuals in the firm are probably Certified Financial Planner accredited	✓
Some useful questions	
Do you have any conflicts of interest you need to declare to me?	✓
Are you a truly fee-based adviser?	✓
Can you show me every charge/cost I will incur if I become a client?	✓
How many other clients with similar assets to me do you handle?	✓
Please describe your approach to creating my wealth plan	✓
Please describe what you believe in from an investment perspective	✓
What are my chances of achieving a successful outcome?	✓
Can I read your investment process document?	✓
How will you show me that I remain on course?	✓
Could I see an example of one of your progress reviews?	✓
Do you ever directly handle my money?	✓
Do you provide an advisory service or can you make decisions on my behalf?	✓
Could I talk to some of your existing clients?	✓
Soft attributes	
You feel comfortable that they know their stuff	✓
They enjoy discussing issues you raise	✓
They provide clear ideas and talk to you in terms that you understand	✓
You feel that they are working for and with you	✓
You feel that you could become professional friends	✓

* Other professional qualifications include: Diploma in Financial Planning (DipPFS), Associateship of the PFS (APFS) or Chartered Financial Planner status.

The Institute of Financial Planning is a well-regarded organisation that is seeking to drive forward the professionalism of the financial planning business. Within their membership, if you look closely and use the criteria above, you will find many of the leading advisers. Perhaps start with accredited firms through the Institute of Financial Planning's website (www.financialplanning.org.uk).

The due diligence that you perform on your adviser is your responsibility. Remember too that hiring an adviser is a process that demands some of your time and decision-making. You cannot abrogate all responsibility to them for your financial well-being. You need to understand and own the strategy that is put in place. They are there to hold your hand over time, monitor and update you on your progress. You need to be engaged in the process as it is your future lifestyle that is at stake.

In the meantime, Table 10.2 provides some pointers on how to locate a financial adviser and some of the questions that you should ask.

10.3 The do-it-yourself option

The DIY option will suit you, either because your investment affairs are pretty simple or you have the time and inclination to undertake the tasks that could otherwise be subcontracted to an investment adviser. Going it alone requires you to set up a workable system for buying, selling and safekeeping the investments that you buy. It will also need to keep a record of the details of each transaction that you undertake to allow you to fill in your tax return appropriately and accurately. The most effective route today for the DIY investor is to open an online brokerage account.

Choosing your investment platform

An online brokerage account becomes the conduit through which to own, safe-keep, record-keep and rebalance your long-term Smarter Portfolio. It allows you to buy funds, ETFs and index-linked gilts at low transaction costs, usually around £10 per trade or less. In some cases you can simply use their fund database and pay a quarterly custody charge. These firms include the likes of Sippdeal (www.sippdeal.co.uk), Hargreaves Lansdown (www.hl.co.uk) and Selftrade (www.selftrade.co.uk) to name a few. There is no shortage of choice. You need to decide which firm is best for you. A few things to check out would be: who owns them, where the assets are custodied, what their charges are and if they charge for inactivity – one of your investment goals!

Once you have set up your accounts you can run through the relatively simple process of transferring any ISA or dealer accounts to the new platform.

Getting started

The generic process for getting started follows along the lines of the list below. Some of these issues are addressed more fully in the sections below.

- Make sure the brokerage firm provides access to the funds/ETFs you wish to own.
- Open an account – Dealing, ISA and Sipp – depending upon what you need.
- Transfer cash or securities from any other accounts. Make sure that the platform you choose allows 'in specie' transfers (securities) or else you may have to cash in your existing investments on which you will suffer costs and possibly taxes.
- Decide your entry strategy, i.e. the time you will take to invest your money, which is different to picking the time you think it is best to enter the market – that is market timing.
- Make the trades – there will not be that many as you will not own many funds or ETFs.
- Invest any income that your portfolio throws off, which it probably will, or make sure that you have selected 'accumulation' shares in the first place. If you are taking income from your portfolio, 'distribution' shares may work better for you.
- Rebalance the assets back to their original mix when they get out of kilter, as they will from time to time. Use cash balances first. More on that later.
- Do the paperwork when it comes to the tax year end, including capital gains and income received (you still receive 'income' from accumulation shares and you need to take this into account).
- That is about it – not too much excitement or glamour!

A small point to remember is that if you are investing regularly work out how much it will cost you as a percentage of your monthly investment – a penny saved is a penny earned. Some platforms allow you to invest regular amounts without cost, others do not.

Making a lump-sum investment

If you are investing a lump sum, perhaps from an inheritance, a bonus or the sale proceeds of your business, you face a dilemma: what happens if equity markets crash after you put your money into them or returns are particularly weak over a long period of time?

It is a real problem, as any investor putting money into equities at the end of 1999 or mid-2007 quickly found out. Imagine that you have £1 million to invest and you decide to put it all into equities; you would be pretty upset if you invested it and within a year or two it was worth only £500,000. Let's do some simple maths: remember that 50% down requires your portfolio to rise by 100%, not 50%, to get back to where it was; also, if your portfolio delivered 5% in real terms a year from that point forwards (our estimate of average real returns from developed market equities), it would take you almost fifteen years to get back to its initial level of purchasing power. This is a very real risk that could damage the outcome of your investing programme. How can you avoid getting hit in this way?

The solution then, if you are concerned about a fall in the equity market and you could live with any gains foregone, is to average your way into the market. You could decide on the number of years that you will do this over and then pick a Smarter Portfolio with a lower growth-oriented asset mix and move up one portfolio a year until you reach your required long-term strategy allocation.

The downside is that you could lose out if the markets forge ahead. It is a risk management issue and one that only you can resolve. In short, own a diverse portfolio and average your way in. Fortunately, it is not so much of a problem if you are building a portfolio using monthly contributions, as you will be averaging in across the whole of your accumulation stage.

Setting up your administration system

Once you are up and running you need to think about how you are going to go about administering your portfolio, with the least fuss and bother. Few of us like paperwork; in fact, for some people the feeling of anxiety about investing is as much to do with handling the administration as it is to do with living with a portfolio. Fortunately today, there are efficient and simple ways to administer a portfolio, particularly if you are a rational, long-term, buy-and-hold investor using index tracker funds and/or exchange-traded funds.

When setting up a portfolio you will have some initial administration to do as well as some regular maintenance work, which can be kept to a minimum. When you buy a fund or ETF, you will need to keep a record of your ownership of it, including: its exact description and any fund code that identifies it; the number of units/shares you own in each fund (active or index) or ETF; any buying and selling of these investments, including how many units/shares were traded and the date and the price at which the transaction took place; and any dividends from equities or coupon payments from bonds that you received. That should all be taken care of by your online brokerage account, if you use one. If not, you will receive contract notes from the fund companies that you need to organise and file appropriately.

In the case of income, you should check if the fund can automatically reinvest it for you to save time and effort. Remember, if you receive cash, you need to put this to work as soon as possible. This class of shares is often called accumulation shares. In the UK you may be liable for tax on any income, if you are a taxable investor, even if it is immediately reinvested.

You will need this information to fill out your tax return, declaring the income received and capital gains that you have realised during the fiscal year if this pot of money is taxable. Fortunately, most of these items are all produced either by brokers or the fund companies themselves. The degree to which you can minimise administration will be a function of the number of investments that you have decided upon for your Smarter Portfolio, the products you have chosen and the platform that you use. Remember, though, that your investment needs should drive your decision-making and not your desire to reduce the administrative hassle.

How you administer your investments will depend upon your own individual circumstances and the vehicles that you use. Time spent thinking about what administrative issues are going to arise from your portfolio and how you are going to handle them will save a lot of time and angst down the road. Here are some pointers that you should bear in mind.

▓ Choosing the right investments is your primary decision, which may dictate the administrative process. Remember that the same products may be sold through a variety of channels and one may be more administratively effective and/or cost-effective than another. Try to keep things as simple and as cheap as possible.

▓ When you receive information from your broker or fund company deal with it immediately. It won't take long. Otherwise, the temptation is to throw it on to the 'I'll do it later' pile and the hurdle of dealing with it becomes greater with each envelope that arrives.

▨ If you are a keen technology user, keep as much information online as possible.

▨ Careful record-keeping is essential and if your filing system is working, finding the information to do your tax return will be far easier for you or anyone you employ to do it.

▨ Do not avoid the admin. Set up an efficient system to control it.

Portfolio maintenance

Portfolio maintenance is made up of three tasks: tracking, monitoring and rebalancing. It should not take you more than a few hours once a year to keep things in order. Figure 10.1 summarises what you will have to deal with. At the end of the day, it is your money and you need to know how much you have, how anyone managing your money is performing and whether your plan is on track to meet your goals.

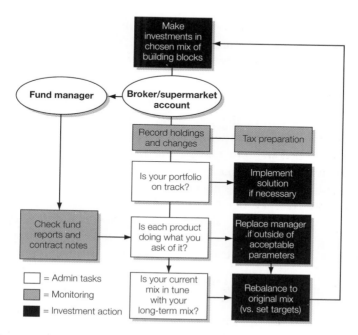

Figure 10.1   **Ongoing tracking, monitoring and rebalancing**

Making sure that you are on track to achieving your goals is important. Working out roughly where your accumulated wealth needs to be in the future, say every couple of years, is a good discipline.

You should only look at your portfolio annually at most; any more frequently and you will probably shock yourself with the inevitable ups and downs. Time does a good job at smoothing out the bumps.

Each year, take a look at how your investments have done against their chosen index. Say, for example, you own a FTSE All-Share index fund – take a look and see what the total expense ratio is now, how closely the fund has tracked the index, how large it is and if there have been any changes in strategy or personnel. In the event that performance is out of line with the market, you may have to take remedial action by replacing the manager or at least keep them under close scrutiny. This is a rare event if you have chosen an index fund carefully. Remember that 'out of line with expectations' means both above and below the benchmark index you have chosen. A manager whose results are better than expected may well be taking more risks than you want him to – beware.

Rebalancing your mix of building blocks

Rebalancing is the process of returning your portfolio back to its original mix, as over time building blocks will generate different levels of return, and the assets in the mix will become skewed in favour of the better-performing asset.

If you believe that markets revert to their long-run average – not a bad assumption to believe in and you would be in good company – then by rebalancing your portfolio, i.e. selling some of the building blocks that have outperformed and buying those that have underperformed, you may be positioning the portfolio appropriately to avoid/capture any mean reversion. It provides a discipline of buying low and selling high. However, there are no certainties that this will pay off over the time frame you are investing over. As such, you should primarily view rebalancing as trying to maintain the risk/reward profile of your portfolio over the time you are invested for and which you chose in the first place. You just have to ignore the fact that, over some time periods and with the benefit of hindsight, it may turn out that it could have been better not to rebalance at all.

Perhaps the most succinct statement on rebalancing comes from David Swensen (2000), who invests for Yale University in the USA:

'Over long periods of time, portfolios allowed to drift tend to contain ever-increasing allocations to risky assets, as higher returns cause riskier positions to crowd out other holdings. The fundamental purpose of rebalancing lies in controlling risk, not enhancing return. Rebalancing trades keeps portfolios at long-term policy targets by reversing deviations resulting from asset class performance differentials. Disciplined rebalancing activity requires a strong stomach and serious staying power.'

He makes the point that in a severe bear market such as 1973–1974 the rebalancing investor was forced to buy more equities as markets continued to fall. Equally, rising equity prices needs a strong stomach as selling equities as part of a rebalance appears, at the time, to be a loser's strategy.

When should you rebalance? That's a question that has no definitive answer. Recent research (Lee, 2008) comes to the following conclusion:

'Aside from avoiding excessive trading, there are no optimal rebalancing rules ... The good news for investors is that without an optimal way to rebalance, the burden of producing returns through optimal rebalancing is lifted. Return generation is again the responsibility of the market ... The optimal rebalancing strategy will differ for each investor, depending on their unique sensitivities to deviations from target allocation, transaction frequency, and tax costs.'

Some investors rebalance every year, which may be reasonable in steady markets. However, it probably makes sense to set a target for rebalancing, for example when the risky assets/defensive assets mix has moved by 10% or more. Too low a target and you will be for ever tinkering with the portfolio and incurring transaction and tax costs; in any case, small deviations are probably statistically insignificant, given all the assumptions that you have made to get to that allocation in the first place. Too high a target and you will expose your portfolio to too much risk, which could be costly. An example of a sensible rebalancing strategy for, say, a 40% defensive and 60% risky growth-oriented mix would be to allow the portfolio to run to 70% in risky assets and 30% in defensive assets and vice versa. Then rebalance.

The tax consequences and trading costs of rebalancing a portfolio need to be taken into consideration. If you sell equities that have gone up in price, you may incur significant capital gains, which may outweigh the added risk of holding a higher proportion of equities than intended. Remember that if you are making regular contributions to an investment plan, you can allocate new contributions into the building block that is underweight. By doing so you can avoid having to crystallise any capital gains in the outperforming asset classes you own. Even if you are not contributing regularly, your portfolio will be throwing off cash in the form of dividends from your shares and coupons from your bonds, which you could use.

10.4 Don't forget about tax

Managing your tax situation well is a very important component of successful investing. As an investor, it makes sense to use any legal tax breaks that you are given by the Chancellor. In most countries there are tax incentives designed to encourage you to invest more for your future and to rely less on the state. Remember that legally paying the taxman at a future date instead of today, or even altogether, can have a significant beneficial effect on your total portfolio returns over the long run. Tax breaks come in a number of forms.

Retirement (pension) savings

In the UK retirement saving is tax efficient, as you are given a tax break for saving into your pension plan. A 40% rate tax payer investing £60 of their pay will get the benefit of £100 in their plan as their contribution is exempt from tax. Apart from these contributions receiving favourable tax treatment, capital gains and some forms of income are largely exempt from tax, although this changes depending on the Chancellor's whim. Pension funds are tax-exempt in many jurisdictions.

ISAs – personal tax shelters

In some jurisdictions, individual investors are provided with tax-deferred or tax-free investment structures. In the UK, for example, you can invest, with taxed income, up to £11,520 per year in an ISA for 2013–2014, which effectively shields you from most income or capital gains tax in the future. You should seriously consider taking advantage of this tax break. The Chancellor is rarely so generous.

Personal allowances

Again, some jurisdictions have allowances that allow you some capital gains tax free. The base cost of your investments, i.e. the price you bought them at, may also be increased over the years, thereby reducing any taxable gains that you must pay tax on later. This is the case in the UK. Remember that these can be used if you find you have to rebalance your portfolio at some time. With a buy-and-hold index fund/ETF strategy, you should have little need to crystallise capital gains, particularly when you are accumulating wealth. The HM Revenue & Customs website (www.hmrc.gov.uk) provides the latest allowances. It does make sense to use up your capital gains allowances as it means the level of unrealised capital gains in your portfolio will be lower over time with less tax to pay if and when you liquidate your portfolio.

Harvesting and offsetting losses

Many jurisdictions allow you to offset capital losses that you make against capital gains. The magnitude and time scale over which losses can be carried forward varies from country to country. Some jurisdictions have rules to stop you from simultaneously selling and repurchasing the same funds, known as bed-and-breakfasting.

Planning upfront how you are going to maximise the tax-efficiency of your investment plan is worthwhile and if you are going to spend money on advice, this is a good place to do so. In general, there are three key points to be made here if you are a taxable investor:

▨ First, maximise the tax breaks that are legally afforded to you by your government. It will make a significant difference to your wealth in the long run.

▨ Second, if you are unsure about what breaks are available to you for each pool of money you are investing and exactly how you can take advantage of these breaks, seek advice from your accountant. Alternatively, phone HM Revenue & Customs, if you are a UK taxpayer, as they are remarkably helpful and efficient.

▨ Finally, your building block mix needs to be driven by your investment needs, not by tax planning. Being tax efficient within the context of your long-term building block mix makes sense.

That's it really for the DIY investor! It really is not too difficult to turn your theoretical portfolio into reality. Good luck!

References

Lee, M. I. (2008) *Rebalancing and Returns*. DFA.

Swensen, D. F. (2000) *Pioneering Portfolio Management*. New York: The Free Press.

Smarter insight

This section provides a deeper insight into some of the key portfolio building blocks that are either useful or probably to be avoided. The more you understand about what is in your portfolio and why other things are not, the more comfortable you are likely to feel.

Chapter 11: Smarter insight – on-menu assets

This chapter provides detail on the building blocks that should form the core of your portfolio. Read carefully and take particular interest in the downside that these could deliver from time to time.

Chapter 12: Smarter insight – off-menu assets

Here you find a balanced view of the challenges and issues that you face in investing in these more esoteric asset classes and strategies. The guile of marketing departments tend to illuminate the upside possibilities, but reality is a tougher master. Hopefully you will be able to decide for yourself why these assets may not be appropriate for you.

11

Smarter insight – on-menu assets

The basic menu for the asset classes that we have decided to use – and those that will be excluded – was established in Chapter 6. It is summarised in Figure 11.1. This chapter provides a bit of a deeper insight into the 'on-menu' with comments on 'off-menu' asset classes and strategies covered in Chapter 12.

11.1 Return Engine asset classes

Before we dive into each of the asset classes in more depth, it makes sense to take a quick look at how different asset classes have performed in both risk and return terms. The challenge we have is that the datasets for global

Figure 11.1   The asset class menu

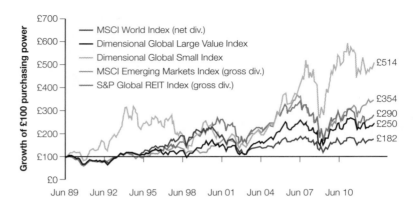

Figure 11.2 Return Engine assets – Growth of £100 after inflation – July 1989 to Dec 2012

REITS and emerging market equities only go back as far as 1989 and 1988 respectively. However, with a little bit of common sense, we can glean some useful insights. Figure 11.2 reveals the growth in purchasing power (i.e. after inflation) of £100 invested in each asset class. No costs have been deducted.

Table 11.1 Summary of Return Engine return and risk characteristics 7/1989 to 4/2013

Data Series	Primary role	Return before inflation*	Return after inflation*	Growth of £1	Risk %	Worst 1 year*	Worst 5 years*	Correlation to global equities
MSCI World Index	Core return	5.9%	2.6%	£1.8	15.7%	−39%	−8%	N/A
Dimensional Global Large Value Index	Return enhancer	8.1%	4.6%	£2.9	18.0%	−40%	−6%	0.9
Dimensional Global Small Index	Return enhancer	7.4%	4.0%	£2.5	17.3%	−38%	−3%	0.9
MSCI Emerging Markets Index	Return enhancer	10.7%	7.2%	£5.1	24.6%	−53%	−14%	0.8
S&P Global REIT Index	Diversifier	9.0%	5.5%	£3.5	17.0%	−43%	−6%	0.7

* Annualised (compound or geometric) rate of return

It is more the journey and the relative position of each asset class that is of interest. During the period under review, the return enhancing asset classes (value, smaller companies and emerging markets) have performed as one might have wished, despite interim periods when each individual asset classes' returns were poor either in an absolute sense, or relative to the broad global market exposure.

Table 11.1 summarises the return and risk of each of these Return Engine asset classes. The one thing that you will notice is that all of them have delivered reasonable inflation plus returns as might be expected, but each is also capable of delivering large downside losses on the journey, often at the same points of market crisis, but not always and not always to the same degree of speed of recovery.

11.2 Core return: developed equity markets

Developed global equity markets represent the core return engine of any portfolio, capturing the dynamism of the companies listed on the markets of developed nations. This represents around 85% of global equity market capitalisation (see Figure 11.3).

The developed markets classification usually comprises 24 markets: Australia, Austria, Belgium, Canada, Denmark, Finland, France, Germany, Greece, Hong Kong, Ireland, Israel, Italy, Japan, Netherlands, New Zealand, Norway, Portugal, Singapore, Spain, Sweden, Switzerland, the United Kingdom and the United States. Korea sits in some developed market indices (FTSE) and not in others (MSCI).

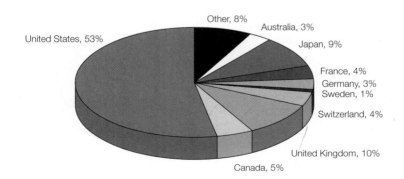

Figure 11.3 **Developed markets by capitalisation**

Source: MSCI 2013 (www.msci.com)

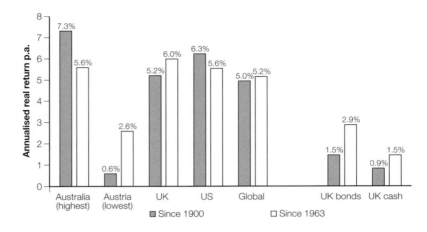

Figure 11.4   Long-term after-inflation returns 1900–2012

Source: Dimson, E., Marsh, P. R. and Staunton, M. (2013)

Past returns

The dataset for the UK and other developed market equities goes back to 1900. As such we have a reasonable time period to understand the broad characteristics associated with being an owner of companies. Figure 11.4 provides insight into the range of returns experienced across markets and over different time periods.

Points of note include the fact that even over long periods of time, a strong equity premium is not assured, as amply demonstrated by the experience of Austria. Global diversification makes sense. Equities have outstripped bonds and cash by a material degree. Their cost of capital is higher – it is more risky to be an owner of companies than a lender. The proportion of time that UK equities have outperformed UK bonds and cash increases with holding periods is illustrated in Table 11.2.

Table 11.2   Equities beat cash and gilts over time: 1900–2011

	Holding period (years)					
Outcome	2	3	4	5	10	18
Equities beat cash	67%	69%	72%	74%	90%	99%
Equities beat gilts	68%	75%	75%	74%	79%	88%

Source: Barclays Equity Gilt Study, 2012

Future returns

As we established earlier in the book, you should earn a reward for the additional risks that you incur from investing in equities as opposed to owning risk-free cash or bonds. You could lose your money, you have no certainty that dividends will be paid, or any certainty that your shares will appreciate. In the pecking order of claims on a company's assets on liquidation, equities are at the bottom of the pile, below secured bankers, bond holders and other creditors; this more risky position (i.e. the higher cost of capital) demands greater reward for investors.

This reward or premium is known as the equity risk premium. Measuring it in the past is simple enough; however, like many arguments in investing, not only are there short-term exceptions to long-run averages, but also different time frames tell different stories. Academics and economists argue ad infinitum about the level of the equity risk premium but as the *Economist* succinctly put it in 2003:

'Yes, over long periods equities have done better than bonds. But there is no equity "premium" – in the sense of a fairly predictable excess over bond returns on which investors can rely ... Searching for a consistent, God-given premium is a fool's errand.'

All I can say, as a practitioner rather than an academic, is that over the long run a premium appears to exist and should do so in the future, otherwise we would simply invest in bonds with lower risk. As the objective of good, simple, long-term investing is giving yourself the greatest chance of success, and equities have a greater chance of delivering long-term real returns than either bonds or cash, if you are a long-term investor you should have a natural bias towards equities.

As investors, we should be reasonably confident that companies operating in free capitalist economies should be able to continue to pay dividends and to increase their profits and collectively generate real growth in a nation's economy over the long term. They have done so in the past over reasonable periods of time. In the long run, we can therefore be reasonably confident that eventually investment returns and market returns will be similar – they have to be.

In the long run, you would expect the return from equities to be related to the growth in dividends as higher corporate profits (i.e. earnings) are generally assumed to lead to higher dividends. At the end of the day, equity returns have to reflect economic reality. That provides us with a simple model for coming up with future long-term rates of return from equities.

In terms of potential levels of return over the next decade, assuming a dividend yield of 3% in the UK and a not unreasonable assumption of earnings growth of 5% in nominal terms and inflation at 3%, and assuming a constant P/E ratio, we get the following estimate of real expected equity return:

3% dividends + 5% earnings growth − 3% inflation = 5% real return

If you believe that the P/E ratio will contract from this point forwards (it would not have been a bad assumption to make by the dispassionate investor in 2000 for example), returns will be lower and vice versa.

Academics and practitioners each have their own view

Other voices in the industry have different opinions. In the case of Dimson, Marsh and Staunton (Dimson et al., 2013), the future equity risk premium above cash is expected to be lower at around 3.0% to 3.5%. JP Morgan Asset Management (my alma mater) on the other hand estimates that the equity risk premium for developed markets is pretty close to long-term history at around 5% (JP Morgan, 2012). No one knows for sure. Perhaps model 5% and 3% and see how it affects you calculations.

Downside risks

Being an owner of equities is always uncertain with respect to the returns that one is going to receive. There is never a 'safe' time to be the owner of equities. You only need to look at Table 11.3 to see how large and frequent the falls experienced over the past 113 years have been for those invested in the UK market.

Table 11.3 Peak-to-trough falls and recoveries for UK equities 1900–2012

Decline (%)	Peak date	Trough date	Recovery date	Decline (year)	Recovery (year)
−64%	Dec-72	Dec-74	Dec-77	2	3
−37%	Dec-99	Dec-02	Dec-05	3	3
−35%	Dec-28	Dec-31	Dec-33	3	2
−30%	Dec-07	Dec-08	Dec-10	1	2
−24%	Dec-36	Dec-40	Dec-42	4	2
−22%	Dec-19	Dec-21	Dec-24	2	3
−15%	Dec-68	Dec-70	Dec-71	2	1
−11%	Dec-46	Dec-49	Dec-51	3	2
−10%	Dec-55	Dec-57	Dec-58	2	1
−10%	Dec-89	Dec-90	Dec-91	1	1

11.3 Return enhancer – emerging market equities

Investing in emerging markets, i.e. economies that are developing from an agricultural to an industrial and service-oriented structure, offers two benefits: first, these markets may be out of sync with the UK and other developed markets, providing a diversification benefit; and second, investors expect higher long-term returns relative to developed equity markets partly due to projected higher growth rates in these economies, but primarily in compensation for the additional risks they take on, i.e. the cost of capital is higher. These material risks include: political instability; currency risk; a lack of open and free markets; higher costs to invest; insufficient legal protection for owners; limited liquidity; and poor corporate governance.

Defining what is an emerging market is not clear cut

No precise definition exists, but measures such as GDP per capita, the regulatory environment and stock market size, steer index providers to a similar set of markets. A single variable of US$25,000 per capita GDP defines the boundary in practice between developed and emerging markets. MSCI, for example, identifies twenty-one emerging markets: Brazil, Chile, China, Colombia, Czech Republic, Egypt, Hungary, India, Indonesia, Korea, Malaysia, Mexico, Morocco, Peru, Philippines, Poland, Russia, South Africa,

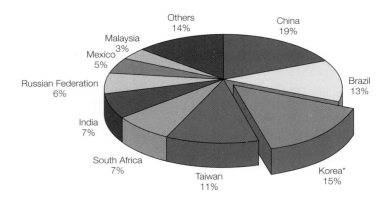

Figure 11.5 **Emerging markets by capitalisation**

Source: MSCI January 2013 (www.msci.com)

* excluded in FTSE EM indices.

Taiwan, Thailand, and Turkey. FTSE however exclude South Korea from their indices.

Emerging markets economies represented around 38% of global GDP at the end of 2010 and are estimated to overtake the output of developed markets before 2020 (*The Economist*, 2011). Over two-thirds of the world's population lives in the emerging economies. Market capitalisation (Figure 11.5) stands at around 30% on a non-float adjusted basis (that is before allowing for what shares are actually free to be bought and sold). On a float adjusted basis (i.e. the actual stocks that are available for foreign investors to own), it represented a little less than 15% of total global equity market capitalisation at the end of 2010. However, Goldman Sachs have estimated that this could be in the region of 20% by 2020 and over 30% by 2030.

Emerging markets may deliver a diversification benefit when combined with developed market equities. However, the correlations between developed markets, such as the UK, and emerging markets, and between emerging markets themselves, have been rising, which reduces the diversification benefit of incorporating emerging markets into portfolios. Figure 11.6 illustrates the point well. It shows the correlation between the MSCI EM Index and the MSCI World Index and between the MSCI Brazil and MSCI China indices.

It has been suggested that the rise in correlations between emerging markets may be due to the increase in funds allocated to emerging markets by global

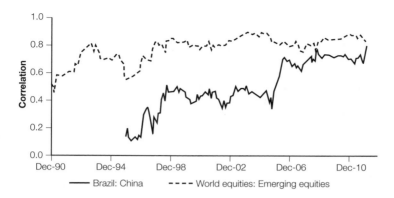

Figure 11.6   **Rolling 3-year correlations have been rising (to December 2012)**

investors, often via broad emerging market funds and ETFs which can be sold quickly due to their liquidity; a crisis in one country or region can spark a wholesale exit from the all emerging markets as the allocation is pared back (Bernstein, 2012).

Past returns

Over the entire period of the emerging market data series (1988–2012) emerging markets returned 13.4% p.a. compared to developed world markets of 7.3%. The outcome is, however, sensitive to start and end dates. You can also see in Figure 11.7 that volatility has been much higher than for developed market equities.

It makes sense to remain broadly diversified across all emerging markets due to the volatile nature of individual emerging markets.

Future returns

The material risks that investors take on in providing capital to companies listed on emerging market bourses should theoretically be compensated. Emerging markets are considerably more volatile than developed markets (25% and 15% respectively from 1988 to 2012). Over the period 2000 to 2009, emerging markets had a beta of 1.3 compared to world equity markets (Dimson et al., 2010). Depending on the ERP for developed markets, this would suggest an incremental risk premium in the region of 1–2% per annum, which is broadly comparable to that adopted by the Yale University

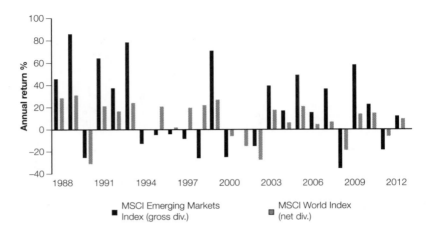

Source: Data from Morningstar EnCorr. All rights reserved.

Figure 11.7 **MSCI Emerging Markets Index vs. MSCI World Index – Jan 1988 to Dec 2012**

Endowment Fund, one of the leading institutional investors and the estimates made by JP Morgan Asset Management in the region of 2.5% (JP Morgan Asset Management, 2012) with an estimated volatility of around 30%, a full 10% above their developed market equity risk assumption. Care is needed in avoiding giving up this potential premium through product costs.

Downside risks

The incremental returns need to be balanced against the incremental risk taken on. Table 11.4 provides insight into the drawdowns seen in emerging market stocks since the data series for the MSCI Emerging Markets Index began in 1988. Drawdowns have been severe and frequent and investors need to be aware of this, particularly at times of spectacular market returns evidenced from time to time.

Due to the volatile nature of emerging market investments and the increasing correlation numbers, allocations to emerging markets should be moderate and based on the expectation, but not the guarantee, of enhanced returns and moderate diversification benefit.

| Table 11.4 | Emerging market equity drawdowns > 10% from 1988 to 2012 |

Decline (%)	Peak date	Trough date	Recovery date	Decline (mths)	Recovery (mths)
−58%	Aug-94	Aug-98	Feb-05	48	78
−45%	Oct-07	Nov-08	Dec-09	13	13
−32%	Jul-90	Nov-90	Mar-91	4	4
−26%	Mar-92	Aug-92	Nov-92	5	3
−22%	Dec-10	Sep-11	NA	9	NA
−15%	Jan-94	Jun-94	Aug-94	5	2
−13%	Apr-06	May-06	Dec-06	1	7
−12%	May-89	Jul-89	Sep-89	2	2
−11%	Feb-90	Mar-90	May-90	1	2
−10%	Sep-88	Nov-88	Feb-89	2	3

11.4 Return enhancer – value equities

As we explored earlier, these are often described as companies that are cheap or undervalued. Perhaps a more apt term for value stocks is distressed stocks. Value stocks are often categorised as weak or underperforming companies, whose stock prices have been written down by the market as a consequence, possibly to below their true or intrinsic value. Financial measures that are frequently applied to value stocks are:

▦ High book-to-market (BtM) (i.e. the underlying value of a company's net assets).

▦ Low price relative to earnings (low P/E ratio) or, in other words, the amount that an investor is willing to pay for each pound of future earnings that the company generates.

▦ High dividend yield, which reflects the payout of cash today as opposed to reinvestment in the business.

On the other hand, growth stocks are companies whose earnings are growing rapidly and appear to have the ability to grow further. Even if growth rates are already high, that will not put off some investors, provided that they believe the market consensus is wrong. In a growth investor's view, earnings growth drives stock price performance and performance is largely independent of the stock value today.

Past returns

Much of the academic work relating to the value premium is from the USA, although the presence of a global value premium is increasingly being researched. In short, the data suggest that a premium exists for investing in value stocks compared with growth stocks and that this is statistically significant. Figure 11.8 illustrates that this is so in both developed and emerging markets.

But there are no guarantees – considerable periods of time can exist, and have existed, over which value stocks have underperformed growth stocks, sometimes to quite an extent, such as in the late 1990s tech boom. From the start of 1997 to the end of 1999 the UK larger cap value shares were beaten by UK large cap growth shares by almost 12% per year. This creates a dilemma: do you try to obtain the value premium by holding more value stocks in your portfolio? If so, are you prepared to sit out what could be lengthy and painful periods of underperformance and hope to be rewarded? It's not recommended that you try to time when to be in value stocks and when to be in growth stocks. As ever with market-timing decisions, the longevity with which value and growth styles can seem seriously out of kilter, combined with rapidity and magnitude of turnarounds, makes this a really tough game to play.

Figure 11.8 **A premium has existed for owning less healthy companies 1/1975 to 4/2013**

Why have value stocks outperformed growth stocks?

That is a good and relevant question. Eugene Fama, a renowned academic explains (Tanous, 1997):

'To me, stock prices are just the prices that produce the expected returns that people require to hold them. If they are growth companies, people are willing to hold them at a lower expected return ... Value stocks may continue to take their knocks. Their prices reflect the fact that they are in poor times. As a result, because people don't want to hold them – in our view because they are riskier – they have higher expected returns.'

A sense of balance is provided by John Bogle (2002) who, with his years of experience and insight, fails to see the existence of the value premium. His thoughts are based largely around his belief in a return-to-mean for markets over time and that costs and additional risks make the victory pyrrhic:

'Place me squarely in the camp of the contrarians who don't accept the inherent superiority of value strategies over growth strategies.'

The thing worth remembering is that the market, for whatever reason, requires that perceived risks are rewarded. If you wish for the higher returns that value stocks, or for that matter small cap stocks (see below), potentially provide, you will be taking on more risk, and this risk in the widest sense will not just be measured by volatility of returns. Place your bets in moderation. If the value premium turns out not to exist then you should end up, over the long term, with a market-like return. So, to some extent, the risk of making an allocation is reduced.

Downside risks

In Chapter 7, Figure 7.3 we looked at the risk that the value premium could be negative (i.e. you would have done worse than simply owning the broad market). In Table 11.5, we look at the peak to trough falls of global value stocks. What you can see is that value stocks have the same capacity to deliver downside shocks of a similar magnitude to the broad market.

Table 11.5 Global value equity drawdowns >10% from 1955–2012					
Decline (%)	Peak date	Trough date	Recovery date	Decline (mths)	Recovery (mths)
−49%	May-07	Feb-09	Feb-11	21	24
−38%	Jan-01	Sep-02	Dec-04	20	27
−36%	Dec-89	Sep-90	Feb-93	9	29
−28%	Sep-87	Nov-87	Dec-88	2	13
−22%	Feb-11	Sep-11	Jan-13	7	16
−21%	May-98	Sep-98	Mar-99	4	6
−13%	Feb-85	Jul-85	Jan-86	5	6
−10%	Sep-79	Mar-80	Aug-80	6	5
−10%	Dec-99	Feb-00	May-00	2	3

Source: Dimensional Global Large Value Index in GBP

11.5 Return enhancer – smaller companies

As we explored earlier, a premium (the small cap (or size) premium as it is known) is paid to investors for the additional risks that they take relative to larger company stocks. Put another way, their cost of capital is higher. Small cap stocks, like value stocks, appear to have characteristics that cannot be diversified away. Thus, according to the manual of investing, the equities of smaller companies (small cap stocks) will outperform those of

Figure 11.9   The small cap premium 1/1975 to 4/2013

larger companies, over time. Some investors try to capture this premium by adding additional exposure in their portfolios, over and above the smaller companies already in the index, to smaller companies. This strategy may work, but it is not guaranteed to succeed. You need to make your own mind up (see Figure 11.9).

However, you would be wise to remember that periods, sometimes as long as twenty years exist, over which you would not have received this premium. The swings between periods of outperformance and underperformance of small cap stocks relative to the market may tempt you into trying to time your entry and exit into small cap stocks to capture the periods of outperformance and avoid periods of underperformance. Pick up the money section of any Sunday paper to see how much pressure there is on you to time markets. Don't be tempted because even the most astute professionals find this hard to do. Being a contrarian is not a route to an emotionally easy life!

Why does the small-cap premium exist?

Now we get to the crux of the debate. I wish I could answer this question, but I cannot. In fact, when you review the discussions and ideas of academics and practitioners in the industry, you see that their views are varied and inconclusive. This should be a warning to you that owning small cap stocks is not a sure thing. However, there does appear to be some form of risk that cannot be diversified away, for which you are apparently being rewarded. My reading of research on this subject would seem to suggest that a premium may exist, but that it is not certain, and it is less convincing than the value premium.

An interview with Eugene Fama (one of the leading academic researchers of value and size effects) by Peter Tanous (1997) about the small cap effect included the following exchange:

Fama: 'The risk in my terms can't be explained by the market. It means that because they move together, there is something about these small stocks that creates an undiversifiable risk. The undiversifiable risk is what you get paid for.'

Tanous: 'What causes that risk?'

Fama: 'You know, that's an embarrassing question because I don't know.'

Even Eugene Fama concludes the following:

'The size premium is, however, weaker and less reliable than the value premium.' (Davis et al., 1999, pub 2009)

Dimson, Marsh and Staunton (2002), leading academics at the London Business School, stated:

'It appears inappropriate to use the term "size effect" to imply that we should automatically expect there to be a small cap premium.'

And finally, John Bogle (2002) again provides us with a balancing viewpoint:

'We see that the long period is punctuated by a whole series of reversion to the mean. Virtually the entire small-cap advantage [in the USA] took place in the first 18 years ... On balance these to-and-fro reversions have cancelled each other out, and since 1945 the returns of large-cap stocks and small-cap stocks have been virtually identical ... So ask yourself whether the evidence to justify the claim that small-cap superiority isn't too fragile a foundation on which to base a long-term strategy.'

Downside risks

My advice would be to make any bets away from the total market with moderation. In the end, if no small cap premium actually exists, you should end up with a market-like return over the longer term, thus mitigating the allocation risk for long-term investors (see Table 11.6).

| Table 11.6 | Global small cap equity drawdowns > 10% from 1955–2012 |

Decline (%)	Peak date	Trough date	Recovery date	Decline (mths)	Recovery (mths)
−46%	Nov-72	Dec-74	Jan-76	25	13
−41%	May-07	Feb-09	Mar-10	21	13
−33%	Aug-00	Jan-03	Jan-04	29	12
−32%	Dec-89	Jan-91	Feb-93	13	25
−30%	Aug-87	Nov-87	Jan-89	3	14
−22%	May-98	Sep-98	Apr-99	4	7
−21%	Mar-70	Jun-70	Feb-71	3	8
−18%	Apr-11	Sep-11	Jan-13	5	16
−16%	Apr-96	Mar-97	Apr-98	11	13
−12%	Feb-85	Jul-85	Dec-85	5	5

Source: Dimensional Global Small Index in GBP

11.6 Commercial property – a diversifier

Commercial property is made up of three key sectors: industrial estates, retail premises and office blocks. This provides diversification away from the residential property market, to which many investors have a high exposure. There is a big difference between owning a shopping mall in Hong Kong, a commercial office in Los Angeles and a retail park in Hamburg compared to a buy-to-let in Fulham. Global commercial property tends to have a moderate correlation to equities, providing a diversification benefit, as property performance is usually linked to rental value growth. This diversification is achieved without the substantial return give-up of holding bonds or cash. It is a useful asset to hold in portfolios.

What are REITs?

REITs are property investment companies that pass through income to shareholders, and thus avoid corporation tax. In the UK, the profits of a REITs property rental business are exempt from tax. One condition that must be met is that 90% of the income of the tax-exempt business is distributed to shareholders within twelve months of the end of the accounting period; in addition, 75% or more of its assets must be investment property and 75% or more of its income must be rental income (HMRC, 2006). REIT details vary across markets but broadly follow the same principles.

In the UK, while listed property companies have long been in existence, the UK REIT regime was only introduced in 2006, with the first REIT being launched in 2007. The advent of REIT regimes around the world is gathering pace and growing confidence exists in their structures, particularly given the way in which REIT structures survived the severe market test associated with the credit crisis.

The corporate structure of real estate holdings, i.e. whether the property is held directly by a fund or owned by a publicly listed company, should have little effect on return and volatility in the long term on an ungeared, apples-to-apples basis. Many investors were blinded by the apparent low volatility that 'bricks and mortar' funds seemed to exhibit, which was simply a consequence of the way in which they were priced. Long-term, publicly listed REITs should deliver comparable returns to bricks and mortar funds. The reality is best summed up by David Swensen (2000: 220):

'The absurd notion that simply changing the form of corporate ownership alters fundamental investment attributes corresponds nicely to the idea of alchemy.

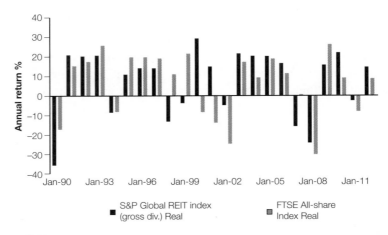

Figure 11.10   Global REIT returns vs UK equity – Jan 1999 to Dec 2012 – real

The higher volatility of REIT shares reflects an appropriate upward adjustment of artificially dampened risk observed in appraisal-based return series.'

Past returns

In terms of economic rationale, property represents a series of cashflows like a bond, made up of the regular payment of rent and the residual value of the building. The more certain the occupancy and length of rental lease, and the quality of the tenant, the lower the volatility of the capital value of the building. As such, buildings with high-quality tenants on long-term leases tend to act more like bonds and are less volatile as the income dominates returns. On the other hand, properties with short-term tenancies, the ultimate being hotels, tend to have more equity-like volatility in their capital value. In the short-term, sentiment and supply and demand will affect the capital values. During the period 7/1989 to 12/2011 the global REIT index delivered a nominal return of 8.6% versus the UK equity markets return of 8.2%. The annualised volatility (risk) numbers were largely comparable at 16.6% and 17.3% respectively (see Figure 11.10).

Future returns

Returns are expected to fall near equities, given its hybrid asset status and the fact that leverage is inherent in the REIT structure. Depending on your view of the equity risk premium for developed markets, REITs could be expected to deliver performance around 1% below equities.

Table 11.7 Global REIT drawdowns > 10% from 1987–2012

Decline (%)	Peak date	Trough date	Recovery date	Decline (mths)	Recovery (mths)
−55%	Jan-07	Feb-09	May-11	25	27
−34%	Aug-89	Oct-90	Nov-92	14	25
−20%	Sep-97	Aug-98	Jun-00	11	22
−16%	Feb-94	Nov-94	Dec-95	9	13
−15%	May-02	Jan-03	Jul-03	8	6
−13%	Jun-11	Sep-11	Jan-12	3	4
−11%	Mar-06	May-06	Sep-06	2	4
−10%	Mar-04	Apr-04	Aug-04	1	4

Source: S&P Global REIT Index (gross div.) TR in GBP

Downside risks

Investing in property is not without its risks. That is why, as an asset class it sits in the Return Engine part of the portfolio. Table 11.7 demonstrates that material drawdowns can and do occur.

11.7 Defensive asset classes

Figure 11.11 provides an insight into the two key asset classes that we use in the Defensive mix – shorter-dated high quality (min AA) bonds and shorter-dated high quality (min AA) inflation linked bonds. The numbers are after inflation and are compared to holding cash. Returns have been higher than expected over this period as governments around the developed world focused on containing inflation in the 1980s and 1990s after the very high inflation of the 1970s. Bond yields fell from as high as 15% or so down to almost 0% delivering investors with both income and capital gains. The future will be less kind, given where yields are today.

You can see from Figure 11.11 overleaf and comparing it with Figure 11.2 (both drawn to the same scale) that Defensive assets are far less volatile, but they can and do have periods when they can lose money. However, they represent a better mix of assets than holding cash which has lost more than 10% purchasing power since the start of 2010.

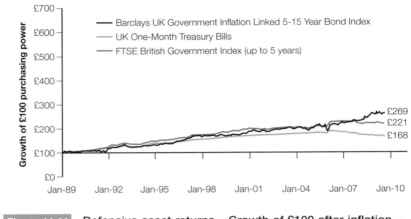

Figure 11.11 **Defensive asset returns – Growth of £100 after inflation – June 1989 to Dec 2012**

11.8 Inflation-linked bonds

The potential damage that inflation can reap on an investor's portfolio needs to be taken seriously. Defensive assets need to perform the role they are charged with robustly and efficiently. As we previously explored, defensive assets play two key roles – defending against equity market trauma and protecting the value of the assets assigned to them, in terms of volatility and purchasing power. Conventional bonds and cash do a poor job of protecting purchasing power as Figure 11.12 illustrates. During the high inflation during the 1970s, holders of cash lost almost a third of their purchasing power.

As such, shorter-dated inflation-linked bonds such as index-linked gilts and index-linked National Savings Certificates (when they are being issued) are therefore strong contenders for low risk assets for most individual investors. Due to their structure, both of these government-backed investments provide low risk to capital from a credit risk perspective. Inflation-linked corporate bonds of high credit quality and those issued by foreign governments when hedged back to GBP, provide inflation proxies.

Index-linked gilts are IOUs issued by the UK government. The principal amount you lend the government is adjusted for the rate of inflation and the interest payable to you twice a year is based on the inflated level of the principal. It is important to note that there is an eight-month lag in the

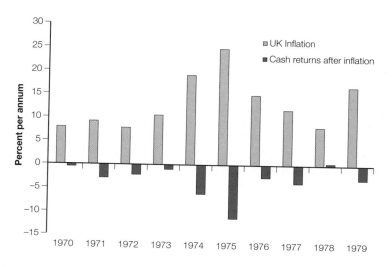

Figure 11.12 **Erosion of purchasing power at times of high inflation**

inflation linking to the Retail Price Index on some current index-linked gilts and a three-month lag on more recent issues (and on all new issues going forwards). This does give rise to the risk on very short-dated gilts that the inflation protection is weak in the event of a rapid inflation spike.

An argument could be made for owning inflation-linked bonds that have a maturity of around five years or so as you then get a relatively low volatility with strong inflation-protection characteristics. If you own them directly and until they mature, you have the certainty that they will deliver inflation-protected capital and interest payments along the way. You can purchase index-linked gilts via most online brokerages if you are a DIY investor.

Your other option is to own a fund or Exchange Traded Fund that invests in them. As you will see, passive products exist for both. The issue you face is that many products tend to replicate the entire market for index-linked gilts, with an average maturity of about twenty years and duration of sixteen years or so. That makes them very volatile. You may want to look at actively managed funds e.g. look at the Morningstar Global Inflation Linked hedged to Sterling category. Pragmatism over dogmatism on this one!

ast returns

The past returns on short and intermediate index linked gilts are set out below. In the past few years they have performed exceptionally well as real yields (remember back to Chapter 6) have fallen as money has flooded towards safe assets, quantitative easing has driven down real yields, growth is benign and pension funds seek to match their inflation-linked liabilities with inflation-linked assets (see Figure 11.13).

Future returns

The simplest and most effective way to estimate the future returns on bonds is to look at their current yields. That makes for unexciting reading. With real yields at or below zero, if you get back the purchasing power that you initially invested, then that will be reasonable over the next ten years. Any more and you will have achieved a positive outcome. Remember – this is the water part of your portfolios – if you need or want return, you will have to look to the Return Engine for it.

Downside risk

The price of inflation linked bonds is driven by the after inflation i.e. real yield demanded by investors (see Table 11.8). Historically this has been in the region of around 2% per annum. Given that real yields are currently around or less than 0 per cent, a rise in yields is likely at some point which will result in a fall in prices – the bond see-saw in practice. The degree to which they will fall will be a function of how far yields rise and the duration of the bonds that you hold. Refer back to Table 6.2 to see the

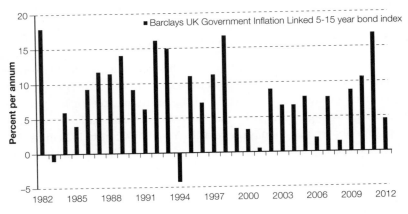

Figure 11.13   **Real returns of index linked gilts**

| Table 11.8 | Index linked gilts – historical attributes 1997 to 2012 |

Index	Periods	Geometric mean (%)	Risk (%)	No drawdowns	Maximum drawdown	Average recovery (m)	Positive months	Negative months
FTSE Index Linked Over 15 Yr TR GBP	179	8.11	9.86	26	−17	3	110	69
FTSE Index Linked All Stocks TR GBP	179	7.25	6.76	29	−13	2	117	62
FTSE Index Linked 5–15 Yr TR GBP	179	7.07	6.33	32	−14	2	119	60
FTSE Index Linked Up to 5 Yr TR GBP	179	5.4	2.75	19	−7	2	149	30

impact. Seven year duration inflation linked bonds and a 2 per cent rise in real yields could result in a 14% or so fall in prices. When the magnitude of future rises is uncertain. Tomorrow, next month or a few years time – who knows?

11.9 Shorter-dated (conventional) bonds

The UK government, some non-UK governments and a number of corporate issuers are deemed to be of very low credit risk (i.e. high credit quality). At times of market crisis, the flight to quality applies, driving yields down and prices up. The risk of an AA rated security defaulting is relatively small. This risk can be mitigated by diversifying issuer risk broadly. It should be noted that any non-GBP currency exposure should be hedged back to Sterling to avoid currency induced volatility in what is intended to be a low volatility part of any investor's portfolio.

Past returns

Looking back over the past thirty-three years, it is evident that high quality short-dated bonds have done a good job of mitigating equity market trauma (see Figure 11.14).

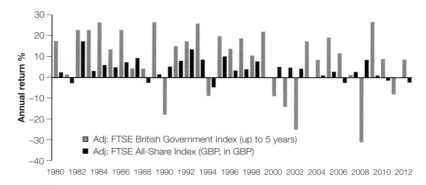

Figure 11.14 High quality short-dated bonds provide strong diversification benefits

Future returns

During periods of unanticipated inflation they may perform poorly as yields rise to compensate investors for higher inflation with a resultant fall in bond prices. During times of deflation, investors should benefit and yields fall; nominal coupons and principal returned at maturity will exhibit greater levels of purchasing power. Returns on shorter-dated AA bonds (no currency exposure) are expected to be unexciting and anything above 1% above the rate of inflation will be a positive outcome.

Downside risk

1994 was a bad year for bond owners as a dramatic rise in yield of 2% resulted in large losses on bond portfolio. It could and most likely will happen again at some point. As ever, rising yields mean falling bond prices. Future inflation threats and a tightening of monetary policy could see material rises in yields. When, and of what magnitude, no-one knows. However, short-dated bonds provide some protection as their price sensitivity is less than longer dated bonds. Price falls of up to 10% are not out with the bounds of reality. Be prepared.'

References

Bernstein, W. (2012) *Skating where the puck was* (ISBN-10: 0988780305; self-published e-books: www.efficientfrontier.com).

Bogle, J. C. (2002) 'The telltale chart', Bogle Financial Markets Research Center (www.vanguard.com).

Davis, J. L., Fama, E. F. and French, K. R. (2009) 'Characteristics, covariances, and average returns: 1929–1997' (February 1999). Center for Research in Security Prices (CRSP) Working Paper No. 471.

Dimson, E., Marsh, P. R. and Staunton, M. (2002) *Triumph of the Optimists: 101 years of global investment data.* Princeton, NJ: Princeton University Press, p. 145.

Dimson, E., Marsh, P. R. and Staunton, M. (2010) *Credit Suisse Global Investment Returns Yearbook, 2010,* 'Emerging markets', p. 6 (www.credit-suisse.com).

Dimson, E., Marsh, P. R. and Staunton, M. (2013) *Credit Suisse Global Investment Returns Yearbook, 2013* (www.credit-suisse.com).

Economist, The (2011) 'Emerging vs. developed economies', 4 August (www.economist.com).

HMRC (2006) www.hmrc.gov.uk/pbr2006/pbrn3.hcm.

J.P. Morgan Asset Management (2012) Long-term Capital Market Assumptions (www.jpmorganinstitutional.com).

Swensen, D. F. (2000) *Pioneering portfolio management.* New York: The Free Press.

Tanous, P. J. (1997) 'An interview with Eugene Fama – Investment gurus'. (http://library.dfaus.com/reprints/interview_fama_tanous).

12

Smarter insight – off-menu assets

A number of investment types have been considered but excluded from the menu, in particular structured products, hedge funds, private equity and commodities, which are all currently receiving wide attention and investor focus. A few thoughts are provided on the main candidates. But in preparation for what you are about to read, take note of what David Swensen of the Yale Endowment has to say on the subject.

'Investors require unusual self-confidence to ignore the widely hyped non-core investments and to embrace the quietly effective core investments.' (David Swensen, 2005: 147)

12.1 Hedge funds

Most investors would readily accept that the hedge fund world is a sophisticated arena. A number of attributes make hedge funds superficially appealing: the promise of returns that are uncorrelated to traditional asset classes; a focus on making and protecting client money; the freedom and flexibility to be long or short of the market, i.e., they can sell the market or stock even if they do not own it, with the hope of buying it back cheaper when it has fallen in price; and the option to use leverage. In fact there is no definitive description of what a hedge fund is. They have been described as a variety of skill-based investment strategies with a broad range of risk and return objectives that take a performance fee. Not all agree. One oft-quoted description, for the more cynical, is that they are simply a compensation strategy masquerading as an investment strategy.

Increasingly, questions are being raised as to what hedge funds are actually offering; recent research suggests that this may in fact be systematic exposure to alternative sources of market-based risks and returns (beta) rather than manager skill (alpha).

The difficulty of understanding the underlying strategies, selecting truly skilful managers (or even competent funds of funds), due diligence, and very high costs (2% annual management fees and 20% performance, plus an additional 1% p.a. and 10% for funds of funds) in what is still a zero-sum game make their inclusion unjustifiable. Let us dig a little deeper.

Scary insights into the hedge fund world

Hedge fund returns that are published and bandied around by hedge fund sales people are simply composites made up from the track records of managers who voluntarily submit returns to various databases. Numbers tend to be packed, as a consequence, with all sorts of biases (self-selection – many funds never even make it to the databases; survivor bias – some fail and fall out; and back-fill bias – where managers back-fill prior performance, which is only likely to happen when performance has been good). Research (Chen et al., 2011) reveals that over the fifteen years of the study to 2009, net returns were around 14% p.a. which sounds good, but when stripped of these biases they were more like 8%, not much different from the US equity market. In the dataset they were looking at (TASS database) they found that 63% of funds were now dead and only 37% had survived!

Interestingly, around two-thirds of returns came from simple market factors (owning bonds and equities) and one-third from manager skill. Costs were very high at an average of around 3.5% p.a. – which is a lot given that 60% of the return is simply delivered by the market. The authors note an important point – that although market beating returns appear to exist, there is no easy way for investors to secure this average and even if you could, you only ended up with a market return as hedge fund managers took all the outperformance for themselves.

Recent insight also comes from a recently published book on the hedge fund industry by an insider, formerly at JP Morgan. Again the issue of industry numbers is raised, both in terms of biases, but also in terms of the asset-weighted returns that investors actually receive compared to the time-weighted returns published by the funds. Some interesting and thought-provoking insights are provided:

■ Between 1998 and 2003 hedge fund returns were positive in aggregate in each year. The industry at that time was small with around $200 billion in assets.

■ Due to its strong performance during the 2000–2003 period (the technology stock crash) the industry attracted assets rapidly.

■ By 2008 it is estimated that hedge fund assets amounted to $2 trillion, a ten-fold increase.

■ The average performance loss in 2008 was –23%.

■ The author estimates that these money flows and the consequent asset-weighted returns, i.e., the returns received by investors based on the timing of their investments, cancelled out all of the profit made in the previous ten-year period!

■ To the end of 2010 investors were still below water, yet hedge fund managers extracted over $100 billion in fees between 2008 and 2010.

■ Hedge fund managers extracted $379 billion for themselves between 1998 and 2008 out of the $449 billion generated above the returns from a cash deposit.

Perhaps the cynics are right on this one. Throw in the fact that even some of the most sophisticated institutional investors find it both hard and resource consuming to run a successful hedge fund programme, it perhaps makes sense to sit back from the hype and believe in the efficacy of a well diversified, sensible mix of traditional investments, returning the bulk of the returns that the markets deliver – the less 'sophisticated', yet highly effective approach that we take.

We should perhaps defer to the words of wisdom from David Swensen (2005: 132) on this one who has been a leading proponent of hedge fund investing at Yale University:

'Casual approaches to hedge fund selection lead to almost certain disappointment. Hedge funds belong in the domain of sophisticated investors who commit significant resources to manager selection ... investors who fail to identify truly superior active managers face a dismal reality.'

12.2 Private equity

Superficially, private equity (leveraged buy-outs and venture capital) appears to provide exciting opportunities for public market-plus returns. In reality, private equity differs from its public equity counterparts in terms of risk, leverage, liquidity, transparency and fees. When these are accounted for, the evidence is more mixed.

Headline performance numbers of private equity investments attract attention, but the reality for investors is often very different. The economic rationale lies, as with any equity investment, in the dividends and increase in the value of the shares of the corporation. However, the higher risks, leverage and costs associated with buy-outs need to be compensated for by superior, hands-on active management skills of private equity firms. This skill appears to be both rare and hard to access.

The alignment of managers' and investors' interests is often put forward as a positive governance attribute. However, as the size of private equity firms has grown, the proportion of revenue that is now derived from the 2% management fee accounts for around two-thirds of revenues (Metrick and Yasuda, 2011).

roblems with the numbers

Looking at industry numbers provides a biased and cloudy view of the reality of private equity. Data is mainly presented in the form of databases of funds that voluntarily submit their return data. It is likely, as with hedge funds, that these databases include material survivor bias to an unquantified degree. Questions are also legitimately raised over the pricing of company investments held by these funds which could result in valuations that are materially different from true market values (Phalippou, 2011). Some question marks also surround the inconsistency of how returns are calculated from firm to firm, generally calculated as an internal rate of return or IRR (Morris, 2010). In addition this form of IRR calculation also implies that the return is achieved on the whole of the investor's cash but fails to take account of cash handed back to investors early and reinvested at an investment rate lower than the IRR. While this may all sound a bit technical, it is a flag that is waving at you warning you of the pitfalls that come with operating in private markets.

etter returns? The jury is still out

The main data history of private equity in the UK comes from the British Venture Capital Association (BVCA). They calculate IRR data on funds across different investment stage and subcategory. During the ten years to December 2009, UK private equity funds (all categories – 328 funds) delivered an IRR of 8.8% p.a. compared to 1.6% from UK equities (BVCA, 2010). The degree of leverage is not readily ascertainable in these figures in order to make an apples-to-apples comparison to public equity market returns. While leverage can act both ways, in a risk asset class, over time it can be expected to increase returns.

It is interesting to note that private equity investment trusts performed significantly worse (–1.3%) over ten years to December 2009, suggesting that marking to market of portfolio assets may make a material difference. Data is not clean and transparent.

In reality, capturing higher returns comes at the price of illiquidity and higher risk. A Yale study of 542 buyout deals illustrated a gross return of 48% compared to that of the market's 17%, and a net 36% after costs. Yet when the effects of leverage differences between these transactions and the public market were taken into account – creating an apples-to-apples comparison – this resulted in the latter outstripping the buyout deals significantly (Swensen, 2005: 134). Return distribution is high between the top and bottom deciles implying that a portfolio approach is a prerequisite, i.e., own lots of funds. For most investors that means a fund of funds approach with the additional 1% management and 10% performance fee on top of fund fees that this implies.

A more recent study of 1,400 private equity funds returns using a higher quality dataset concludes that it is likely that US private equity has outperformed the US public equity market, by around 3% p.a. (Harris et. al., 2013). The results vary depending upon which private equity database is used and which public equity benchmark is used (buyouts tend to be smaller companies than those in the S&P 500). According to this study, venture capital funds outperformed in the 1990s but underperformed in the 2000s.

Leverage has in the past accounted for more than 50% of returns (Acharya et al., 2011). But in the face of the ongoing deleveraging of financial institutions, the opportunity for financial engineering has diminished and true improvement of the operating businesses will be a prerequisite for strong returns. Not all private equity managers have these skills.

Fallacious arguments are sometimes put forward that private equity has a low correlation to public equities. This is most likely attributable to the naïve use of performance numbers that are masked by stale pricing of privately held assets. US venture capital returns have been shown to be highly correlated to the NASDAQ market in the US making it a poor diversifier (Landmark Partners, 2009).

Accessing private equity in practice

High costs, particularly of fund of fund structures, decrease the upside opportunity. For the individual investor, the benefits of private equity are outweighed by the practical problems of entry, diversification and manager selection – even of fund of fund managers. Liquidity is also a potential issue as investors are required to lock up their money over a period of up to ten years. This creates challenges for rebalancing assets at times of material market movements, which was a material issue for major US endowments during the credit crisis.

These risks are compounded by the fact that only the top decile of managers is likely to deliver returns that compensate for these additional risks. Research indicates that only 3% are top quartile more than 75% of the time (Asset Alternatives, 2001). This implies the need for superior manager selection skills, access to top manager funds, which is often restricted, and high investor asset levels for direct access and appropriate levels of diversification. As David Swensen, CIO of the Yale University Endowment and one of the most astute institutional investors around, and who runs one of the most admired private equity programmes, states:

'Only top quartile, or top decile funds produce returns sufficient to compensate for private equity's greater illiquidity and higher risks. In the absence of truly superior fund selection skills (or extraordinary luck) investors should stay far, far away from private equity investments.'

es, damned lies and peer group comparisons

The lack of clarity around how performance relative to peer groups is presented makes above-average manager selection decidedly difficult. A piece of research (Gottschalg, 2009) looking into the old joke that *'75% of all funds claim to be in the top quartile'*, is surprisingly close to the truth. It reveals that canny selection of starting dates and comparison to different performance benchmarks, which have different performance results, allows 66% of funds to be able to claim that they are top quartile!

All in all, private equity is a pretty difficult place to play. Remember that simply hoping that it will work out is not a reason for getting involved!

2.3 Structured products

You will have walked past the big glass windows of the banks and building societies in your local high street and noticed the advertisements enticing you to invest in 'principal protected, stock market participation' products. Maybe some readers will have even felt tempted to invest in one – after all, why not take a punt on the equity market without risking any money? What could be more appealing than that, particularly when deposits are yielding next to nothing and equity markets are all over the place? It all seems so simple. So simple in fact that £42 billion of UK investors' money is currently invested in such 'structured products', as they are known.

Sophisticated and complex investment products, created and peddled by intelligent professionals are often seen as valuable opportunities not to be missed. Perhaps a better working rule of thumb is that the long-term value of an investment opportunity should, as a starting point, be viewed as being inversely related to its sophistication and complexity.

What is in the bank's window?

Let us take a look at the simple investment product the bank is selling in its window. In its simplest form, you hand over cash to the bank, which buys a bond (or uses some other means to ensure that your initial amount invested is 'safe'). Instead of paying interest on this money, it promises to provide you with a specified return pay-off. This is usually based on a formula such that if an event, X, occurs, you will receive Y per cent of the gains of market Z. An example might be that if at the end of five years the FTSE 100 index is above its starting level (event X), you will receive 100% (Y) of the return of this index (Z). If it does not occur, you will get your money back at the end of the fixed term of the product. At the outset, you know exactly what your possible outcomes are. All fees have already been accounted for in the pay-off structure. So far, so simple, although not all payoffs are quite so readily understandable in practice.

It gets more tricky though

The upside return is delivered via the purchase of a derivative contract linked to an asset class index, often an equity index, such as the FTSE 100 index which tracks the price level of the 100 largest UK listed companies (getting a bit more complex), usually in the form of a call option, although this could be a SWAP or a futures contract (oh dear), priced using an option pricing model such as Black-Scholes that takes into account factors such as the strike price of the option, the price today, the implied volatility of the index and the time to expiry (help!).

Hopefully you get the point – the mechanics of this 'simple' product are actually quite sophisticated and complex. Investment banks employ bright, ambitious people on big packages to structure these products. Scope exists for some tricky pricing too, given that the average adviser, let alone retail investor, will have little chance of truly understanding the underlying costs involved. Research indicates that even simple structured products can be grossly mispriced with investors paying up to 10% above their true value (i.e. profit for the issuer). The more complex the pay-off structure, the harder the sums are!

urely they would not take advantage?

In the 1990s, 'ROF' became an infamous acronym. It was used to describe the amount of fees that an institution could get away with charging its clients i.e. the 'Rip Off Factor', coined originally by some Bankers Trust employees, who were eventually taken to court by Procter & Gamble, one of their clients. This is how it was reported at the time by *Businessweek*:

'It's Nov. 2, 1993, and two employees of Bankers Trust Co. are discussing a leveraged derivative deal the bank had recently sold to Procter & Gamble Co. "They would never know. They would never be able to know how much money was taken out of that," says one employee, referring to the huge profits the bank stood to make on the transaction. "Never, no way, no way" replies her colleague.'

But that was 1992, surely things are better now? Sadly not. The Financial Services Authority (FSA), the UK's financial regulator, recently reviewed the practices of several institutions that account for 50% or so of all structured products sold in the UK. The FSA's head of conduct supervision commented (FT.com, 2011):

'Many of the problems we found with the product design process were rooted in the fact that the firms are focusing too much on their own commercial interests rather than the outcomes they are delivering to consumers.'

Little changes, it would appear. It is worth noting too that the popularity of these types of products to banks, building societies and insurance companies, is driven not only by the direct pricing benefits to the issuer of the product, but because they represent a cheap source of funding for the institution.

rom an outcome perspective it's tricky too

While the 'if X set of events occurs you will receive Y' pay-off outcome can be easily grasped, there is no probability estimate attached to this set of events occurring. It is no good knowing that there are two outcomes possible, but no idea of the chance of one happening over the other. Pay-off structures are often more complex. For example, the return promise may be 150% of the upside of the equity market, but this is offered with less security of principal, or perhaps multiple events are included in the pay-off formula. This makes the probability assessment far more difficult.

Given the limited lifespan of these products, estimating the finishing level of the FTSE 100 in five years time is taking an active bet on the market, which is notoriously difficult to do well. An intuitive *'well it should be higher, but I won't lose much if it is not'* is not really the foundation of a sensible and robust approach to investing.

What happened to your dividends?

Dividends are the regular cash payment made to shareholders, as part of the compensation for taking on the risk of ownership. The other component of compensation is a rise in the price of the shares of the company. An important insight into equity investing is that share price rises alone have historically only just delivered a return higher than inflation. It is the reinvestment of cash dividends back into the market that accounts for the bulk of the attractive returns that equities have, and are expected to deliver, over time.

If we go back to the products being sold in bank windows, they usually promise to deliver only the 'price return' of the index, such as the FTSE 100, rather than a 'total return' index where reinvested dividends are included. With dividend yields around 3%, over the lifespan of a five-year product, an investor would give up 15% compared to equity investments where dividends are included. Looked at in another way, this is a 15% cushion for an investor taking on the full risk of equities, by simply buying an equity index tracker fund. Rolling from one structured product to the next gives up this important long-term driver of returns.

Principal protection

Promising to give you your capital back sounds like a reasonable deal if Plan A does not come off (for example, the FTSE 100 ends lower over five years than its start point). Try telling that to the owners of the $18 billion invested globally in structured products issued by Lehman Brothers, who lost most of their money. By placing your money onto the balance sheet of banks and other financial institutions, you are opening yourself up to the risk that they go bust. That is not a trivial decision to make, particularly as some products sit outside of UK investor protection schemes.

Alternatively, assume that Plan A does not come off but the issuer is still in business and they give you back the £100 you initially invested. If inflation had been at the levels we have seen over the past five years, your initial £100 would be worth only £85.

Here's a quote to round off this section from a former economist at the SEC, the US's equivalent to the FSA in the UK (Wargo, 2008):

'They are horrible investments for retail investors ... Simple portfolios of bonds, stocks or the S&P 500 will beat structured products 99.5% of the time because of the heavy profit built into the pricing.'

So, perhaps the next time you pass that bank or building society window, look away!

2.4 Gold

Gold has always been an asset that has attracted significant attention, particularly as a store of value at times of extreme uncertainty. A case can certainly be made for holding some physical gold, perhaps in the form of coins or ingots, in the liquidity reserves of those who fear the breakdown of fiat currencies at times of extreme market events such as those surrounding the collapse of Lehman Brothers. In the extreme collapse of the financial system, paper gold (e.g. via a gold fund) would be less favourable given the counterparty risk of failure and inability to access the value of the gold. This is a purely personal decision that sits outside a long-term investment portfolio.

oes it have a strategic role in your portfolio?

The theoretical case for a positive real return from gold is weak. It is a commodity, and returns come from changes in the spot price over time, based on supply and demand. Gold offers a net negative yield due to the cost of insurance and storage (potentially offset by any gold lending revenues). Many would suggest that investing in gold is a speculative bet. Given the lack of cash flow, common valuation models are not useful. Valuations based on purchasing power relative to items such as loaves of bread and barrels of oil are sometimes used to try and gauge levels of over- or under-valuation.

Attempts to establish the real rate of return include estimating the rates of global economic growth (around 3% p.a. from 1980 to 2009) and the rate of increase of 'above ground' gold (around 1.5% p.a.) would give a long-term real return of 1.5%, but this depends entirely on the assumptions for the two variables. The stock of global gold is around 170,000 metric tons, representing a cube 68 feet along each side.

Warren Buffett (2012) puts the case succinctly against gold, positioned against equities:

'This type of investment requires an expanding pool of buyers, who, in turn, are enticed because they believe that the buying pool will expand still further. Owners are not inspired by what the asset itself can produce – it will remain lifeless forever – but rather by the belief that others will desire it more avidly in the future ... Gold, however, has two significant shortcomings, being neither of much use or procreative. True, gold has some industrial and decorative utility, but the demand for these purposes is both limited and incapable of soaking up new production. Meanwhile, if you own one ounce of gold for eternity, you will still only own one ounce at its end.'

Enough said!

12.5 Commodity futures

The commodity boom during the mid-2000s raised investor awareness of commodities. As ever, many chased returns as commodity prices rose on the back of Western consumer demand and production delivered by countries such as China and India. In many respects the true argument that surrounds this less well known and understood investment is one of risk reduction, not return, as we will explore. To begin to understand the introduction we need to take a step back and think what is going on when we say we are going to invest in commodities. What do we really mean?

The first point to note is that direct commodity prices are unlikely to deliver long-term real returns as they make up the inflation basket. Second, it is likely that any short-term imbalances in supply and demand are likely to even out over time. It is perhaps imprudent then to believe that commodity prices themselves will be the source of long-term real returns, as many investors do. In addition, direct investment in commodities is impractical for individual investors, as the consequences of taking delivery of a million barrels of crude oil are undesirable.

For that reason many commodity funds were launched that invested in the shares of companies involved in the extraction and processing of commodities. This is a leveraged play on the underlying commodity price, with the danger that the share price and the commodity price become disconnected. Perhaps the firm's strategy is poor, or its employee relations pitiful, or the management team weak. Success becomes an active management risk and should be excluded, for the many reasons we covered at the start of the book. You own these firms in any case in a well diversified global portfolio, e.g. BP.

That leaves us with commodity futures funds, which have the potential to be a useful addition to the asset class menu, as they appear to provide the opportunity of real returns and are uncorrelated with bonds and equities. This is despite the fact that each individual commodity future in itself is a more or less zero sum bet (i.e. there is little real value in it).

What is a futures contract?

A futures contract involves two people: traditionally, on one side is a hedger, like a farmer looking to lock in the price of his crop, such as wheat, at some point in the future, and on the other side of this contract is a speculator who is looking to take on the price risk, making money if the price of wheat rises and a loss if the price of wheat falls. The futures contract reflects a recognised quantity of the commodity and the expiry date. Futures are rarely held to maturity as you then have the obligation of taking delivery of the commodity. Gains or losses are settled.

Where do commodity futures returns come from?

Given, as we said above, commodity prices will be comparable to inflation in the long term and that supply and demand imbalances will even out over time, at first glance you would be forgiven for wondering what all the fuss is about. Commodity futures fund returns do not come from underlying cash generation that comes with being an owner of a company or a lender to it, but from the properties of the futures markets and the ownership of a basket of futures contracts. If you are intrigued, then read on (if not, then exclude them from your growth-oriented assets, substituting them for equities).

Recent research concludes that investment into a diversified basket of commodity futures has historically produced strong real returns (Gorton and Rouwenhorst, 2004) and may well do so again in the future, given some of the underlying characteristics of a diversified basket of uncorrelated futures contracts.

Returns come from two main sources: the return on collateral provided against which futures contracts are purchased and from the 'commodity strategy' premium (Ibbotson Associates, 2006), which is made up of an insurance-like premium and what is known as a rebalancing bonus. Understanding what each element is, and its likelihood of being captured going forwards, presents a more robust approach over the naïve extrapolation of historical data, or the simplistic expectation of an upward movement of commodity prices.

The insurance premium represents compensation for accepting the risk of unexpected deflationary commodity price movements from those wishing to hedge this position; it is paid through the futures contract being lower than the expected spot price – a situation described by Keynes as 'normal backwardation', a rather bizarre term to those on the outside of the futures markets. However, with the weight of money flowing into commodity futures, this could be expected to decrease, perhaps entirely, entering into a state of 'cantango' where the futures price is actually above the expected spot price; although recent research suggests that 'backwardation' may be the consequence of low inventory levels (Gorton et al., 2007).

The rebalancing bonus represents the return benefit that is accrued by owning a basket of uncorrelated/low-correlated individual futures (agricultural products, oil, metals, etc.) with high standard deviation that is rebalanced regularly. Even if the net excess return on each individual futures contract is zero (implying no insurance premium), a reasonable excess return can potentially be generated by regular rebalancing of the basket (a buy-low-sell-high strategy).

The contribution of each element is debated, with some arguing that the return is primarily due to the insurance premium (Gorton and Rouwenhorst, 2004) and others arguing for the rebalancing bonus (Erb and Harvey, 2006). It is likely that all these factors, in some proportion, contribute to the historical excess return evidenced. The rebalancing bonus alone and the uncorrelated nature of the basket's returns to equities and bonds make this a potentially attractive diversification asset class in the context of a portfolio. The conclusions that can be drawn from the research are as follows: commodities do not offer investors a consistent risk premium; commodity volatility is comparable to that of large company US stocks; the risks of large outlying losses is not excessive; and commodities are uncorrelated with bonds and equities (Kat and Oomen, 2006).

The decision to exclude them from portfolios

Even in the absence of any real return, the uncorrelated nature of commodities should drive down risk, freeing up the risk budget to be spent elsewhere, i.e. adding higher-risk assets in search of returns. Recent research appears to indicate that correlations between commodity futures and traditional financial assets have remained unchanged over the past fifteen years despite the upsurge in interest and investment in commodities (Buyuksahin et al., 2007). So, while a case can be made for their inclusion, material issues surround their product structures. Without going into more detail, the return stream from commodity futures is provided by an investment bank by way of a swap agreement. This introduces both counterparty risk (if the swap provider fails) along with a number of conflicts of interest inherent in the structure. The FSA and other regulators are not entirely happy with these 'synthetic' products. Perhaps place them on your 'watch list'.

References

Acharya, V. V., Hahn, M. and Kehoe, C. (2011) 'Corporate governance and value creation: evidence from private equity' (http://pages.stern.nyu.edu).

Asset Alternatives (2001) 'Single investor private equity fund of funds: why compromise?' quoted in: D. Söhnholz, *FERI Private Equity* (www.altassets.net).

Buffett, W. (2012) 'Why stocks beat gold and bonds', *Fortune*, 9 February.

Buyuksahin, B., Haigh, M. and Robe, M. (2007) 'Commodities and equities: "a market of one"?' 31 December (http://ssrn.com).

BVCA (2010) 'Private Equity and Venture Capital Performance Measurement Survey, 2010' (www.BVCA.com).

Chen, P., Ibbotson, R. and Zhu, K. (2011) 'The ABCs of hedge funds: Alphas, Betas, and Costs', *Financial Analysts Journal*, vol. 67, no. 1 (January).

Erb, C. B. and Harvey, C. R. (2006) 'The tactical and strategic value of commodity futures', Social Science Research Network Working Paper, 12 January.

FT.com (2011) 'FSA finds weaknesses in structured products', 2 November 2011.

Gorton, G. B. and Rouwenhorst, K. G. (2004) 'Fact and fantasies about commodities futures'. NBER Working Paper Series, Working Paper 10595, National Bureau of Economic Research.

Gorton, G. B., Hayashi, F. and Rouwenhorst, K. G. (2007) 'The fundamentals of commodity futures returns', Yale ICF Working Paper 07–08.

Gottschalg, O. (2009) 'Why more than 25% of funds claim top quartile performance', A Buyout Research Program Research Brief (www.peracs.com/report/Top%20Quartile.pdf).

Harris, R. S., Jenkinson, T. and Kaplan, S. N. (2013) 'Private equity performance: what do we know?' (2 April). Fama-Miller Working Paper; Chicago Booth Research Paper No. 11-44; Darden Business School Working Paper No. 1932316 (http://ssrn.com/abstract=1932316).

Ibbotson Associates (2006) *Strategic Asset Allocation and Commodities*. Commissioned by PIMCO.

Kat, H. M. and Oomen, R. C.A. (2006) 'What every investor should know about commodities'. Part II Multivariate Return Analysis, AIRC Working Paper Series.

Landmark Partners (2009) 'Venture Capital: Hope is Not a Strategy'.

Metrick, A. and Yasuda, A. (2011) 'The economics of private equity funds', Swedish Institute for Financial Research Conference on The Economics of the Private Equity Market; Review of Financial Studies, Vol. 23, pp. 2303–41 (http://ssrn.com/abstract=996334).

Morris, P. (2010) 'Private equity, public loss?',Centre for the Study of Financial Innovation, July.

Phalippou, L. (2011) 'Why is the evidence on private equity performance so confusing?' (www.ssrn.com).

Swensen, D. F. (2005) *Unconventional Success*. New York: The Free Press.

Wargo, B. (2008) 'The fever for structured products', March (WealthManagement.com), March 2008.

Conclusion

This book has, I hope, been useful to you, both in getting you into a smarter investing mindset and in allowing you to decide what type of portfolio makes sense, and how you can put this into practice. If you take anything away from this book, then let it be these six points:

1 Getting the mix of investment building blocks right is the most critical factor. Balance equity risks with high quality shorter-dated bonds. Remember that diversification makes good sense and is the only free lunch that investing provides you. Spread your portfolio into a number of building blocks to create a portfolio that will help you through the seasons.

2 Remember that risk and return go hand in hand with few, if any, exceptions. If it looks too good to be true, it probably is.

3 Make a pact with yourself only to make investment choices that increase your chances of being successful. Remember that you are always aiming to lose the fewest points relative to the market, which means controlling all costs at every point of the process.

4 Stick with your chosen mix at all times and rebalance your portfolio if the proportions move significantly out of line using cash flows from the portfolio or additional contributions wherever possible.

5 Implement the portfolio using low-cost index funds (or exchange-traded funds) as the default vehicle to give yourself the greatest chance of capturing the bulk of the market returns that each of your portfolio building blocks delivers. Use active managers if index funds or equivalent are not available or where they can truly convince you, on terms that you set, that they have the people, process and commitment to deliver market-beating returns for you in the future. If you are not sure, do not risk it – index!

6 Try your hardest to control your emotions: avoid feeling covetous of building blocks doing better than your own; do not be tempted by greed or paralysed by fear. If you have been diligent in establishing your investment portfolio (1–4 above) then, when times get tough, as they will, choose to do nothing as your default strategy!

Finally, be confident that you are now a smarter investor by following the *smarter investing* approach. Enjoy your investing and the wealth it brings you, with any luck!

Bibliography

Often when it comes to investment books the bibliography is long enough to keep you going for a lifetime. I have decided to take a different tack and include on a very limited number of books and other sources. These have made a real impact on me and I would urge you to take a look too, if you want to learn more.

Website

Sensible Investing TV – www.sensibleinvesting.tv

This website has been backed by one of my clients, Barnett Ravenscroft Wealth Management. The aim of the station is to provide a well-argued, independent and robust position on why passive investing is an effective way for consumers to invest money and to provide an ongoing insight into, and understanding of, a range of industry related issues that affect consumers looking to invest their money. An example is the very clear, three-part video blog on the RDR aimed at the consumer that is on the site.

While the site has been sponsored by BRWM, the ethos is not one of promoting the firm but of getting the message out there to the general public. It is, by a long shot, the best collection of video evidence supporting a passive approach. Amongst those interviewed as part of the programme, were: Jack Bogle, Burton Malkiel, Charles Ellis, Eugene Fama, Ken French, William Sharpe, and William Bernstein to name a few. These are some of the key thinkers referenced throughout the book.

Take a look – it is worth a few minutes of your time.

Screenshot of Sensible Investing TV home page

Source: Sensible Investing TV

sightful books

The books below have influenced my thinking over the years and I thank the authors for putting their knowledge and ideas on to paper for all of us to share. I am only naming four books. Read them all and you will be well rewarded. None of them is too technical for the interested lay person and all are very well written.

Winning the Loser's Game, Charles D. Ellis, McGraw-Hill, 2002 (ISBN 0–07–138767–6).

This is an excellent book that I read in 1994, and wished I had done sooner. It is Charles Ellis' insight into the *'losing-the-fewest points'* strategy that underpins the philosophy that we developed – an easy and entertaining read.

The Little Book of Common Sense Investing, John C. Bogle, John Wiley & Sons, 2010 (ISBN 978-0-470-10210-7).

John Bogle is the grandfather of sensible, low cost investing. He has written several key books on investing and the state of both the investment industry and capitalism in general. This short book contains the essence of his thinking and makes a very compelling case for a 'losing the fewest points' approach. A 'must read' book.

The Little Book of Behavioral Investing, James Montier, John Wiley & Sons, 2010 (ISBN 978-0-470-68602-7).

This is a brilliant insight into how the mind is constantly trying to make us do things that are detrimental to our wealth. By understanding the scale of the problem, we at least have an insight into how we can limit some of the damage. It is a master class on the subject and deserves to be read by every investor – they will be richer (both financially and mentally) for doing so.

Pioneering Portfolio Management, David F. Swensen, The Free Press, 2000 (ISBN 0-684-86443-6).

David Swensen is the Chief Investment Officer at Yale University in the USA and is responsible for the management of the University's endowment fund. He is one of the most progressive thinkers in the business, with a clear philosophy of where his team can and cannot add value. Yale has been at the forefront of the move into alternative investment products such as private equity and absolute return strategies (hedge funds). The book is an excellent read for those of you who want to see what a leading investment team is doing and to understand the role and drawbacks of a wide range of traditional and alternative asset classes. This is the most technical of the four books, but still easily understandable.

Appendix 1: Your risk profile

As you have already discovered, emotions have the capacity to destroy hard won investment returns as they tend to lead you astray; they tempt you to get into things that perhaps you should not at the peak and make you exit otherwise sensible long-term investments at the lows. While we would all like to think that we are capable of rational behaviour and avoid such obvious wealth destroying strategies, the empirical evidence is that most investors do not. What we can do though is to identify portfolios that sit within our risk comfort zone, where we have a greater chance of standing firm. This chapter helps you to understand how you can identify your risk comfort zone.

What is your risk profile?

As investors, we all need to understand and feel comfortable with where we sit emotionally with the favourable outcomes we desire (such as retiring early, being able to fund a stable and enjoyable lifestyle in retirement, etc.) against the less favourable outcomes that we may experience along the way in terms of weak performance, potential losses, and possibly not even reaching our goals at all. Simply put, it is the point beyond which you are likely to harbour thoughts of bailing out of your investment strategy – not a wise thing to do.

This personal, emotional stance is what is generally referred to as your 'risk profile'. It is a relatively stable psychometric trait that is not really affected by the prevailing market conditions. Your financial risk profile is a consequence of your genetics, as well as your own learned values, motivations and attitudes towards financial risks. Interestingly, it appears that there is some positive correlation with the level of your income, your wealth and your education (i.e. the higher they are, the higher your risk tolerance is likely to be) and negatively with being in a partnership and the number of people that rely on you. This is perhaps intuitive.

Whilst an investor's risk profile remains largely consistent across time, it may change slowly over time through increased education, experience and changing circumstances, although the influence of these are somewhat uncertain and unresearched. Take a look at Figure A1.1. It illustrates some research work that was undertaken using the period between May 1999 and December 2008 (Davey, 2009), which captures the last desperate moments of the technology boom and subsequent bust, the rise in the markets from 2003 to 2007 and the slump from the end of 2007. The global equity markets are overlaid on top of the average risk profile from the UK, USA, Australia and New Zealand. The conclusion is obvious: risk tolerance is a pretty stable trait.

Average risk tolerance scores vs. global equity markets (May 1999 – Dec 2009)

Figure A1.1   Risk tolerance appears to be stable despite market crashes

Source: Risk tolerance – data from UK, US, Australia and New Zealand FinaMetrica © Copyright all rights reserved 2009.
Global equities – MSCI (www.msci.com)

Ascertaining your risk profile

If you have ever used an adviser then you will no doubt have been subjected to some form of questionnaire or discussion about your 'attitude to risk'. Not surprising given its importance and the regulator's requirement for advisers to do so:

'Ascertaining a private customer's true attitude to risk is critical for any adviser in assessing suitability and making an investment recommendation.' FSA, 2008

Unfortunately, much of the advice industry seems to operate on a self-assessment basis, asking nonsensical questions such as *'what would you say your attitude to risk is?'* or *'do you like to jump out of aeroplanes?'* to arrive at a score or statement such as 'low risk taker', or 'moderate risk taker' – whatever that means.

Psychometrics – a more professional approach

Psychometrics is the field of study concerned with the theory and technique of psychological assessment, which includes the measurement of knowledge, abilities, attitudes and personality traits. It uses measurement instruments such as questionnaires and tests that are structured to deliver valid and reliable outputs.

You may well be familiar with psychometric tests and may have even undertaken some yourself; in fact, over 95% of the FTSE 100 companies use psychometric testing to select their staff, as do the police, the civil service, airlines and even football clubs such as AC Milan (*Guardian*, 2002). Basic psychometric testing was developed during the Second World War to try to identify the jobs that would best suit different women entering the workforce in support of the war effort and the resulting Myers-Briggs test is still widely in use today.

The construction of a risk profile test – let's call it a questionnaire, as it sounds less intimidating – therefore requires far more than just putting together a list of ten questions to score. In the same way you would not ask an adviser to service your car, don't ask them to create a psychometric test themselves! The same applies if you are not intending to use an adviser – seek out a professional psychometric risk profiling tool – they do exist.

When I work with my clients (leading firms who manage the wealth of individuals and families) they occasionally say that some clients have a reluctance to undertake the tests at first, worrying that there are right and wrong answers or that they will be judged on the results in some way. In fact (and perhaps unlike doing a psychometric test for a job interview where the outcome may be detrimental to your chances), undertaking a risk profiling test can only be beneficial. If you have a 'low' risk profile score that is no better or worse than having a 'high' risk profile score – you will simply be in a position to make better, more informed choices. That is the secret to successful investing and what this book is all about. Almost without fail, all of their clients who take these psychometric risk profiling tests and talk through the implications find them to be an exceptionally valuable part of the investment process.

Fortunately a number of psychometric risk profiling tests are available online. Broadly, you pay a small fee and complete the questionnaire, which should be in plain English and very straightforward, and will most likely consist of 25–30 multiple choice questions and answers as the accuracy increases with the greater number of questions asked (Krus and Helmstader,

1987). Once complete, most will provide a detailed written report that relates specifically to your profile and explores the implications of your answers. The better ones will provide a suggestion as to the appropriate level of 'risky' assets (which you can generally read as equities at this point) that you can emotionally tolerate.

The results provide a catalyst for thinking hard about your risk profile within a framework that makes sense; it does not provide the 'right' answer; it does not mean that you should invest in a portfolio with this level of 'risky' assets; but it does provide the start to useful thinking and dialogue. The next step is to work out how much risk you need to take to reach your financial goals (Appendix 2) and how much you can afford to lose (look at the Figures in Chapter 8). Use this useful tool, not to think for you, but to help you think.

FinaMetrica – a market leader

When it comes to deciding which tool to use, your choice is limited, which is a good thing, particularly if within that choice strong solutions exist. Fortunately that is the case. One of the most highly regarded, long standing and widely used is FinaMetrica (www.MyRiskTolerance.com). This tool was developed in conjunction with the University of New South Wales Applied Psychology Unit and has been available since 1998. It exceeds international standards for psychometric tests of this kind and is widely used by leading advisers around the world including the USA, Australia and the UK (Davey and Resnik, 2008). The answers to the questionnaire are scored and the outcome is a risk tolerance score that translates into a comfort/discomfort range for 'risky' (equity-like) assets. To date around 450,000 investors have used this questionnaire. In fact, the vast majority of my innovative and proactive clients use FinaMetrica with their clients and were doing so long before I worked with them.

Take a look at the website and read some of the interesting background comments and articles and consider completing the questionnaire – it may be some of the best money you spend.

Others exist too, although I have no first-hand knowledge of their efficacy or methodology, and they are often embedded in the software used by advisers and are not available to those investing directly.

References

Davey, G. (2009) 'Risk tolerance revisited', FinaMetrica Pty Limited (www.riskprofiling.com).

Davey, G. and Resnik, P. (2008) 'Risk tolerance, risk profiling and the financial planning process', FinaMetrica Pty Limited (www.riskprofiling.com).

FSA (2008) www.fsa.gov.uk.

Guardian (2002) http://jobs.guardian.co.uk/careers/200256/356292/psychometric-testing-podcast.

Krus, D. J. and Helmstader, G. C. (1987) 'The relationship between correlation and internal consistency notions of test reliability', *Educational and Psychological Measurement*.

Appendix 2: Goal planning

Let's spend a little time thinking about how to turn the question 'Where do I start?' into a definite plan of action. The answer is that you start right here; in the next few minutes you should have a pretty fair idea of what you should be doing.

Well thought-out goals underpin success

Understanding what you want from your investing is the critical starting point of any investment programme; being able clearly to articulate these goals will help you and any one else assisting you, to tackle the issues you face. One of the constants that I found in my discussions with clients over the years is that many of them have only vague notions about what they want to achieve with their money and relatively few have a precise set of articulated goals.

In many ways that is not really very surprising. We find it easy to think emotionally about our vision: 'I want to be comfortable in my retirement'; 'I want to be involved in more philanthropic works'; or 'I want to provide my children with financial security', but find it harder to articulate in much more detail what we really want our money to do for us, such as

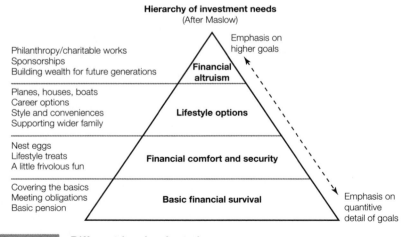

Figure A2.1 **Different levels of needs**

Source: Maslow 1970 (adapted)

'I need a £1.2 million pool when I retire to generate an income equivalent to £50,000 in today's money (before tax) giving me a standard of living that is comfortable, without having to worry about running out of money before I die'.

Looking at your own goals in this way may help you to understand them a little better. Your focus may be on investment goals towards the top of the pyramid in Figure A2.1, if you are already financially secure, or your focus may be towards the bottom of the pyramid, as you strive to put in place some financial security for yourself and your family. Most institutional investors such as pension plans, endowments, foundations and corporate treasurers have basic financial survival goals.

At the lower levels of the hierarchy, attention to the nitty-gritty detail of time, contributions, rates of return (and their associated uncertainty) and the size of your investment pot is more critical because the consequence of not being successful has serious repercussions. Those at higher levels have the luxury of being able to concentrate on higher-level objectives such as maintaining or increasing their purchasing power over the long run, and may need less detail in their planning.

General goals for individuals

As you read through each of the generic goals below, think hard about those that are relevant to you.

Basic financial survival – retirement

Increasingly, people are having to plan and invest for their own retirement as traditional defined benefit (final salary) schemes, where your benefits are defined as a function of your time with the company and your final salary, become unavailable to employees. Many are rightly concerned with being able to generate an acceptable level of income for their retirement. Common goals may be to 'avoid being poor' or 'to be able to enjoy ourselves in our retirement' or to 'feel comfortable that we can live how we do now, for the rest of our lives'.

Today, with the ever-growing influence of defined contribution pension plans (where a set monthly contribution is made by an employer, into an employee's individual pension pot), you alone are responsible for investing to satisfy your basic financial survival. All of the investment responsibility and investment risk is on your shoulders, and getting your investing programme right, i.e., giving yourself the greatest chance of having the right level of purchasing power available at the right time, is critical.

Basic financial survival – school/university fees

'I want to be able to give my children the best education I can,' is a common goal for some parents, which is often achieved by building reserves to meet school and university fees, through regular savings plans as the children grow up. Fortunately, many schools provide indications of future expected fees; the downside is that these seem to be growing faster than inflation. How important this is to you, only you will know.

Nest eggs

'I want to put something aside for a rainy day', 'We want to be able to afford a few small luxuries in our retirement', or 'It's good knowing that there is a little extra' are all familiar investment visions. These types of goals often apply to investors who have sufficient sources of income to take care of their basic financial survival and represent funds to provide an additional layer of security.

Lifestyle options

'I want to be free to pursue the things that I want to do' and 'I want to be able to have some fun with my wider family' are examples of higher-level goals. No one is at risk of being hungry or not being able to afford their heating bills, but these goals are as important to those fortunate enough to be in this position as any other investor's goals, even if they are not, in an absolute sense, as critical.

Philanthropic works

Fortunately for society, there are many investors who use their wealth for philanthropic purposes. 'I would like to set up a foundation to provide annual scholarships …' and 'We would like to provide a trust to maintain …' are philanthropic objectives, for investors who feel that their other financial needs have been taken care of and they would like to put their wealth to good use within society or their local community.

Five steps in defining your goals

Sitting down and thinking hard about what you want your wealth to achieve may feel like a daunting and tiresome proposition. But a little time spent thinking about and planning what you want to achieve is time well spent. This task is made easier by dividing it into five manageable steps (see Table A2.1).

■ Step 1: Divide your plan into appropriate pools – retirement, school fees, fun, etc.

■ Step 2: State your vision for each – what are you trying to achieve? A comfortable retirement? A pot to pay for all of the school and university fees for your children from 12 to 22 years of age?

■ Step 3: Define your investment horizon for each pool – the link between your investment horizon and your portfolio of investments is explored in depth in Chapter 8.

■ Step 4: Consider the consequences of not achieving your goals – how much will it hurt? Is it an essential goal or icing on the cake?

■ Step 5: Explain your goals in financial terms – at some point you need to translate your vision in Step 2 into hard numbers.

Basic financial survival goals – doing the maths

You need to work out what the nitty-gritty numbers that underlie your emotional investment goals are, however boring that may sound. This is not difficult if you think about it logically.

Table A2.1 Work out your five-step plan

Step	Pot 1
Step 1: Investment pools	Retirement income
Step 2: Vision	Comfortable retirement
Step 3: Horizon	30 years to retirement at 65 Live until at least 95!
Step 4: Consequences	Critical. Need at least half the income target (£15,000)
Step 5: Goals in financial terms	Detailed calculations required.
	Need £30,000 income

At this point, some people throw their arms up in horror. Do not panic! With a few simple calculations you can begin to get a rough idea of what you should be aiming for. Most of the maths is done and the results are set out in the tables that follow. These provide estimates to help you to understand the task in hand and some of the challenges that you face. Do not switch off at this point, however tempted you are! The example we will use is based around saving for retirement, but the tables and approach can be used to suit most goals.

Getting started is straightforward. Take a minute to study Figure A2.2. You can see that there are a number of questions that need answers. It is simply a matter of working through the questions and using the tables provided and some simple calculations to get some ball-park figures.

Estimating how much to save for retirement

You may be surprised just how much you need to accumulate and how much you will need to save regularly to get there – but get there you will, with a little planning and a sensible portfolio. You need to answer the following questions for yourself.

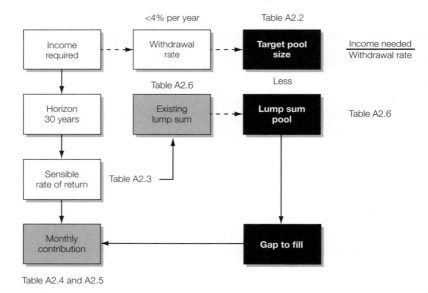

Figure A2.2 The road map for financial goals

Question 1: How much income do I need?

The goal of investing for retirement is to be pretty sure that you will be able to pay yourself an acceptable level of income that keeps pace with inflation throughout your retirement, so the first thing is to decide how much income you will require. Thinking in terms of the income you require in terms of today's money is the easiest way to look at things: 'I need 75% of my salary today to live comfortably'.

This is a good way to think because it allows you to talk about things in today's money terms and know what your income will buy you. It is hard to conceive how comfortable your retirement will be unless you factor in the effects of inflation. Will an income of £80,000 a year in tomorrow's devalued money provide a comfortable retirement? Not if a loaf of bread costs £15 and a pint of beer £35! To allow yourself the ability to talk about things you want in the future, in today's money terms, you must always use real, i.e., post-inflation, returns in any calculations you make. Using real returns on the asset side of your personal balance sheet allows you to ignore inflation on the liability side. Throughout the rest of this book, we will use real returns.

Sit down with a piece of paper and decide what level of income you need. Remember to allow for any state or other pensions or sources of income that you will have. Use the level of income you decide for the remainder of this section. I leave it to you to work out how much this represents!

Question 2: How large does my target pool need to be?

A significant challenge is that we do not know how long we will live and therefore cannot be certain how quickly we can spend the capital. Obviously, if you spend your capital over time, your target pool size does not need to be as large as if you wish to preserve the purchasing power of your capital pool. You have three options on retirement:

■ Maintain the purchasing power of your portfolio and your income. This implies that you withdraw an income that is equal to or less than the real return generated by your portfolio. Given that we are living longer, perhaps into our nineties, this is a sensible approach, particularly if it represents the bulk of your retirement income. Although as the US comedian Henny Youngman once said: *'I went to the bank today and I have all the money I need ... if I die tomorrow.'*

Table A2.2 How large does your target pool need to be?

Withdrawal rate p.a.	Income required							
	£10,000	£20,000	£30,000	£40,000	£50,000	£60,000	£70,000	£80,000
2%	£500,000	£1,000,000	£1,500,000	£2,000,000	£2,500,000	£3,000,000	£3,500,000	£4,000,000
3%	£333,333	£666,667	£1,000,000	£1,333,333	£1,666,667	£2,000,000	£2,333,333	£2,666,667
4%	£250,000	£500,000	£750,000	£1,000,000	£1,250,000	£1,500,000	£1,750,000	£2,000,000
5%	£200,000	£400,000	£600,000	£800,000	£1,000,000	£1,200,000	£1,400,000	£1,600,000
6%	£166,667	£333,333	£500,000	£666,667	£833,333	£1,000,000	£1,166,667	£1,333,333

Source: Albion Strategic Consulting

= You have a serious danger of running out of money

- Pay yourself an income that includes capital, using up the capital over a designated period of time. This is an option suitable for some. However, trying to predict when exactly you might run out of money is not easy with unpredictable markets and longevity.

- Use some or all of the accumulated pool to buy an income from an insurance company in the form of an annuity. Basically, you hand over your money in return for an income for the remainder of your life. They now hold the risk of you outliving the standard mortality tables and you take the risk that you die sooner and your estate loses monies that would have existed by controlling these assets yourself.

As a general rule of thumb, you should withdraw 4% or less from your portfolio (well balanced between equities and bonds), if you want to avoid the possibility you will run out of money before you die, as this represents the level of real returns that such a mix of investments would hope (but is not certain) to achieve.

The level of income required divided by the withdrawal rate defines how much money needs to be in your target pool at the end of your accumulation period. Table A2.2 provides an indication of the size of pool you require at different rates of withdrawal, to generate your required annual, pre-tax income. You can see that in real terms these pool sizes can be frighteningly large (and appear even bigger in before-inflation terms) and just how valuable non-contributory final salary schemes really are.

Do not be discouraged by the magnitude of the task. As you will see from later tables, the combined effect of compounding of moderate returns over time and regular drip feeding of contributions into your pot have the ability to create substantial wealth.

Question 3: How long will I invest for?

At first glance that appears an easy question to answer, perhaps picking your sixty-fifth birthday, the normal 'retirement' age in the UK, as the end of your accumulation phase (unless of course the Chancellor decides we all need to work longer). In reality, as organisations narrow rapidly near the top, and loyalty to long-serving employees fails, you should perhaps consider that being in gainful, full employment at sixty, let alone sixty-seven, is no longer going to be the norm. Perhaps you should consider having more in your pot at an earlier stage (say fifty-five perhaps), which means investing higher, regular contributions, to provide security and flexibility in your later working years; working if you choose, or when you can.

| Table A2.3 | Reasonable return expectations |

Smarter Portfolio	0	20	40	60	80	100
Expected real return*	1%	2%	3%	4%	5%	6%
Portfolio risk %	5%	6%	9%	13%	17%	21%
*Rounded estimates						

10 year horizon	0	20	40	60	80	100
Return > 0%	75%	85%	85%	85%	85%	80%
Return > 1%	50%	70%	75%	75%	80%	75%
Return > 2%	25%	50%	65%	70%	70%	70%
Return > 3%	10%	30%	50%	60%	65%	70%
Return > 4%	5%	15%	35%	50%	60%	65%
Return > 5%	0%	5%	25%	40%	50%	55%
Return > 6%	0%	0%	15%	30%	45%	50%

20 year horizon	0	20	40	60	80	100
Return > 0%	80%	95%	90%	90%	90%	90%
Return > 1%	50%	80%	85%	85%	85%	85%
Return > 2%	20%	50%	70%	75%	80%	80%
Return > 3%	5%	25%	50%	65%	70%	75%
Return > 4%	0%	5%	30%	50%	60%	65%
Return > 5%	0%	0%	15%	35%	50%	60%
Return > 6%	0%	0%	5%	25%	40%	50%

30 year horizon	0	20	40	60	80	100
Return > 0%	85%	95%	95%	95%	95%	95%
Return > 1%	50%	80%	90%	90%	90%	90%
Return > 2%	15%	50%	75%	80%	85%	85%
Return > 3%	0%	20%	50%	65%	75%	80%
Return > 4%	0%	5%	25%	50%	65%	70%
Return > 5%	0%	0%	10%	35%	50%	60%
Return > 6%	0%	0%	5%	20%	40%	50%

Note: Based on Monte Carlo simulations using the 'conservative' estimate for after-inflation returns and expected portfolio risk.

Question 4: What portfolio returns are reasonable to use?

This is probably the most used, abused and misunderstood area of investing. Overly optimistic estimates of return will always come back to haunt you, as they did the endowment mortgage sales industry. You may be lucky and get higher returns or unlucky and get lower returns than you expect from your portfolio; even over long periods of time, returns can vary significantly from their averages. Understanding your chances of achieving an acceptable rate of return from your portfolio is therefore critical (see Table A2.3).

Question 5: What contributions will I need to make?

At this point, you know what income you need, have worked out what target pool size you are aiming for with a given withdrawal rate, and have chosen a rate of return that has a reasonable chance of being achieved over the time that you will be investing for. You now need to work out how much you should contribute every month.

The pot of money you end up with is a function of the regular contributions you make, the time over which you make them and the real return that your portfolio generates. Many would-be investors become too focused on the rate of return that their portfolio will achieve, even though you cannot control this with any certainty – the best you can do is to choose a rate that gives you a reasonable chance of success, but with no guarantees. On the other hand, time (in some cases) and the contributions you make may well be variable and can play a significant role in increasing the chances of a successful outcome. As they are in your control, they are all the more valuable.

There are two approaches tackling the question of contributions.

Table A2.4   Approximate monthly contributions to build £1,000,000

Years	Real rate of return							
	1%	2%	3%	4%	5%	6%	7%	8%
10	£8,000	£7,600	£7,300	£6,900	£6,600	£6,300	£6,000	£5,800
20	£3,800	£3,400	£3,100	£2,800	£2,500	£2,300	£2,000	£1,800
30	£2,400	£2,100	£1,800	£1,500	£1,300	£1,100	£900	£800

Source: Albion Strategic Consulting

Approach 1: Contributions to build £1,000,000

This first approach calculates the monthly contributions that you would need to make to accumulate £1,000,000 of purchasing power, depending on your investment horizon and the real rates of return you expect from your portfolio. You can scale the contributions up or down depending on your target pool size. For example, to accumulate £1 million at 4% over thirty years you would have to contribute approximately £1,500 a month. To build £300,000, then multiply £1,500 by £300,000/£1,000,000 or 30%, to give £450 a month. Take a look back at Table A2.3 before you choose a rate in Table A2.4 above.

Approach 2: Pool size based on monthly contributions

The second approach estimates how large the target pool will be depending on the level of monthly contributions that you make at different rates of expected real returns and the investment period (Table A2.5). Again, see what the effect is on your potential pool if returns are worse than you expect. Remember to take into account any tax relief on the contributions you make. Running a few 'what if?' scenarios using these tables will be time well spent.

Table A2.5   How large will your target pool be?

Real return	Monthly contribution							
2%	**£100**	**£200**	**£400**	**£600**	**£800**	**£1,000**	**£1,500**	**£2,000**
10 Years	£15,000	£25,000	£55,000	£80,000	£105,000	£130,000	£195,000	£265,000
20 Years	£30,000	£60,000	£115,000	£175,000	£235,000	£290,000	£435,000	£585,000
30 Years	£50,000	£95,000	£195,000	£290,000	£390,000	£485,000	£730,000	£975,000
3%	**£100**	**£200**	**£400**	**£600**	**£800**	**£1,000**	**£1,500**	**£2,000**
10 Years	£15,000	£30,000	£55,000	£85,000	£110,000	£140,000	£205,000	£275,000
20 Years	£30,000	£65,000	£130,000	£195,000	£260,000	£320,000	£485,000	£645,000
30 Years	£55,000	£115,000	£230,000	£345,000	£455,000	£570,000	£855,000	£1,140,000
4%	**£100**	**£200**	**£400**	**£600**	**£800**	**£1,000**	**£1,500**	**£2,000**
10 Years	£15,000	£30,000	£60,000	£85,000	£115,000	£145,000	£215,000	£290,000
20 Years	£35,000	£70,000	£145,000	£215,000	£285,000	£355,000	£535,000	£715,000
30 Years	£65,000	£135,000	£270,000	£405,000	£540,000	£675,000	£1,010,000	£1,345,000
5%	**£100**	**£200**	**£400**	**£600**	**£800**	**£1,000**	**£1,500**	**£2,000**
10 Years	£15,000	£30,000	£60,000	£90,000	£120,000	£150,000	£225,000	£300,000
20 Years	£40,000	£80,000	£160,000	£240,000	£315,000	£395,000	£595,000	£795,000
30 Years	£80,000	£160,000	£320,000	£480,000	£640,000	£795,000	£1,195,000	£1,595,000

Increasing your chances of success

At the end of the day, there will always be some uncertainty. However, you can control most of the elements involved: you can choose a rate of return that has a high chance of being achieved; pay in higher contributions to compensate for this lower rate of return; and if necessary either scale back your goals or extend the investment period. Perhaps these are unpalatable actions, but all are preferable to a long retirement spent scrimping and saving to meet basic needs. I leave it up to you at this point to decide.

Lump-sum investing

Your investment programme may consist of making a lump-sum investment, perhaps due to monies acquired through the sale of a business, an inheritance, work-related bonuses, or the sale of a property. In this case, the end value of an investment pool is based on three things: the amount you invest as a lump sum, the time it is invested for, and the real rate of return from the mix of portfolio building blocks used. This would also apply to any capital you already have in your investment pool, and to which you will make additional regular contributions.

You can see the effect of time and return on the purchasing power of £1 in Table A2.6. You can multiply any lump sum investment that you plan to make by this number. Choose your investment horizon and the real rate of return that gives a suitable chance of success.

A caveat to using the numbers

Always bear in mind that using these outputs only provides rough figures and cannot fully describe the uncertainty of the markets that you face. You can never be certain of the returns in advance, although by choosing a rate of return that has a good chance of being achieved over your investment horizon using Table A2.3 is a start. You can hope that your investments

Table A2.6 The effect of time and return on lump-sum investments

Growth of £1	Expected real return							
Years	1%	2%	3%	4%	5%	6%	7%	8%
10	£1.1	£1.2	£1.3	£1.5	£1.6	£1.8	£2.0	£2.2
20	£1.2	£1.5	£1.8	£2.2	£2.7	£3.2	£3.9	£4.7
30	£1.3	£1.8	£2.4	£3.2	£4.3	£5.7	£7.6	£10.1

$$\textit{Final value} = \frac{\text{annual contributions} \quad [(1 + \text{rate of return})^{\text{Number of years}} - 1)]}{\text{Rate of return}}$$

$$\textit{Annual contributions} = \frac{(\text{final value x rate of return})}{[(1 + \text{rate of return})^{\wedge \text{Number of years}} - 1)]}$$

$$\textit{Pool size} = \frac{\text{required income}}{\text{withdrawal rate}}$$

Where ^ = to the power of

Figure A2.3   **Formulae for your own calculations**

achieve such returns and, if they do, then these numbers will give you an indication of what to expect.

Remember, too, that any contributions that you make need to be scaled up, in real life, to reflect the nominal amount you need to invest. You can use an inflation index to do this simply. Finally, remember that investing will cost you. Build in investing costs into your expected returns. If you use index funds, then 0.5% a year in costs is a reasonably conservative deduction.

The danger of using simplistic models like the ones above is that they can lull you into a false sense of security. Be smart and think about some of their limitations. At this point you at least have a reasonable chance of finding the right ballpark for your financial targets.

Other useful calculations

In Figure A2.3, if you are interested, you will find the formulae to calculate basic estimates for your own investment plan. You probably need to use a spreadsheet, as the calculations are laborious using a calculator. Always bear in mind the limitations of such calculations. They do, however, provide you with a useful tool to look at the consequences of different courses of action, allowing you to make decisions aligned more closely with your goals.

References

Maslow, A. (1970) 'A theory of motivation', in: *Motivation and personality*, 1st edn. Upper Saddle River, NJ: Pearson Education.

Appendix 3

Data series used in Smarter Portfolios simulation

Expected attributes	Real return %	Source/Permissions
Equity assets		
Global developed equity (market)	MSCI World Index (net div.)	Morningstar EnCorr. All rights reserved.
Global developed equity (value) to 12/1993	Dimensional Global Large Value Index	Courtesy of Dimensional Fund Advisers
Global developed equity (value) from 1/1994	Dimensional Global Value Index	Courtesy of Dimensional Fund Advisers
Global developed equity (smaller companies)	Dimensional Global Small Index	Courtesy of Dimensional Fund Advisers
Emerging markets (market)	MSCI Emerging Markets Index (gross div.)	Morningstar EnCorr. All rights reserved.
Emerging markets (value) to 12/1993	Dimensional Emerging Markets Value Index	Courtesy of Dimensional Fund Advisers
Emerging markets (smaller companies) to 12/1993	Dimensional Emerging Markets Small Index	Courtesy of Dimensional Fund Advisers
Emerging markets (value & smaller companies) from 1/1994	Dimensional Emerging Markets Targeted Value Index	Courtesy of Dimensional Fund Advisers
Global commercial property to 6/1989	FTSE NAREIT Equity REITs TR Index	Morningstar EnCorr. All rights reserved.
Global commercial property	S&P Global REIT Index (gross div.)	Morningstar EnCorr. All rights reserved.
Fixed income assets		
Short-dated (min AA) bonds	FTSE British Government Index (up to 5 years)	Morningstar EnCorr. All rights reserved.
UK index linked gilts (0-5)	FTSE British Government Inflation lInked Index (up to 5 years)	Morningstar EnCorr. All rights reserved.
UK index linked gilts (5-15)	Barclays UK Government Inflation Linked 5-15 Year Bond	Morningstar EnCorr. All rights reserved.
Adjustment data		
Cash	UK 1 Month T-Bill	Bank of England
Inflation	UK Retail Price Index (UK RPI)	Bank of England

Simulation methodology

Data period from 7/1989 to 12/2012 unless otherwise stated.

Monthly data – total returns (income and capital).

Adjusted for inflation, where stated, using UK RPI.

Rebalanced once every 12 months.

No transaction or product costs have been deducted.

Index